JOHN **WESLEY'S** TEACHINGS

Also by Thomas C. Oden

VOLUME 1

GOD AND PROVIDENCE

JOHN WESLEY'S
TEACHINGS

THOMAS C. ODEN

ZONDERVAN

John Wesley's Teachings, Volume 1
Copyright © 2012 by Thomas C. Oden

Volumes 1 and 2 are revised and expanded from *John Wesley's Scriptural Christianity*
Copyright © 1994 by Thomas C. Oden

This title is also available as a Zondervan ebook.

Requests for information should be addressed to:

Zondervan, 3900 *Sparks Dr. SE, Grand Rapids, Michigan 49546*

Library of Congress Cataloging-in-Publication Data

Oden, Thomas C.
    John Wesley's teachings / Thomas C. Oden.
       v. cm.
    Rev. ed. of: John Wesley's scriptural Christianity. c1994.
    Includes bibliographical references and indexes.
    Contents: v. 1. God and providence— v. 2. Christ and salvation— v. 3. The practice of pastoral care— v. 4. Issues of ethics and society.
    ISBN 978-0-310-32815-5 (softcover)
    1. Wesley, John, 1703-1791. 2. Theology, Doctrinal. 3. Methodist Church—Doctrines. 4. Theology, Doctrinal—History—18th century. 5. Methodist Church—Doctrines—History— 18th century. I. Oden, Thomas C. John Wesley's scriptural Christianity. II. Title.
    BX8331.3.O35 2012
    230'.7092—dc23   2012001655

Cover design: John Hamilton Design
Cover image: Corbis® Images
Interior design: Beth Shagene
Edited by Katya Covrett and Laura Dodge Weller

Printed in the United States of America

HB 11.27.2020

To major partners in dialogue on Wesley, many of them my former graduate students in the Wesley Seminars at Drew University over the years who are now teaching and writing in this and related fields. I have benefited from their dialogue in ways beyond telling.

Prof. Kenneth Collins of Asbury Theological Seminary, Wilmore, Kentucky

Prof. John Tyson of Houghton College, Houghton, New York

Chancellor Christopher Hall of Eastern University and dean of Palmer Theological Seminary, St. Davids, Pennsylvania

Dr. Joel Elowsky of Concordia University – Milwaukee, Mequon, Wisconsin

President David Eaton of Wesleyan University, Bartlesville, Oklahoma

Prof. Donald Thorsen of Azusa Pacific School of Theology, Azusa, California

Prof. Leicester Longden of Dubuque Theological Seminary, Dubuque, Iowa

Prof. Stephen Seamands of Asbury Theological Seminary, Wilmore, Kentucky

Dr. Thomas Buchan of Asbury Theological Seminary, Orlando, Florida

Prof. David Ford of St. Tikhon's Theological Orthodox Seminary, South Canaan, Pennsylvania

Dr. Michael Christensen of Drew Theological School, Madison, New Jersey

Prof. William Ury of Wesley Biblical Seminary, Jackson, Mississippi

Prof. Kelley Steve McCormick of Nazarene Theological Seminary, Kansas City, Missouri

Prof. Kenneth Brewer of Somerset Christian College, Zarephath, New Jersey

Prof. Christopher Bounds of Indiana Wesleyan University, Marion, Indiana

Dr. Stephen Flick of Wesley Biblical Seminary, Jackson, Mississippi

Dean Leroy Lindsey of the OMS Biblical Seminary of Mexico, Mexico City

Prof. Woodrow Whidden of Andrews University, Berrien Springs, Michigan

Dr. Gunshick Shim, district superintendent in New York United Methodist Conference, Long Island, New York

The late Father Jeffrey Finch, translator for *Ancient Christian Commentary on Scripture*

Contents

VOLUME ONE
God and Providence

E. Sin and Death

1. Distinguishing Temporal Death from Spiritual Death
2. Whether Redemption in Christ Makes Up for Losses Suffered in Adam
3. The Westminster Catechism on Original Sin

F. Adam's Headship with Eve's Cooperation

1. Adam as a Public Person: On Federal Headship
2. The Consequence of Adam's Fall for Subsequent Human History
3. The Abyss into Which Humanity Plunged
4. Distinguishing Original Sin from Actual Sin

G. Answering Questions on the Insidious Spread of Sin

1. The Intergenerational Sociality of Sin
2. The Communication of the Sin of Adam and Eve to All Humanity
3. Whether Loss of Communion with God Sharpens the Sting of Unexplained Suffering
4. Whether There Remains a Natural Tendency to Sin
5. Whether Guilt May be Imputed from One to Another

H. The Hidden Link between Redemption and Original Sin

1. Original Sin and New Birth
2. Reframing Wesley's Doctrine within Contemporary Culture

I. Conclusion

Preface

This is a reader's guide to John Wesley's teaching. It introduces his thought on the basic tenets of Christian teaching on God and providence (volume 1), Christ and salvation (volume 2), pastoral theology (volume 3), and ethics and society (volume 4). These are ordered in accord with Wesley's own organization of subject matter. They are arranged in the familiar sequence of classic consensual Christian teaching to which he adhered. The exposition presents a plain account of Wesley's works and thrives on constant citation from Wesley's own texts.

My task has been to clarify Wesley's explicit intent in everyday modern English. This intent can be checked by reading the text itself, well marked in the notes. I have reduced the archaisms and ambiguities to communicate his meaning as clearly as possible to a contemporary audience.

Tracking References to the Major Editions

The preferred scholarly edition of *The Works of John Wesley* is the Oxford/Abingdon Bicentennial edition (Oxford: 1975 – 83; Nashville: 1984 –), signified by B.[1]

The most frequently reproduced edition, often still the only one appearing on library and pastoral bookshelves, is the Thomas Jackson edition, first published in 1829 – 31, signified by J for Jackson. Thus, whenever B or J appears in the footnotes, the reader is being directed to either the Bicentennial edition (B) or the Jackson edition (J). This is necessary because the reader may have access to one but not both editions. Many more copies of the Jackson edition have been distributed than the Bicentennial edition.

Here are the key guidelines for the scholarly apparatus:

- Volume references in Arabic numerals refer to the Bicentennial edition. Volume references in uppercase Roman numerals refer to the Jackson edition.
- Both the Bicentennial edition (B) and the Jackson edition (J) are available in searchable CD-ROMs or online. In the case of B, the current disk is still incomplete, awaiting print publication of many volumes.
- Distinguishing a B reference from a J reference is easy: If the first digit is an

[1]In rare cases where Sugden's edition of the *Standard Sermons* (see Abbreviations: *SS*) is quoted, the reader's attention is directed especially to his annotations.

Arabic numeral, the reference is to B. If the first digit is an uppercase Roman numeral, the reference is to J. A reference to B 4:133 indicates the Bicentennial edition, volume 4, page 133. But a reference to J IV:133 indicates the Jackson edition, volume 4 (IV), page 133.

- In cases where a new homily is being introduced in order to be discussed more fully, I have referenced in parentheses the Bicentennial edition (B) in this conventional order: the homily number, the date of the homily, and the volume and page references in the Bicentennial edition. Where the Jackson edition (J) is referenced, I have listed the homily number and the volume and page references in Jackson.
- At times the homily numbers appear in a different order and number in the Bicentennial than in the Jackson edition.[2]

My purpose is to assist those who wish to access handily the proper text in the available edition. Readers will more frequently be working out of either J or B but ordinarily not both. For convenience, we cite both editions. An appendix titled "Alphabetical Correlation of the Sermons in the Jackson and Bicentennial Editions" can be found at the back of all volumes. Those who are doing scholarly research work are advised to work with the Bicentennial edition whenever possible.

On Biblical References

Though Wesley expressed abiding gratitude for the King James Version of the Bible, especially in its value for common worship, his study text was normally in the original language. In citing the lead text for his homilies, I ordinarily cite the King James Authorized text (KJV) from which Wesley was preaching or writing, unless specified otherwise.

When he published his own translation of the New Testament, many references in the Authorized Version of 1611 were altered to communicate with his plain-speaking audience of the 1700s. There is no reason to think that Wesley regarded his own English rendering of the Greek as definitive for future centuries of English readers for whom the language protocols and usages would have shifted as they normally do over decades.

Those who might assume that Wesley himself was constantly working out of the King James Version do well to recall that Wesley read the Greek New Testament fluently. He studied it daily in his early morning and evening meditations.

On Other Editions of Wesley's Works

The only collected edition published during Wesley's lifetime was the 32-volume Bristol edition of *The Works of the Rev. John Wesley* (Bristol, UK: William Pine, 1771 – 74).

---

[2]"The Trouble and Rest of Good Men" appears as Sermon 109 in the Bicentennial edition (B #109), and as Sermon 127 in the Jackson edition (J #127). The numbering is often the same but in some instances is different.

The second edition of *The Works of the Rev. John Wesley* was edited by Joseph Benson (17 vols., London: Conference Offices, 1809 – 13; republished in New York and Philadelphia in 10 volumes, 1826 – 27).

The most-used third edition of *The Works of the Rev. John Wesley*, edited by Thomas Jackson (14 vols., London, 1829 – 31), has been frequently reprinted in America and is employed here as one of two major available editions of Wesley's Works.[3]

Prior to the Bicentennial edition, the editions that presented an annotated editorial apparatus to the works of Wesley, with scholarly introductions according to modern standards, were Nehemiah Curnock's edition of *The Journal of John Wesley* (see *JJW* in Abbreviations) in 1916, Edward H. Sugden's edition of the *Standard Sermons* (see *SS*) in 1921, John Telford's edition of the *Letters of John Wesley* (see *LJW*) in 1931, and Albert C. Outler's selection of Wesley's key writings (see *JWO*) in 1964. These are all commended here. The Oxford/Abingdon Bicentennial edition (see B in Abbreviations)[4] will stand for generations to come as the definitive edition.

Wesley's Patrimony

Wesley left behind an enormous corpus of literature. This vast body includes 151 teaching homilies, six decades of journals (1735 – 91), manuscript diaries, eight volumes of letters, essays, doctrinal tracts, occasional writings, and prefaces. The untold numbers of hymns were mostly written by John's brother Charles but were edited by John. These were the fruits of their editing and publishing over a very long time span. It is difficult to think of a single figure in the eighteenth century who left behind such a massive body of work as did John Wesley.

This series seeks to deliver to the nonprofessional reader the gist of the whole of Wesley's patrimony in systematic order. It provides a window into the basic wisdom of his Christian teaching. While it cannot claim to be comprehensive, it seeks to include core insights from all of these varied genres of literature.

This is why we need multiple volumes to examine this massive range of Wesley's works. A shorter series would threaten to cut off essential parts. For readers who want to investigate only one doctrine or idea, the Further Reading in each section will make these searches more accessible.

---

[3]That Telford, Sugden, Curnock, and Jackson (see Abbreviations) are hardly mentioned in the Bicentennial edition of the Sermons remains a puzzle. They all contain useful notes pertinent to this study. The American edition, edited by John Emory, was published in New York in 1831, based on the Jackson edition. In many libraries, the Jackson edition is the only one available.

[4]When "Articles of Religion" (Art.) are indicated, I am referring to Wesley's own recension of the Twenty-Four Articles (to which the 1784 American Methodist Church added a twenty-fifth), derived and edited down from the Anglican Thirty-Nine Articles. The Articles have played a central role in the American Wesleyan doctrinal traditions. They are included in the constitutions of most church bodies of the Wesleyan tradition. When Confession (Confes.) is referenced, I am indicating the summary of Wesleyan faith set forth in the 1962 Confession of the Evangelical United Brethren, which by a constitutionally restrictive rule has become a doctrinal standard of the United Methodist Church. A reference to the first article of the Confession appears as Confes. 1.

On This Edition

Zondervan has a distinguished reputation as a publisher of reference works and classics, many of them bound in multivolume editions. My hope is that this series will become a sufficiently useful resource for lay and professional readers that it will be in due time made available digitally for international readers for decades to come. Nothing like this text-by-text review of the content of Wesley's teaching exists in Wesley studies.

In 1994 Zondervan published my earlier study of Wesley's doctrine under the title *John Wesley's Scriptural Christianity: A Plain Exposition of His Teaching on Christian Doctrine (JWSC)*. In this present edition, much of the content of that single volume is now expanded and extensively revised, quadrupling the information presented in the earlier single volume.

Abbreviations

ACCS	*The Ancient Christian Commentary on Scripture.* Edited by Thomas C. Oden. Downers Grove, IL: InterVarsity, 1997–2010.
AHR	*American Historical Review.*
AM	*Arminian Magazine.*
Art.	Twenty-Five Articles of Religion.
AS	*Asbury Seminarian.*
B	Bicentennial edition of *The Works of John Wesley.* Edited by Frank Baker and Richard Heitzenrater. Oxford: Clarendon, and New York: Oxford University Press, 1975–83; Nashville: Abingdon, 1984–; in print: vols. 1, 2, 3, 4, 7, 18, 19, 20, 21, 22, 23, 24.
BCP	Book of Common Prayer.
BETS	*Bulletin of the Evangelical Theological Society.*
Bull.	Bulletin.
CCD	"A Clear and Concise Demonstration of the Divine Inspiration of Holy Scripture."
CH	*A Collection of Hymns for the Use of the People Called Methodists,* vol. 7 of the Bicentennial edition.
Chr.	Christian.
ChrCent	*Christian Century.*
CL	A Christian Library.
COC	*Creeds of the Churches: A Reader in Christian Doctrine.* Edited by John H. Leith. Atlanta: John Knox, 1982.
Confes.	1962 Confession of the Evangelical United Brethren.
CWT	Robert W. Burtner and Robert E. Chiles. *A Compend of Wesley's Theology.* Nashville: Abingdon, 1954.
Diss.	Dissertation.
DOS	*The Doctrine of Original Sin according to Scripture, Reason, and Experience.*
DPF	"Dialogue between a Predestinarian and His Friend."

DSF	"The Doctrine of Salvation, Faith and Good Works Extracted from the Homilies of the Church of England."
DSWT	Thomas C. Oden. *Doctrinal Standards in the Wesleyan Tradition.* Grand Rapids: Zondervan, 1988.
EA	"An Earnest Appeal to Men of Reason and Religion."
ENNT	*Explanatory Notes upon the New Testament.*
ENOT	*Explanatory Notes upon the Old Testament.*
EQ	*Evangelical Quarterly.*
ETS	Evangelical Theological Society.
EWT	Paul Mickey. *Essentials of Wesleyan Theology.* Grand Rapids: Zondervan, 1980.
FA	"A Farther Appeal to Men of Reason and Religion."
FAP	Francis Asbury Press, Zondervan.
FB	Howard A. Slaatte. *Fire in the Brand: Introduction to the Creative Work and Theology of John Wesley.* New York: Exposition, 1963.
FW	Kenneth Collins. *A Faithful Witness: John Wesley's Homiletical Theology.* Wilmore, KY: Wesleyan Heritage, 1993.
FWAT	Mildred Bangs Wynkoop. *Foundations of Wesleyan-Arminian Theology.* Kansas City, MO: Beacon Hill, 1967.
HSP	*Hymns and Sacred Poems.*
J	Jackson edition of Wesley's Works. Edited by Thomas Jackson, 1829 – 32. The 1872 edition has been reprinted in many 14-volume American editions (Eerdmans, Zondervan, Christian Book Distributors, et al.); digitally available on Wesley.nnu.edu.
Int	*Interpretation — Journal of Bible and Theology.*
JBR	*Journal of Bible and Religion.*
JJW	*The Journal of John Wesley.* Edited by Nehemiah Curnock. 8 vols. London: Epworth, 1916.
JTS	*Journal of Theological Studies.*
JWO	*John Wesley.* Edited by Albert C. Outler. Library of Protestant Theology. New York: Oxford University Press, 1964.
JWPH	Robert Monk. *John Wesley: His Puritan Heritage.* Nashville: Abingdon, 1966.
JWSC	Thomas C. Oden. *John Wesley's Scriptural Christianity: A Plain Exposition of His Teaching on Christian Doctrine.* Grand Rapids: Zondervan, 1994.
JWTT	Colin Williams. *John Wesley's Theology Today.* Nashville: Abingdon, 1960.
KJV	King James Version.

LCM   Letter to the Rev. Dr. Conyers Middleton (January 4, 1749).

LJW   *Letters of John Wesley.* Edited by John Telford. 8 vols. London: Epworth, 1931.

LLBL   A Letter to the Right Reverend Lord Bishop of London.

LPC   Letter on Preaching Christ (same as Letter to an Evangelical Layman, December 20, 1751).

LQHR   *London Quarterly and Holborn Review.*

LS   Thomas C. Oden. *Life in the Spirit.* San Francisco: HarperSanFrancisco, 1992.

MH   *Methodist History.*

Minutes "Minutes of Some Late Conversations between the Rev. Mr. Wesley and Others."

MLS   *Martin Luther: Selections from His Writings.* Edited by John Dillenberger. New York: Doubleday, 1961.

MM   *Methodist Magazine.*

MOB   William M. Arnett. "John Wesley: Man of One Book." PhD diss., Drew University, 1954.

MPL   *Patrologia latina (Patrologiae cursus completus: Series latina).* Edited by J.-P. Migne. 217 vols. Paris: 1844–64.

MQR   *Methodist Quarterly Review.*

MR   *Methodist Review.*

NDM   Reinhold Niebuhr. *The Nature and Destiny of Man.* 2 vols. New York: Scribner, 1941, 1943.

NIV   New International Version

NRSV   New Revised Standard Version.

NT   New Testament.

OED   *Oxford English Dictionary.*

OT   Old Testament.

PACP   *A Plain Account of Christian Perfection.*

PCC   "Predestination Calmly Considered."

PM   *Preacher's Magazine.*

Pref.   Preface.

Publ.   Publishing, Publishers.

PW   *Poetical Works of Charles Wesley and John Wesley.* Edited by George Osborn. 13 vols. London: Wesleyan Methodist Conference, 1868–72.

PWHS   *Proceedings of the Wesley Historical Society.*

Q   Quarterly.

QR   *Quarterly Review.*

RC   Roman Catholic.

RE   *Realencyklopädie für protestantische Theologie und Kirche.* Edited by
          J. J. Herzog and A. Hauck. 24 vols. Leipzig: J. H. Hinrichs, 1896 – 1913.

RJW   George Croft Cell. *The Rediscovery of John Wesley.* New York: Henry
          Holt, 1935.

RL   *Religion in Life.*

SS   *Wesley's Standard Sermons.* Edited by Edward H. Sugden.
          2 vols. London: Epworth, 1921; 3rd ed., 1951.

SSO   John Wesley. *Sermons on Several Occasions.* 3 vols. London: W. Strahan,
          1746.

SSM   *Sunday Service of the Methodists of the United States of America* (1784).
          Edited by Edward C. Hobbs. Nashville: Methodist Student Movement,
          1956.

TCNT   Twentieth Century New Testament.

TIRC   "Thoughts on the Imputation of the Righteousness of Christ."

TJW   William R. Cannon. *Theology of John Wesley: With Special Reference
          to the Doctrine of Justification.* New York: Abingdon, 1946.

TUN   "Thoughts upon Necessity."

UMC   United Methodist Church.

unpubl.   Unpublished.

WC   John Deschner. *Wesley's Christology.* Grand Rapids: Zondervan, 1989.

WHS   Lycurgus M. Starkey. *The Work of the Holy Spirit.* Nashville: Abingdon,
          1962.

WMM   *Wesleyan Methodist Magazine.*

WQ   Donald Thorsen. *The Wesleyan Quadrilateral: Scripture, Tradition,
          Reason, and Experience as a Model of Evangelical Theology.* Grand
          Rapids: Zondervan, 1990.

WQR   *Wesleyan Quarterly Review*

WRE   John W. Prince. *Wesley on Religious Education.* New York: Methodist
          Book Concern, 1926.

WS   Harald G. A. Lindström. *Wesley and Sanctification.* Nashville:
          Abingdon, 1946.

WTH   Albert C. Outler. *The Wesleyan Theological Heritage: Essays of Albert
          C. Outler.* Edited by Thomas C. Oden and Leicester R. Longden. Grand
          Rapids: Zondervan, 1991.

WTJ   *Wesleyan Theological Journal.*

XXV   Twenty-Five Articles. Adapted from the *Sunday Service* of 1784.

XXXIX   Anglican Thirty-Nine Articles of Religion.

Introduction

A. The Teaching Homily as Christian Doctrine

In his address to readers of his collected works of 1771, Wesley made a preliminary attempt at a rough sequential organization of his instructional homilies: "I wanted to methodize these tracts, *to range them under proper heads*, placing those together which were on similar subjects, and in such order that one might illustrate another.... There is *scarce any subject of importance, either in practical or controversial divinity, which is not treated* of more or less, either professedly or occasionally."[1] Wesley's own careful ordering of his work is the systematic design on which we will build.

1. The Scope of Wesley's Teaching

No major Christian doctrine is neglected in Wesley's teaching. Key classic teaching topics are treated with remarkable internal consistency. My objective is to set forth the implicit inner cohesion of these diverse points of Wesley's teaching.

There is an intuitive sense of order in this wide range of homilies and essays. My task is to organize Wesley's teaching in a sequence natural to his own design and consistent with the classic Christian tradition to which he appealed. Wesley did not invent this systematic sequence. He was the grateful inheritor of the well-known order of salvation in ancient Christian teaching. This order can be seen implicitly in the Council of Nicaea and in the consensus-bearing texts of Cyril of Jerusalem, John of Damascus, Thomas Aquinas, and John Calvin. Among Anglican divines, it is prominent in Thomas Cranmer, John Jewel, and John Pearson.

I will show that the whole range of classic *loci* (points of theology) appears in Wesley's large body of writings, but they are not easily recognized as a systematic whole because of the nature of the teaching homily, which focused on a single text of sacred Scripture. Only a few of these *loci*, notably original sin and the way of salvation, are dealt with at great length historically and systematically.

Wesley's intent was not to write a comprehensive ecclesial theology, such as that of Richard Hooker, or a commentary on the creed, such as that of John Pearson

---

[1]"Preface to the Third Edition," J I:3, in a brief address "To the Reader" in the thirty-two duodecima volumes of 1774, italics added.

before him, but to speak plainly to his connection[2] of spiritual formation on all major themes of Christian teaching.

2. The Teaching Homily

Wesley taught his connection by published homilies. The earliest of these were collected and frequently published as his *Standard Sermons* (in various editions numbering forty-eight, fifty-two, and fifty-three).

The way Christian doctrine was taught by eighteenth-century Anglican divines was through published teaching sermons, not rococo tomes on specific doctrines. Wesley was born and bred in this Anglican centrist tradition of homiletic instruction.

The notion of an established, reliably transmitted book of homilies was a familiar pattern of the English church tradition (following Thomas Cranmer, Lancelot Andrewes, John Jewel, and Matthew Parker). This book was a collection of prepared thematic teaching sermons designed to instruct congregations on received Christian doctrine.[3] Wesley followed this two-hundred-year Anglican tradition by modestly offering his own tutorial homilies to those in his direct connection of spiritual formation.[4]

3. The Whole Compass of Divinity

We do not have from Wesley's hand, as from Calvin's or Suarez's or Melanchthon's, a definitive systematic theology in the sense of a comprehensive and sequential organization of the topics of theology. With Wesley, what we have are occasional instructional homilies, many preached numerous times on his lengthy journeys through England, Scotland, and Ireland. Though not organized as systematic theology, these homilies were designed for standard doctrinal instruction, published for future reference, and clearly intended to inform the entire curriculum of evangelical studies on the "whole compass of divinity."[5]

Among the charges made against Wesley in his lifetime,[6] which he answered in detail, was the indictment by Roland Hill, who thought that Wesley remained "absolutely unsettled with regard to every fundamental doctrine of the gospel," and that "no two disputants in the Schools can be more opposite to each other than he

---

[2]The British archaic spelling *connexion* is dear to astute insiders. It is rarely in use except among traditional British Methodists. Because it appears awkward to modern readers, I will not insist on the archaic form.

[3]*LJW* 1:305, 312; 3:382; 4:125–26, 379–81; JWO 119–33, 204–6, 417; FA, B 11:175, cf. 279. See also John Cosin and Jeremy Taylor.

[4]The root word of *homily* is *homos*, the same root from which our terms *homogeneity*, *homogenize*, and *homoousian* come. A *homilios* is an assembly, and a *homilia* is an intentional, reflective, deliberate, considered instruction to gathered hearers. Since so many have a distasteful aversion to the very word *sermon*, tarred by a long history of browbeating, legalistic emotivism, I prefer the more descriptive term *teaching homily* as a contemporary dynamic equivalent. Cf. *FW* 11–14.

[5]*LJW* 4:181; 5:326.

[6]Among other complaints, Wesley was charged with contradictions, inconsistencies (B 9:56, 375), evasions (B 9:374–75), and hypocrisy (B 9:304).

is to himself."[7] Wesley wrote detailed and amusing responses to critics Roland Hill, Conyers Middleton, and George Lavington to demonstrate the consistency of his teaching over his long life. He defended himself against charges of internal incongruities and took pains to demonstrate that the supposed discrepancies that others thought they had identified were based on the eighteenth-century reader's hasty misstatement or failure to grasp his intent.[8]

Neither Wesley nor his successors ever issued an edition of his published works deliberately sequenced in the order of standard points of classic systematic theology.[9] My task is to show the systematic cohesion and range of his homilies and essays. If this task had been undertaken decades ago, Wesley might have been earlier acknowledged as a major Protestant thinker rather than as his stereotype of pragmatic organizer so characteristic of nineteenth-century interpreters.

To those who imagine that Wesley lacked a systematic mind,[10] I will show that every major point of classic Christian teaching is addressed in his instructional homilies, supplemented by his essays, journals, prefaces, and letters, with minimal lapses and incongruities.[11] Within the scope of his fifty-plus years of writing, Wesley covered virtually every pivotal issue of Christian theology, Christology, soteriology, ecclesiology, pastoral care, and ethics. It is difficult to find any major question of Christian doctrine that he grossly disregarded.

Though there is nothing in Wesley or most other Anglican sources that has the structural appearance of the ponderous dogmatic style of the seventeenth-century Lutheran or Reformed orthodox dogmatics, still no essential article of faith is left unattended, as we will see.[12]

B. Wesley's Evangelical Connection of Spiritual Formation

1. The Connection

To stand "in Wesley's connection" traditionally has meant that one looks to him

---

[7]"Some Remarks of Mr. Hill's 'Review of All the Doctrines Taught by Mr. John Wesley,'" J X:377, quoting Roland Hill.

[8]"Some Remarks of Mr. Hill's 'Review of All the Doctrines Taught by Mr. John Wesley,'" J X:381. In response to Hill, Wesley patiently refuted 101 specific arguments arranged under twenty-four headings. As an experienced former teacher of logic, he did not lack confidence that he could "unravel truth and falsehood, although artfully twisted together."

[9]With the swollen shelves of Wesley studies in history archives, it is surprising that no previous writer has attempted the task presented in this series: a plain exposition of the core arguments of his teaching, explicated text by text in his own words, with an attempt to cover his major writings.

[10]John Deschner, who has written the definitive work on Wesley's Christology, maintains that "Wesley's theology is not a settled system of doctrine, as Calvin's or Schleiermacher's theologies are. It is rather the effort of an energetic mind to organize for popular use the principal elements of a message" (WC 14). Cf. Albert C. Outler, "John Wesley: Folk-Theologian," Theology Today 34 (1977): 150–66. The most eminent interpreters of Wesley — George Croft Cell, Albert Outler, Thomas Langford, John Deschner, Richard Heitzenrater, and Donald Thorsen — are all uncomfortable with the claim that Wesley was a systematic theologian. They tend to regard it as a stretch of the imagination to view Wesley under the rubric of dogmatician or systematic theological teacher or exacting catechist. My purpose is to show that this is more plausible than usually thought.

[11]LJW 5:326.

[12]For doctrinal summaries, see JWO 183–85, 386ff.

...iritual formation. Hundreds of thousands of believers in the eighteenth and nineteenth centuries stood faithfully within this connection, some with greater or lesser distance. The entire early Methodist Movement was voluntarily and personally mentored by this remarkable pastoral guide. Wesley gave himself unreservedly to the pastoral care of thousands in countless English, Irish, Welsh, and Scottish villages, traveling incessantly to serve the interests of believers' spiritual maturation.

Many today remain obliquely in Wesley's evangelical connection or remnants of it, though more distanced by time and history. Some who remain committed to the churches resulting from his ministry are now asking how they might again be formed by his wisdom, the truth of his message, and the joyful integrity of his outlook. Others not in the Wesleyan family of evangelical churches can benefit by seeing in Wesley a godly leader of special spiritual power.

It is remarkable that persons thoroughly immersed in modern consciousness still seek to reappropriate Wesley's counsel, not only by means of his writings and sermons, but also by attending to the roots from which he drew strength — especially the patristic, Anglican, holiness, and Reformed traditions. Untold numbers of people around the globe have been personally formed by his spirit, even when unaware of it.

2. The Scope of the Wesleyan Connection Today

The family of churches Wesley's ministry spawned is vast and worldwide. It includes not only the eight-million-member United Methodist Church (larger than combined Lutheran and Episcopalian bodies in the United States) but also a conspicuous assortment of worldwide church bodies that have spun off from Methodist and holiness revival preaching.

Chief among these are the Wesleyan Church, the Free Methodist Church, the Church of the Nazarene, the Salvation Army, the African Methodist Episcopal Church, and the AME Zion Church traditions. Even more numerous worldwide are many forms of charismatic and Pentecostal communities that preach entire sanctification, assurance, and holy living. Notably, the African-Initiated Churches movement in Africa has profuse echoes of Wesley's teaching. Wesley's teaching is among the major prototypes of modern global evangelical theology. No serious account of the history of world evangelical thought could omit Wesley.

C. My Purpose

1. Why I Write on Wesley: A Note on Vocation

A personal vocational note may help some readers get in touch with my motivation for doing this study.

My vocation since 1970 has been centered on the recovery of classic Christian teaching, especially in its early phases in the patristic period. Over many years, a significant part of that vocation has been teaching candidates for ordination in this tradition. This has extended to providing scholarly resources for the larger Wesleyan family of churches, and evangelicals generally, especially those seeking to recover their vital historic roots.

This is why I write. It is not merely an incidental part of my vocation, nor disrelated to that aspect of my vocation that has focused in recent years on postmodern orthodoxy and classical consensual Christianity.[13]

In the 1980s and early 1990s, I worked steadily on a systematic theology that was grounded in classic, historic Christian teaching. That three-volume work has now been thoroughly revised in a one-volume edition titled *Classic Christianity: A Systematic Theology* (San Francisco: HarperCollins, 2009). Since 1979 I have earnestly pledged to my readers that I intend to propose nothing original as if it might be some improvement on apostolic teaching and its early exegesis.

After seventeen years of editing the *Ancient Christian Commentary on Scripture*, focused on patristic texts,[14] I turn again to the same tree of classic Christianity in its eighteenth-century evangelical form. Its modern expression is the community of faith into which I was born, baptized, and ordained. Many years after I was ordained, I was reborn into this faith.

I want to show how a particular branch of that patristic tradition, Wesleyan theology, has grown out of the same root of ancient ecumenical teaching. Wesley's eighteenth-century movement corresponds closely with classic fourth-century consensus Christian teaching. Wesley's teaching springs out of what he called, in lowercase, the catholic spirit.[15]

I see these two tasks — patristic exegesis and Wesleyan preaching — not as conflicted but as complementary. Both projects are close to the center of my vocation: the rediscovery of ancient ecumenical theology and the recovery of classical Christianity within my own evolving Wesleyan tradition.[16] This correlation has been neglected in the secondary literature. Many of Wesley's ultramodern interpreters are focused on accommodating Wesley in ways congenial to contemporary audiences. Some have entirely recast Wesley in terms of liberation theology or process theology or gender studies in a way that leaves Wesley himself only vaguely

---

[13]As one who grew up on the prairie, I have for three and a half decades been teaching in the New York area, with the dust of the Oklahoma plains still under my eyelids. Working in the shadow of the prototype international cosmopolis, I find myself located by ordination in the heart of Protestantism's second-largest denomination, teaching in one of its leading academic institutions. Inwardly this feels to me to be some sort of hidden providence beyond mere human artifice, which places on me a weighty challenge and opportunity to remain faithful not only to Wesley but also to Wesley's current organizational elites.

[14]Thomas C. Oden, ed., *Ancient Christian Commentary on Scripture*, 29 vols. (Downers Grove, IL: InterVarsity, 1993–2010).

[15]I promised my readers in my systematic theology that I would not foist off Arminian or Wesleyan or even Protestant thinking. I pledged nothing new that would pretend to override the wisdom of classic Christianity. In these volumes I continue that pledge.

[16]I do not want my readers to draw the unintended conclusion that I have abandoned my longstanding consensual patristic classical effort as I now refocus on my own Wesleyan tradition as a modern expression of ancient ecumenical teaching.

recognizable. My mission is to let him speak for himself in his own language to modern believers.

2. Clear Exposition

Two reference points are constantly correlated in what follows: the text itself and our contemporary language situation to which I believe the text still speaks.

My aim is to offer a present-day interpretation and exposition of Wesley's teaching in contemporary language, deliberately seeking to be expressly accountable to his own text.

Two worldviews are constantly linked in what follows: the text itself, written for an eighteenth-century audience, and our contemporary language situation, to which I believe the text still speaks.

If the method is inductively expository, its inherent order is instinctively systematic. My modest task is merely to arrange and explicate Wesley's texts in the prevailing classic order of the ancient Christian writers, but with the special imprint of Wesley's own priorities, colloquialisms, idioms, and predilections.[17] By "classic order" I mean the chain of theological reasoning generally found in the tradition from Irenaeus and Cyril of Jerusalem through John of Damascus and Thomas Aquinas to John Calvin and John Pearson.[18]

3. Adhering to Primary Sources

I have deliberately focused on primary sources in this study, leaving it to others, especially those with more historical than systematic interests, to pursue developmental questions concerning Wesley's theological and biographical transformations in their social contexts.[19] However intriguing the psychological, social, and historical-critical approaches may be to me, they have a track record of not yielding profound theological insights. These insights require tested methods of exegesis according to the analogy of faith, as Wesley insisted. They apply the criteria of internal coherence, unity, and continuity of apostolic and canonical testimony, and a conciliatory attitude. The hermeneutical method of this study is to work more with the intratextual theological truth of the primary text itself than with the history of its development.[20]

---

[17]There is surprisingly little repetition in Wesley when the sequence is viewed economically in this traditional order. As a writer and an editor, he was a stickler for economy of style.

[18]The expository method has not been comprehensively applied to Wesley's writings. The leading recent interpreters of Wesley — Albert Outler, Frank Baker, and Richard Heitzenrater — have wisely sought to place him in historical context. They have left open the field for simple exposition. Of those who have tried to provide a general account of Wesley's theology, see Further Reading at the end of this section.

[19]Other scholars are currently making significant inquiries into Wesley's theology, notably Randy Maddox, Kenneth Collins, Theodore Runyon, and William Abraham. They are skilled in and intent on entering into the vast arena of secondary literature on Wesley to assess its adequacy, a worthy task that I do not here attempt.

[20]Though I commend the work of colleagues who prefer to engage the secondary literature, the more I read it, the more I come to see that it has put upon itself the limitations of hyper-historicism. A

This method exists in tension to some extent with some Reformed evangelicals who, without a thorough reading of Wesley's own writings, may tend to caricature him (against his explicit wish) as Pelagian or lacking a sound doctrine of grace. Some Lutherans cannot imagine that Wesley grasped justification by grace through faith. Some Anglicans remember only one thing about Wesley, and that is that he reluctantly permitted the separation of Methodism from the Church of England. They forget the fact that he himself remained Anglican all his life and resisted precisely that separation with all his might. Most of all, Wesley's own texts resist those Wesleyans who so sentimentalize and idealize his pragmatic skills that he is not taken seriously as an independent thinker.

D. History and Doctrine

1. The Chief Mentor of Modern Wesley Studies

These volumes stand in a singular relation of appreciation to the work of my incomparable mentor Albert C. Outler — complementary, sympathetic, and grateful. I have spent most of my professional life as a systematic theologian with avid interests in early Christianity. Outler spent his as a historical theologian with avid interests in ecumenical teaching, ancient and modern. My method is primarily systematic; Outler's was primarily historical. These are complementary methods.

The theological method underlying this study weighs in more heavily on divine revelation as a premise of a wholesome historical inquiry, since the meaning of universal history is the overarching subject of the discipline of theology. Outler's method has weighed in more heavily on historical inquiry without neglecting theological implications. This is why I remain grateful for Outler's enormous contribution but still remain less bound to critical historical methods that commonly have a constricted view of evidence. In all my writings since the 1970s, I have sought to expand the range of evidence to include "revelation as history" (Pannenberg). This is a method that is consistent with Wesley's teachings, although I did not fully grasp it until reading Cyril the Great.

The following attempt seeks to order Wesley's thought cohesively, comprehensively, and systematically. This is a task that my beloved teacher Albert Outler never aspired to do, and in fact may have looked upon somewhat disdainfully.

Outler's vocation was to provide an exhaustive placement of Wesley in his historical context, showing his sources and accurately describing his thought in its historical-autobiographical development, which he did in an exemplary way. My modest attempt stands on his shoulders. It presupposes his work and the work of other historians in this recent period that he described as the "Third Phase" of Wesley studies, a phase whose methods have been dominated by historians, who,

---

complementary emphasis is now needed: empathic exposition of theological themes in Wesley draws directly from his own texts rather than from contemporary historians. Here the focus is deliberately on the primary texts themselves.

though brilliant, have not wished to enter into the plausibility of Wesley's exposition of the plain sense of sacred Scripture.[21]

2. Whether Wesley Was a Systematic Theologian

I have never aspired to being a historian in the sense that Élie Halévy, V. H. H. Green, and Richard Heitzenrater are primarily historians. I am unapologetically an orthodox scholar with respect to classic texts, with lifelong interests in historical wisdom. I work unashamedly according to the methods of classic Christian exegesis, which form the foundation of all that we today call a theology of revelation.[22] If historians sometimes assume that such a task is implausible or even impossible, my purpose is to show its viability in a particular arena: Wesley's teaching.[23] Albert Outler made Wesley accessible to Wesleyans as a folk theologian. I seek to make Wesley accessible to non-Wesleyans as a wise teacher of classic Christianity.

Without denying or ignoring the intriguing question of how Wesley's theology developed and changed over time, my question is fashioned differently: To what degree, if any, does the gist of the whole of Wesley's theological contribution admit of consistent cohesion, with viable, organic conception and design?[24]

Those who begin by insisting that the percentage is zero will have to be convinced by the Wesley texts themselves. If the percentage is anything above zero, then the burden of proof rests on the expositor to show textually that there indeed is in the primary text a solid core of cohesive teaching.[25] That is my assignment.

---

[21]I am restless both with those historians who cannot take Wesley seriously as a theologian and with those theologians who refuse to see Wesley in his historical-intellectual context.

[22]If some may misinterpret my intent as claiming too much for Wesley as systematician, let me refine the point more modestly: Wesley was an evangelical preacher whose intellectual temperament exhibited a steady concern for cohesion and consistency grounded in a wide database. On this score, I think Wesley is not so overtly systematic as Aquinas or Calvin or Barth, but more so than Luther or Newman, and equally so with Cranmer and Edwards.

[23]The method of this study resists a strong tendency among some recent historians to restrict historical knowledge to scientific and empirical evidences in a way that dismisses all talk of revelation. Wesley was tutored by Oxford historians who did not narrow historical evidences in this way. Some historians today are prone to caricature orthodox Christian teachers as always prematurely jumping to conclusions, overleaping piles of evidence, missing developmental complexities, and overlooking contextual influences. Orthodox Christian teachers have a wider database than do modern historians, since they do not narrow historical knowledge to empirical and scientific models of knowing. Modern historians are often fixated on picking up ephemeral pieces of evidence but never grasping the larger picture, always too hesitant to make judgments about how the changing views of a person cohere through their mutations. Some are fixated on the specifics of the context so much that the wisdom that motivated them to take a historical figure seriously has become diffused. In Wesley studies I admire the excellent work of rigorous historians such as Albert Outler, Frank Baker, Richard Heitzenrater, Alan K. Walz, and my esteemed colleagues at Drew University — Kenneth E. Rowe and Charles Yrigoyen. I think their splendid work still yearns for a larger presentation of evidence that can be based only on the premises most dear to Wesley: divine revelation and the authority of apostolic teaching for understanding universal history.

[24]The most systematically ignored aspect of the secondary literature on Wesley's teaching is the triune frame of his theology, embracing his ordering of discipline, sacrament, pastoral practice, and moral reasoning. In the section on the Trinity in this volume (pp. 56 – 64), I will show how important this was to him, and how triune reasoning is saturated throughout the entire enterprise, in his doctrines of God the Creator, God the Son, and God the Holy Spirit.

[25]Focal questions to be pursued are the following: Does Wesley's teaching illumine the evangelical

Wesley has been prematurely dismissed as unsystematic on the ground that his writings were largely occasional and not ordered in a methodical, systematic manner.[26] My objective is to show that all of his occasional writings indeed had a cohesive and implicitly systematic core. That core is textually available to anyone who cares to examine it fairly.

Wesley is a special sort of systematic theologian — his interrelated reflections emerge directly out of his wide range of active pastoral relationships. This is especially noticeable in his letters, where pastoral and moral advice and spiritual admonition abound yet integrate into a connected pattern of deliberate reflection. Readers who look for a systematic theologian strongly grounded in pastoral care will find it more in Wesley than in Friedrich Schleiermacher or Karl Barth, who ostensibly might otherwise appear to be more systematic. The remainder of this series, in fact, will be devoted to the *pastoral* and *moral* aspects of Wesley's teaching.

One further whimsical note: though Wesley is often imagined to be unduly sober and humorless, I have found many engaging passages where he radiates brilliant sparks of wit and comic perception. Rather than merge them into a separate section on humor, I have decided to let them lie quietly in the text, awaiting the reader's unanticipated discovery. There is no other motive greater in my mind than proactively sharing with readers the steady joy I have found in reading Wesley, which centers in taking pleasure in the good news of God's own coming.

3. How to Make Practical Use of This Study

It is customary in a preface to sketch the ways in which the work has practical utility or moral relevance. This series, for example, may be practically used for devotional reading, for moral reflection, or even for topical sermon preparation. Even more so, it will serve as a reference work for identifying the range of Wesley's ideas and opinions. The indexes and Further Reading sections will be the guide to the reader who is particularly interested in a topic, whether on ecological recovery, moral relativism, enthusiasm, catholicity, experience, paradise, final justification, providence, or any of countless other topics. These may intrigue the curious, inspire the devout, or give courage to those weary in well doing.

Wesley's teaching awaits being fruitfully applied to numerous pressing issues of contemporary society, such as addictive behaviors, poverty, and punk nihilism.

---

pastoral task today? How fully developed are his doctrines of creation, providence, the triune God, theological method, sin and grace, justification and sanctification, Word and sacraments, and eschatology? It is commonly acknowledged that Wesley gave explicit attention to selected areas of theology such as soteriology and ecclesiology, and the work of the Holy Spirit, but to what extent did Wesley attend sufficiently to the wider range of theological questions so as to be rightly regarded as a reliable guide to Christian doctrine as a whole? Is it possible to sort out Wesley's essays, sermons, and occasional writings in terms of the categories of classical doctrines of systematic theology and survey them generally in a brief scope?

[26]It need not count against the cohesive thought of a writer that he is capable of occasional writings in which specific challenges are answered, provided those occasional writings are consistent with the larger literary whole. The attempts to explain this cohesion through various theories of Wesley's development have often resulted in an unnecessary fragmentation of that wholeness.

Instead, I prefer to alert readers to what is most likely to be enjoyed from these pages: Wesley's good sense, practical wisdom, and nonspeculative earthy realism.

Further Reading on Wesley's Theology

Overviews of Wesley's Theology

Baker, Frank. "The Doctrines in the Discipline." In *From Wesley to Asbury: Studies in Early American Methodism*, 162–82. Durham, NC: Duke University Press, 1976.

Burwash, Nathaniel. *Wesley's Doctrinal Standards*. Introduction. Toronto: William Briggs, 1881; reprint, Salem, OH: Schmul, 1967.

Campbell, Ted A. *Methodist Doctrine: The Essentials*. Nashville: Abingdon, 1999.

Cannon, William R. *Theology of John Wesley: With Special Reference to the Doctrine of Justification*. New York: Abingdon, 1946.

Cell, George C. *The Rediscovery of John Wesley*. New York: Henry Holt, 1935.

Coke, Thomas, and Francis Asbury. *The Doctrines and Discipline of the Methodist Episcopal Church in America*. Philadelphia: Henry Tuckniss, 1798.

Collins, Kenneth J. *A Faithful Witness: John Wesley's Homiletical Theology*. Wilmore, KY: Wesleyan Heritage, 1993.

———. *The Theology of John Wesley: Holy Love and the Shape of Grace*. Nashville: Abingdon, 2007.

———. *Wesley on Salvation*. Grand Rapids: Zondervan, 1989.

Harper, Steve. *John Wesley's Message for Today*. Grand Rapids: Zondervan, 1983.

Lee, Umphrey. *John Wesley and Modern Religion*. Nashville: Cokesbury, 1936.

Mickey, Paul. *Essentials of Wesleyan Theology*. Grand Rapids: Zondervan, 1980.

Norwood, Frederick A. "Roots and Structure of Wesley's Theology." In *The Story of American Methodism*, chap. 3. Nashville: Abingdon, 1974.

Outler, Albert C. "John Wesley as Theologian: Then and Now." *MH* 12, no. 4 (1974): 64–82.

———. "Toward a Reappraisal of John Wesley as Theologian." *Perkins School of Theology Journal* 14, no. 2 (1961): 5–14.

———, ed. *John Wesley*. Introduction, 3–33. Library of Protestant Theology. New York: Oxford University Press, 1964.

Pope, William Burt. *A Compendium of Christian Theology*. 3 vols. London: Wesleyan Methodist Book-Room, 1880.

Ralston, Thomas N. *Elements of Divinity*. New York: Abingdon, 1924.

Slaatte, Howard A. *Fire in the Brand: Introduction to the Creative Work and Theology of John Wesley*. New York: Exposition, 1963.

Sugden, Edward H. *Wesley's Standard Sermons*. London: Epworth, 1921; 3rd ed., 1951. See introduction and annotations.

Summers, Thomas O. *Systematic Theology*. 2 vols. Edited by J. J. Tigert. Nashville: Methodist Publishing House South, 1888.

Watson, Philip. *The Message of the Wesleys.* New York: Macmillan, 1964.

Watson, Richard. *Theological Institutes.* 2 vols. New York: Mason and Lane, 1836, 1840; edited by John M'Clintock, New York: Carlton & Porter, 1850.

Williams, Colin W. *John Wesley's Theology Today.* Nashville: Abingdon, 1960.

Systematic Theologies Largely Based on Wesley's Theology

Banks, John S. *A Manual of Christian Doctrine.* 1st American edition. Edited by J. J. Tigert. Nashville: Lamar & Barton, 1924.

Binney, Amos, with Daniel Steele. *Theological Compend Improved.* New York: Phillips and Hunt, 1875.

Burwash, Nathaniel. *Manual of Christian Theology.* 2 vols. London: Horace Marshall, 1900.

Gamertsfelder, S. *Systematic Theology.* Harrisburg, PA: Evangelical Publishing House, 1952.

Merrill, Stephen M. *Aspects of Christian Experience.* New York: Methodist Book Concern, 1862.

Miley, John. *Systematic Theology.* Reprint, Peabody, MA: Hendrickson, 1989.

Miner, Raymond. *Systematic Theology.* 2 vols. Cincinnati: Hitchcock and Walden, 1877–79.

Outler, Albert C. *Theology in the Wesleyan Spirit.* Nashville: Tidings, 1975.

Pope, William Burt. *A Compendium of Christian Theology.* 3 vols. London: Wesleyan Methodist Book-Room, 1880.

Ralston, Thomas N. *Elements of Divinity.* New York: Abingdon, 1924.

Summers, Thomas O. *Systematic Theology.* 2 vols. Edited by J. J. Tigert. Nashville: Methodist Publishing House South, 1888.

Tillett, Wilbur. *Personal Salvation.* Nashville: Barbee and Smith, 1902.

Watson, Richard. *Theological Institutes.* 2 vols. New York: Mason and Lane, 1836, 1840; edited by John M'Clintock, New York: Carlton & Porter, 1850.

Weaver, Jonathan. *Christian Theology.* Dayton, OH: United Brethren Publishing House, 1900.

Wynkoop, Mildred Bangs. *Foundations of Wesleyan-Arminian Theology.* Kansas City, MO: Beacon Hill, 1967.

The Relation of Wesley's Theology to His Biography

Clarke, Adam. *Memoirs of the Wesley Family.* London: J. & T. Clarke, 1823.

Coke, Thomas, and Henry Moore. *The Life of the Rev. John Wesley, A.M.* London: G. Paramore, 1792.

Gambold, John. "The Character of Mr. John Wesley." *MM* 21 (1798).

Green, Vivian H. H. *The Young Mr. Wesley.* London: Edward Arnold, 1961.

Heitzenrater, Richard P. *The Elusive Mr. Wesley.* 2 vols. Nashville: Abingdon, 1984.

———. *Mirror and Memory: Reflections on Early Methodism.* Nashville: Abingdon, 1989.

Schmidt, Martin. *John Wesley: A Theological Biography.* 2 vols. in 3. Nashville: Abingdon, 1963–73.

Tuttle, Robert. *John Wesley: His Life and Theology.* Grand Rapids: Zondervan, 1978.

Tyerman, Luke. *The Life and Times of the Rev. John Wesley.* 3 vols. New York: Harper, 1872.

Bibliographical Resources

Baker, Frank, comp. *A Union Catalogue of the Publications of John and Charles Wesley.* Durham, NC: Duke University Press, 1966.

————. "Unfolding John Wesley: A Survey of Twenty Years' Study in Wesley's Thought." *QR* 1, no. 1 (1980).

Bassett, Paul M. "Finding the Real John Wesley." *Christianity Today* 28, no. 16 (1984).

Green, Richard. *The Works of John and Charles Wesley: A Bibliography.* 2nd ed. New York: AMS, 1906.

Jarboe, Betty M. *John and Charles Wesley: A Bibliography.* Metuchen, NJ: Scarecrow, 1987.

Jones, Arthur E. *A Union Checklist of Editions of the Publications of John and Charles Wesley: Based upon the "Works of John and Charles Wesley: A Bibliography" by Richard Green (1906).* Madison, NJ: Drew University, 1960.

Rowe, Kenneth E. *Methodist Union Catalogue.* Metuchen, NJ: Scarecrow, 1975 – .

Humor in Wesley

Crawford, Robert C. "John Wesley's Humour." *WMM* 157 (1934): 313 – 15.

Foster, Henry J. "Wesley's Humour." *WMM* 126 (1903): 446 – 49.

Page, W. Scott. "Wesley and the Sense of Humour." *MR* (1906): 13.

Perkins, J. P. "The Humour of John Wesley." *WMM* 143 (1920): 697 – 98.

VOLUME ONE

GOD AND PROVIDENCE

JOHN WESLEY'S
TEACHINGS

CHAPTER 1

God

In a series of homilies from his mature years, Wesley entered into a meticulous, detailed consideration of the divine attributes, especially the eternity, omnipresence, and unity of God. Though sparse, these homilies convey sufficient argument to indicate the main lines of Wesley's doctrine of God.

A. Attributes of God

The ancient Christian writers and the earliest ecumenical councils formed the foundation for the Anglican evangelicalism that Wesley affirmed. He was also very close to classic Protestant sources — Luther and Augsburg, Calvin and the Heidelberg Confession — regarding the knowledge and attributes of God.

Wesley summarized key points of the doctrine of God he had received in his renowned "Letter to a Roman Catholic": "As I am assured that there is an infinite and independent Being and that it is impossible there should be more than one, so I believe that this one God is the Father of all things," especially of self-determining rational creatures, and that this one "is in a peculiar manner the Father of those whom he regenerates by his Spirit, whom he adopts in his Son as coheirs with him."[1] The eternity of God received more explicit treatment in Homily #54, "On Eternity."

1. The Eternity of God

a. Eternity Past and Future

The text of the homily "On Eternity" is Psalm 90:2: "From everlasting to everlasting, thou art God" [Homily #54 (1789), B 2:358 – 72; J #54, VI:189 – 98].

As immensity is boundless space, so eternity is "boundless duration."[2] As omnipresence refers to God's relation to space, as present in every location, eternity refers to God's sovereign relation to time. God is intimately present in every moment.

There was no time when God was not. There will be no time when God will not be.[3] If eternity is from everlasting to everlasting, it can be thought of as

---

[1]"A Letter to a Roman Catholic," JWO 494.
[2]"On Eternity," B 2:358, sec. 1.
[3]"On Eternity," B 2:359, J VI:189 – 98, sec. 3; JWO 455.

distinguishable in two directions: (1) *Eternity past* is that duration that reaches *from everlasting*, eternity before creation, time viewed as before, the eternity that precedes this now and all past nows, which Wesley calls *a parte ante*. (2) *Eternity yet to come* is the duration that reaches *to everlasting*, which will have no end, the whole of time after now, everything eternally on the future side of now (*a parte post*).[4]

Time viewed synoptically is a "fragment of eternity broken off at both ends."[5] The eternity of God embraces and surrounds time. Time is that portion of duration that begins when the world begins and ends when the world comes to its final days. We do not see all of time, but only a momentary glimpse, which we call the present.[6]

b. Eternity as Decision Now

The faithful stand before God in a way that keeps them in the presence of eternity. When faith receives God as the Lord of time, everything is changed, all relationships are reshaped, all are reborn, all things become new. Social and ethical responsibility come from that change of heart of each person one by one, in due time affecting the flow of the political order and economic life. Only the renewed, whole person who is serious about eternity is rightly prepared to work effectively to make a better society.

Wesley offered a practical way of thinking personally about the eternity of God by placing his hearer imaginatively on the brink of a here-and-now decision: *think of yourself as deciding now for or against eternal life*. Each hearer is invited to enter now into an unending relationship with the Eternal by choosing a happy eternity, a life of eternal blessedness, or the misery of missing what is eternally good and worthy of worship. This is the choice being offered in the emerging reign of God. This decision is being made implicitly every temporal moment. It is hidden tacitly in every single human experience of time.

This continuing act of choosing has vast consequences for human happiness. It is no exaggeration to view human existence as deciding every moment toward the joy of eternal life or the despair of eternal emptiness.[7] Only when we think of ourselves as standing on the edge of either a happy or a pitiable eternity does present life become meaningful and serious. "The Creator bids thee now stretch out thy hand either to the one or to the other."[8]

Even if we doubt this, we can test the hypothesis that our personal lives will continue beyond bodily death in eternity. We all have a high stake in our relation to our eternal future. This premise alone has the latent power of transforming human actions.

---

[4]"On Eternity," B 2:362, J VI:189–98, sec. 7; cf. "The Unity of the Divine Being," 4:60, proem.

[5]"On Eternity," B 2:360, J VI:189–98, sec. 3; "On Predestination," B 3:416–17, sec. 5; Augustine, *Confessions* 11–12.

[6]"The Imperfection of Human Knowledge," B 2:570, J VI:339, sec. 1.3.

[7]"Human Life a Dream," B 4:108–19; J VII:318–25.

[8]"On Eternity," B 2:368–71, secs. 17–19.

2. Time

a. The Fleet Flow of Time

Every moment of time has the fleeting character of beginning and ending. That is what characterizes it as time.[9] It is not a sad thought that time, which had a finite beginning in God and which has a fleeting present, will have a consummate ending in God. The faithful know that the Sovereign over time is in process of duly completing and fittingly refinishing the good but fallen creation. Nothing that happens within the distortions of history has power to undo God's long-range eternal purpose within time.[10]

It is evident that we experience our living souls only as embodied within space. Similarly, we experience eternity only from within the crunch of time. This is why we who are so enmeshed in time and its demands are so permeated with finitude. We have great difficulty in grasping the very concept of eternity because of this condition of being so wrapped up in time. Our human awareness, as creatures of fleeting time, can form only a veiled idea of eternity, and that only by fragile analogies. As God is immense beyond any conceivable finite immensity, so eternity is infinite beyond any imaginable duration of time.[11]

Time remains for temporal minds an ever-flowing mystery. There is no nontemporal moment or place for the finite mind to step away, as if to depart from time, to think trans-temporally about time, as if we had a point outside time to perceive time. Time is an uncommon mystery. It is difficult to wrap our minds around precisely because we are creatures lodged in time. It is right here in time that we are called to understand ourselves within the frame of reference of eternity, living life in this world as if accountable to the giver of time.[12]

b. God in the Now

What divides past and future is now, the infinitely fleeting moment that can never be possessed as a fixed entity. We can never capture or hold a moment except in the tenuous form of memory. This is why temporal life is rightly compared to a dream.[13]

What we call "now" keeps on vanishing, eluding our grasp, changing its face. Yet the present is the only position from which anyone can ever know or see the world, through the tiny keyhole of this constantly disappearing moment we call "now." This fleeting present lies "between two eternities."[14] The moment we say "now," we have already lost the now in which we just said "now." We have this little splinter of ongoing time, which itself is a continuing refraction of the eternal.[15]

---

[9]B 2:360.

[10]B 2:358 – 70, 420 – 24; 3:196 – 97.

[11]"On Eternity," B 2:360, secs. 4 – 5.

[12]"On Eternity," B 2:360 – 61, secs. 4 – 6.

[13]"Human Life a Dream," B 4:109 – 14, secs. 1 – 9.

[14]"On Eternity," B 2:360, sec. 4.

[15]The Platonic idea that time is the unfolding expression of eternity is taken captive by Christ in the incarnation. It is a powerful idea, in Wesley's view, that what we are experiencing right now is precisely *eternity entering time*, as seen by biblical revelation in the nativity of the Son.

God meets us in time, but as the incomparable Creator of time, God is not bound by time. Only one who is simultaneously present with every moment of time can fully know the future and past reaches of eternity.[16] That one we call God.

c. Knowing Time from within Time

God is radically different from creatures in that God inhabits all eternity, whereas creatures inhabit fleeting successive temporal moments held together by memory and imagination.

Since God has a present relation to all past and future moments, God can know time in a far larger way than our knowing. The whole of time is beyond our knowing.

God's complete memory and foreknowledge of time do not coercively predetermine events to come or arbitrarily undo events that have occurred.[17] God's relation to the future and past is entirely different from ours.

Time-drenched minds have limited access through *memory* to their personal past and to their future through *imagination*. Meanwhile, the eternal God is always already present to the past. God embraces the entirety of all times.

Harder to conceive is the premise that God is present to all future moments, a premise essential to the Christian teaching of the eternal God — that God already knows the future because he is eternally present to all moments. "Strictly speaking, there is no 'fore'knowledge, no more than 'after'knowledge with God: but all things are known to Him as present from eternity to eternity."[18]

This does not mean that God determines the future so as to ignore or arbitrarily overrule human freedom. Divine foreknowledge does not imply predetermination. It simply means that God knows what outcomes the freedom of creatures will bring, because he dwells in the future. The omniscient God knows how the free choices of creatures will interplay with incalculable contingencies, because he has accompanied every step of every hypothetical choice. God has become paradoxically revealed in history as having already secured final outcomes that are still in process of unfolding in the decisions of free creatures in time.[19] Nothing is taken away from the reality of human choice by the fact that God dwells in the future as well as the now.

d. Whether Spiritual Creatures Have a Beginning in Time

The human soul (*psuche, anima*) is the living aspect of human existence in time. Through conception and birth we are entrusted with soul, which is to say a life, an enlivening of flesh. The soul is generated in sexual procreation as a gift of God. Once given, *psuche* continues to exist beyond death as a relation with the eternal Life-giver. Jewish and Christian Scriptures promise that the soul will be reunited with the body in the resurrection on the last day. The soul is created and hence is

---

[16]"On Eternity," B 2:366 – 70, secs. 14 – 18.
[17]"On Eternity," B 2:359, sec. 3.
[18]*ENNT* on 1 Peter 1:2; "On Predestination," B 2:420, sec. 15.
[19]"On Eternity," B 2:360f., secs. 4 – 5.

not eternal in time past; but having been created, it does not finally come to nothing in death.

A corpse is a body without life — that is, no soul resides in the body. Death is defined as the separation of life (that which God breathes into the body) from the body. When the motion of the body ceases, its cardiovascular movement and breathing cease. The life or soul breathed into the body by God leaves the body but thereby does not simply end; it awaits a final reckoning. That end-time event is called the general resurrection. What happens at the end of history is the mystery of bodily resurrection in a glorified body that transcends simple physicality and yet is a resurrection of the same body. Death does not end the life of the soul or even finally of the body, since in the resurrection, body and soul are reunited.[20]

e. Whether Material Creation Is Eternal

Matter is not eternal, since matter is created. Yet matter once created will not be annihilated but will finally be transformed so as to mirror once again the beauty and goodness of the original creation. Once God makes matter, he permits it to continually change, but not so as to be exterminated. The Almighty has sufficient power, of course, to annihilate atoms, but no reason to do so.[21]

Wesley argued for the durability of atomic matter through whatever cosmic changes occur. Though creatures may lose their present form, every subparticle of every atom endures, even while being transmuted, under one form or other, to the fulfillment of time in eternity. Even diamonds, the hardest of physical substances, may under extreme heat be turned to dust, yet as dust they continue.[22]

No creature shares with God the attribute of eternal aseity. This means that God's being is necessary being. It exists without beginning. "Yet there is no absurdity in supposing that all creatures are eternal *a parte post*. All matter indeed is continually changing ... but that it is changeable does in nowise imply that it is perishable. The substance may remain one and the same, though under innumerable different forms."[23]

The promised new creation implies not the eradication of the old but its transformation. What is promised is a new heaven and new earth where nothing has been destroyed, a full renovation without annihilation. It "will melt" but "*not perish*."[24] As matter changes in form but with its substance remaining through different forms, so in the case of the soul does life remain after death, yet in a different spiritual form.[25]

f. How Faith Transforms the Temporal World

The remedy for human despair over ever-passing time is faith. That means

---

[20]"On Eternity," B 2:361, sec. 6.
[21]"On Eternity," B 2:362, sec. 7.
[22]Ibid.
[23]"On Eternity," B 2:360, sec. 7.
[24]"On Eternity," B 2:361, sec. 7, italics added.
[25]"On Eternity," B 2:361–63, sec. 7.

coming by grace to trust in the trustability of the Eternal One who gives life. Whether the soul is eternally happy or self-alienated hinges on whether a person trusts in the trustworthiness of God who comes before and after all things.

Faith walks continually in the awareness of the unseen Eternal One, meditating daily on that one who does not pass, who puts all things temporal in fitting proportion and perspective.[26]

God presides over every individual life as patiently as over the whole universe. Each of us has a short time to live in a bodily sense, perhaps a few decades at most, perhaps no time at all, since even the young and healthy are vulnerable to accident and illness. But no one, however vulnerable, is deprived of some level of recognition that time is coming and going. The decisive frame of reference in which to understand our own brief lives is eternity, a thought both sobering and exhilarating.[27]

g. How Faith Requires Decision

This vision of eternity calls each hearer to a here-and-now choice with eternal consequences.[28] Rather than offering a speculative theory of eternity, Wesley asked his hearers personally and earnestly, if your life is indeed cast within time, which stands always in relation to the eternal, what are you choosing to do with it? Eternity places a decisive challenge before our lives, calls us to a specific decision: a relation of eternal happiness with the eternal Life-giver, or a relation of eternal misery in turning away from that eternal happiness. We are rational creatures and have the power to choose. How we live out our lives in this sphere is decisive for eternity.[29]

Evangelical preaching leads to a single point: each of us is now making a decision about eternity. Now is the time to place our time in relation to eternity. The gospel provides a way. Now, after all, is the only moment we concretely experience. There is a great difference between the soul that lives forever happily glorifying God, even amid the loss of creaturely goods, and the soul that mourns forever the loss of creaturely goods and resents the Giver for those losses.[30]

No one becomes eternally happy or miserable except by his or her own choice.[31] Grace provides choice with constant options to move toward the truth. There is no pretemporal divine decree that condemns us to unhappiness or determines us absolutely to happiness so as to circumvent human freedom.

Those who participate by faith in the eternal life of God through the Son are taken up into a blessed eternity. If the "happy life" is to share in the creative willing and working of God in history, the miserable life is its opposite, separated from God's own life, alienated from it entirely. When we choose temporal values over the Creator, the Source and End of all finite values, then our lives become miserable

---

[26]"On Eternity," B 2:368 – 72, sec. 17.

[27]"On Eternity," B 2:368 – 71, secs. 17 – 19.

[28]B 1:549; 2:286, 296 – 97; 4:327, 402.

[29]"On Redeeming the Time," B 3:322 – 32; cf. Charles Wesley, "Awake, Thou That Sleepest," B 1:142 – 58.

[30]"On Eternity," B 2:368 – 72, secs. 17 – 20.

[31]"On Eternity," B 2:372, sec. 20.

because they are ill-timed, out of proper focus, off target. In consequence of the primitive fall of humanity, this off-centeredness has become our pervasive condition and will remain our human condition till nature is changed by grace.[32]

Closely parallel with the eternity of God is the omnipresence of God, which Wesley took up in Homily #118.

3. The Omnipresence of God

The text of "On the Omnipresence of God" is Jeremiah 23:24: "Do not I fill heaven and earth?" [Homily #118 (1788), B 4:39–47; J #118, VII:238–44].

Finite minds are incapable of fully grasping God's omnipresence, because the knower remains finitely localized in each and every perception.

a. Whether God Is Present Everywhere

Even when fleeing from God, we find ourselves meeting the one from whom we flee (Ps. 139). "There is no point of space, whether within or without the bounds of creation, where God is not."[33] Wesley challenged deistic rationalists who argued that God first created then abandoned the world to its own devices, leaving the Creator functionally absent from the world.

God's holiness addresses and pervades the whole of creation — spiritual and physical: "'Do not I fill heaven and earth?' declares the LORD" (Jer. 23:24 NIV). Both the unseen world of the spirit and the seen world of physical creation are penetrated by God's eternal presence. As Jonah discovered, there is no place to hide from the presence of the one who creates and sustains all spatial locations.[34] The faithful celebrate the abode of God as both transcending and embracing all time and space.[35]

Take a grain of sand in your hand. Compare its magnitude not just with a sand dune but with the whole of space. Compared to the boundlessness of God, this world of space stands in the same relation as the millionth part of a grain of sand stands to known space. Yet even with such immensity, the cosmos remains measurable and bounded. All its physical expressions are finite, hence next to nothing in relation to the infinite.[36] Time and space are transcended by the boundlessness of God.

The Giver and Measurer of space cannot be measured by spatial quantities. However one might imagine the cosmic immensity, God is present at every discrete point, from the smallest speck, the tiniest sparrow, every niche of time and space, to the uttermost parts of the seas and heavens, and unknown galaxies.[37]

b. Whether There Are Other Universes

Are other universes possible? Whether space is filled with matter, we do not

---

[32]"On Eternity," B 2:368–72, secs. 17–20.
[33]"On the Omnipresence of God," B 4:42, sec. 1.1.
[34]"On the Omnipresence of God," B 4:42, sec. 1.1; 4:39–47; J VII:238–44.
[35]*LJW* 5:300; B 1:123–24; 2:502, 538–39, 569–70; 4:39–50.
[36]"On the Omnipresence of God," B 4:42, secs. 1.2, 3; cf. quotation from Cyprian in "What Is Man?" Ps. 8:3–4, B 3:458, sec. 2.3.
[37]"The Imperfection of Human Knowledge," B 2:570, J VI:338, sec. 1.2.

know empirically, but we can know by the analogy of faith that whatever space exists is forever accompanied by God the Creator, "who fills everything in every way" (Eph. 1:23 NIV).

Suppose we imagine a space beyond knowable spaces. Wesley toyed with the fantasy as to whether some hypothesized "space beyond space" might be conceived. Suppose we could imagine the entire extent of the cosmos — would there then be any space outside the cosmos? If there is, that too would be bounded by the boundlessness of God, for God as singular Creator transcends all conceivable worlds.

Even if we posit myriad other creations about which we know nothing, the same reasoning applies. The one God is present to all possible creations imaginable. God is not merely the Creator of the universe we see, but of all that can be conceived. Otherwise, God would not be that necessary one than which no greater being can be conceived. No created order is conceivable without positing a creator. There is no cosmic design without a designer.[38]

The omnipresent God is as attentive to and enabling of the tiniest atomic element, as of the whole cosmos, sustaining each and governing all, influencing the aggregate noncoercively without destroying the free will of rational creatures. When God gives humans freedom, it is not an abandonment to the coercive forces of nature. It is not a deceit that only pretends to but does not offer viable self-determining freedom.[39]

c. Whether God Can Be Conceived as without the World

To posit a world without God is to posit nothing, for there cannot be an effect without a cause.

The world minus God adds up entirely to nothing. God minus the world remains completely God. Nothing has been subtracted from God by the absence of a particular world. God's existence is not dependent on the world's existence; otherwise, some creature would become bizarrely necessary to the Creator.[40]

Suppose we fantasize the premise that only God exists and not any world. That of course is a dream that could only be dreamed by a free personal agent living in an actual world. So that idea is intrinsically absurd. We can entertain such fantasies only because a tangible world has indeed been created. But even granting such a fantastic premise, God would remain the incomparable Creator still able to choose to create or not create any such conceivable world, which would remain dependent in every moment of time and space on the sustaining power of the Creator.[41]

This radically distinguishes the Judeo-Christian naming of God from all pantheisms. All pantheistic views presume a source of being continuous with or inseparable from the world or reducible to the world itself. The result is the irrationality that God is the world. If God is the world, then the accompanying illusion is that the

---

[38]"On the Omnipresence of God," B 4:42–43, sec. 2.
[39]"On the Omnipresence of God," B 4:42–44, sec. 2.
[40]"On the Omnipresence of God," B 4:43–44, sec. 2; J VII:238–44.
[41]"On the Omnipresence of God," B 4:44; cf. 2:13.

world is viewed as God's body. This is not merely a conceptual error but a profound sin of the mind that at root is a distorted act of idolatrous willing.[42] All notions of the self-sufficiency of matter or of the oozing or emanating of matter from God are notions foreign to the Hebrew Bible and the New Testament. All conceivable reductions of God to creaturely being, whether by skeptical naturalism or animistic nativism or earth-mother vitalism or philosophical pantheism, are sharply repudiated.[43]

Some cannot imagine God without a world. They insist that since God's overflowing love is by some external necessity bound to be creative, God cannot be conceived except in relation to a creation. Wesley answered that a supposed "creator" who from the outset remains dependent upon the world thus "created" (so to speak) is not the Creator attested in Scripture who created "heaven and earth" — the creedal way of pointing synoptically to all that has been created. "Where no creature is, still God is there. The presence or absence of any or all creatures makes no difference with regard to him."[44] It is this precise point that put Wesley in tension with some views that later would be called process theology. Those who view the world as the body of God cannot find a precedent in Wesley. Those who wish to exalt nature by viewing it as identical with God rather than creature, or who bind the world and God intrinsically together according to the analogy of body and mind, find few affinities with Wesley's firm tenet of divine omnipresence.[45]

d. Whether God Can Be Almighty without Being Omnipresent

To imagine any space entirely beyond God's influence is to deny the witness of Scripture and creed to "God the Father Almighty." To confess "God Almighty" is to acknowledge at the same time the omnipresence of God.[46] There can be no serious affirmation of unsurpassable divine power that does not at the same time imply that God is pervasively present in the world. No human actor can act where the actor is not present.[47] No unsurpassable competent being will be found acting unless that being is present. Hence the intrinsic relation of omnipotence with omnipresence. One cannot be imagined without the other.

Some empiricists may attempt to look at God as an object, as if analogous to chemical components or biological structures. But God does not yield to flat measurable observation, because God is spirit, transcending materiality and natural causality. The study of creation is not a mode of inquiry in which facts can be established in the same way that empirical conclusions can be drawn by using scientific method substantiated through experimentation with repeatable physical measurements.

Those who behold God do so with spiritual senses. The Creator gives rational

---

[42]Letter to William Law, January 6, 1756, *LJW* 3:343–45.

[43]Ibid., *LJW* 3:332–42.

[44]"On the Omnipresence of God," B 4:43, J VII:240–41, sec. 2.3.

[45]"On the Omnipresence of God," B 4:42–45, sec. 2.

[46]*LJW* 3:343–44; 5:365; 8:153; B 1:589; 2:540–41; 4:320–21.

[47]"The Unity of the Divine Being," B 4:61–62, secs. 3–4; *LJW* 6:49.

creatures not only our familiar physical senses[48] but also by providence through the means of grace a spiritual sensibility, a capacity to receive his self-disclosure. This sensibility grows through prayer, sacrament, sacrificial service, the reading of Scripture, and spiritual discipline.[49]

e. Moral Consequences of Divine Omnipresence

No one can speak rightly of the attributes of God while ignoring their moral implications. The teaching of divine omnipresence has powerful consequences for interpersonal relationships. It shapes our dealings with others. The very thought of God's omnipresence calls us to moral attentiveness to what we are currently saying and feeling. It is as if we are being held up immediately before the all-seeing, all-knowing God who fills even secret spaces.

If we live out our lives daily in the presence of God, that presence impinges powerfully on each here-and-now moral choice. The serious beholder of space, whether in macrocosm or microcosm, acknowledges with awe that God meets us in every meeting, each moment, each twinkling of the eye, every millimeter of space. God is with us.[50] Emmanuel, the Song of the incarnation, is the grand historical Illuminator of the blunter rational idea of omnipresence.

The very idea of the omnipresence of God draws each beholder toward a lively awareness of God's personal presence with us. In the light of the gospel, this means being drawn toward the enjoyment of the reconciled divine companionship. This is accompanied by the wonder of being a responsibly free human agent in a world in which God accompanies us in every moment of time and space. Each believer is called to "take captive every thought to make it obedient to Christ" (2 Cor. 10:5 NIV), rejoicing in God's continuing presence accompanying each present moment.

The resulting moral implication: measure each moral choice in relation to the simple fact of the eternal divine presence. Behavior is transformed, speech reshaped, thinking reconfigured in relation to this omnipresent Companion. God gives himself to us to make life happy again, as once again rooted in its true center instead of in transient idolatries. Believers are called to "spare no pains to preserve always a deep, a continual, a lively, and a joyful sense of God's gracious presence."[51]

Those in Wesley's connection of spiritual formation can easily see, by reasonable inference, the rudiments of other divine attributes from these substantive discussions of omnipresence and eternity.[52] One of these divine attributes is the oneness of God.

4. The Unity of the Divine Being

The text of "The Unity of the Divine Being" is Mark 12:32: "There is one God" [Homily #120 (1789), B 4:61–71; J #114, VII:264–73].

---

[48]Concerning the empirical knowledge derived from the senses, see B 4:29–30, 49–51, 200; 11:56–57.

[49]"On the Omnipresence of God," B 4:42–45, sec. 2.

[50]"On Divine Providence," B 2:539, J VI:316, sec. 11.

[51]"On the Omnipresence of God," B 4:47, sec. 3.6.

[52]CH 7:370.

a. The Unity of Humanity

The idea of the unity of humanity is a consequence of the premise of the unity of God. It is only because God is one that we can glimpse the oneness of rational creatures amid the vast diversities of human cultures.

The personal and ethical expression of that centeredness is the love of the tangible, definite, particular one nearby (the neighbor) as we love ourselves in response to the love of God. Where many gods are worshiped, we can be sure that neither the true God is worshiped nor the unity of humanity grasped.[53]

The guiding text on the unity of God is Mark 12:32, where a detractor having asked Jesus about the most important commandment heard his reply from Hebrew Scripture: "'Hear, O Israel: The Lord our God, the Lord is one. Love the Lord your God with all your heart and with all your soul and with all your mind and with all your strength.' The second is this: 'Love your neighbor as yourself.' There is no commandment greater than these" (Mark 12:29 – 31 NIV; cf. Deut. 6:4, 5).

b. The Unity of the Divine Attributes

God's being is known from God's own acts in history. God is known from what he does. We discover God's character by recalling the long story in Scripture of the disclosure of his character in human history.[54]

Though the divine unity is manifested by complementary attributes, all unite and cohere in God's own life. God is eternal without ceasing to be omnipresent, omnipresent without ceasing to be empathic, all-knowing without ceasing to engender freedom. Each divine attribute is complementary to other divine attributes.[55]

c. The Divine Necessity

Some attributes can be ascribed only to God and not in any way to creatures. Other divine attributes are said to be relational attributes because they pertain to the *relation* God has with creation and creatures while remaining omnipresent, omnipotent, and omniscient.[56]

The attributes of divine necessity and unbegottenness cannot be simply conveyed to creatures or unilaterally transferred to finite, dependent, prejudiced mortals. For this reason, they are called incommunicable attributes.[57] Finite minds and bodies can never be in themselves necessary, since all creatures are contingent on their creation. The divine attribute of aseity (underived being or self-sufficiency) cannot be relocated or communicated or made analogous with anything that characterizes radically derived, dependent human existence.[58]

---

[53]"The Unity of the Divine Being," B 4:61, J VII:264–73, secs. 1–3.
[54]"The Unity of the Divine Being," B 4:61, secs. 1–3.
[55]"The Unity of the Divine Being," B 4:61–64, secs. 2–9.
[56]*LJW* 3:343–44; 5:365; 8:153; B 1:589; 2:540–41; 4:320–21.
[57]*LJW* 2:71; 5:231.
[58]"The Unity of the Divine Being," B 4:61, sec. 2.

5. Relational Attributes: Goodness, Mercy, Holiness, Spirit

a. Divine Attributes Pertaining to God's Relation with Creatures

All living creatures have their being in time within narrow bounds marked by birth and death. God transcends time by experiencing eternal simultaneity with all events of time. God alone is omnipresent to all other presents, so as to be aware of all conceivable pasts, in all conceivable aspects, and all conceivable futures.[59]

Being God is incommunicable to finite minds in the sense that finite minds cannot know as fully as God knows. Only God knows how to be God. God alone is omniscient. God knows not simply the part as we know the part, but he knows intensively and extensively the whole of what has occurred. He knows all that is yet to occur and all that is occurring in any conceivable moment of time and space. That premise does not rule out human freedom but speaks of an infinitely free one as human freedom's Companion and Enabler, foreknowing but not foreordaining free acts of will.[60]

What are these communicable divine attributes—those in which finite creatures are called to share to some extent with the being of God? These divine attributes are proximately communicated to others: veracity, compassion,[61] justice,[62] and spirituality.[63]

b. Goodness, Mercy, and Holiness

The mercy of God, for example, is a characteristic of God that he wishes to share with us and calls us to share with others.[64] God alone is infinitely good, the Giver of other goods, in a goodness beyond finite bounds, abundant in beneficence, as incomparable in goodness as in power and knowing. No less than seventeen hymns from the 1780 *Collection of Hymns for the Use of the People Called Methodists* are focused on "Describing the Goodness of God."[65] The most fitting response to the goodness of God in creation is a grateful life of communicating goodness to others.[66]

God alone is incomparably holy.[67] In the presence of this Holy One, we who have abused our God-given freedom feel intensely any hint of unholiness in our lives. Scripture calls that awareness "conscience." God has allowed us to share in his holiness, even if only negatively, by allowing us to feel the difference between our goodness and his unsurpassable goodness. Similarly, the Holy One who is incomparably merciful calls us to be merciful.[68]

59"The Unity of the Divine Being," B 4:61, sec. 3.
60"The Unity of the Divine Being," B 4:61–62, J VII:264–73, secs. 3–6.
61B 1:274–75; 2:422–35; JWO 226f., 385–86, 469–70.
62*LJW* 3:345; B1:344–45; 2:12–13; 4:285f.; JWO 435–37, 451–52.
63"The Unity of the Divine Being," B 4:62–65, secs. 7–11.
64B 2:411, 424, 434; 4:62–63.
65*CH* 7:107–28.
66*LJW* 8:153.
67"The Unity of the Divine Being," secs. 5–6.
68"The Unity of the Divine Being," B 4:62, sec. 7.

c. God Is Spirit

The basic Hebraic analogy for "Spirit" is wind moving without being seen, yet knowable by the spiritual senses. God is not seen as other objects are seen yet is proximately knowable just as the wind is knowable even if not seen.

To affirm with Scripture that God is Spirit is to deny that he can be reduced to matter. As Spirit, God is not an object visible to our eyes, not reducible to finite causality or corporeal matter or material determinants. While sustaining nature in time, God is not reducible to nature. While making natural causality reliable, God remains the ground and premise of its reliability.[69]

God creates not only all matter but also the whole range of spiritual creatures that transcend matter, all living beings in heaven and on earth, including the whole of angelic creation, humanity, and human history with all their variable possibilities. God creates persons with the proximate capacity to refract his own being, unity, mercy, justice, spirituality, and love.[70]

6. God, Happiness, and Religion

a. God's Happiness

Wesley's reasoning about each divine attribute has a practical moral focus. Proper contemplation of God's attributes always aims practically at human happiness. This is a notion prominently accented in Wesley's instructional homilies and is a conspicuous feature of his teaching.[71]

God intends from the beginning to enable the happiness of creatures to that full extent to which each creature is capable. The moral order is provided for the happiness of creatures.[72] The purpose of creation is the sheer joy of God in creating companionable creatures to share his own goodness to the full extent that creatures are capable of sharing it.[73] It is our skewed freedom that absurdly distorts and upsets that order. God does not create the world for the sake of the damnation or alienation of rational creatures.[74]

God exceedingly enjoys the work of creation. Its whole aspect elicits God's approval and redounds to God's glory.[75] God "made all things to be happy." Our freedom is made to be happy in God. God created companionate, free, self-determining personal beings in order that God's own freedom might be shared in and enjoyed. This happiness is God's intention for every creature, even as wise parenting seeks the true happiness of the family.[76]

---

[69]"On the Omnipresence of God," B 4:45, sec. 2.8.
[70]"The Unity of the Divine Being," B 4:63, sec. 8.
[71]B 4:209.
[72]B 1:35, 223 – 24; 2:195 – 96; 3:533 – 34; 4:300 – 301, 305.
[73]Varying degrees of happiness are proportional to degrees of faith active in love. B 4:286.
[74]"The Unity of the Divine Being," B 4:63, sec. 9.
[75]B 9:39 – 40; JWO 450 – 51.
[76]"The Unity of the Divine Being," B 4:63 – 65, secs. 9 – 11.

b. God's Benevolence Disregarded by Man's Idolatry

What stands in the way of happiness? We treat the finite goods of creation as if they are absolute goods. Idolatry is the disordering of human choice, the twisting of human freedom away from its ordered good toward its disordered fall from goodness.[77] An idol is any good creature or relation that we pretend is absolute. We worship and adore these created goods in the place of the Giver of all things.[78]

The seemingly irreversible problem that emerges everywhere in human history is summarized in the term *sin*. Those who have been offered freedom have a disastrous history of being prone to barter it away.[79]

God does not make things bad or prone innately to evil. Only good comes from God's hand as created. We receive these good gifts freely and then pretend that the creation itself is the source of our goodness and happiness. We love the creature more than the Creator. That sin is prone to evil is a result not of its having been created in this way but of its own willing. The will becomes bound to act as idolatrous freedom would have it.[80]

Human nature is simultaneously a composite of opposites: finitude and freedom. Freedom is capable of transcending finitude but wills to become bound to it. We become living souls housed in dying bodies. Our story is one of spirit contending with flesh. We are given freedom out of the divine goodness on the proviso that we exercise our powers responsibly. That capacity becomes distorted either downhill in the direction of sensuality or uphill in the direction of pride. In our acts of excessive sensuality, we become weighted down with body and its limitations. We pretend that we have no self-transcending spirit.[81] Oppositely, in our pride we pretend that we are the center of the universe, as if we have no body, no grounding finitude. Good things, which are intended for ordered human happiness, become through the exercise of freedom idolatrously disordered toward sensuality and pride.[82]

7. True and False Religion

a. Three Forms of False Religion

Even our religious sensibilities and our native proneness to worship enter into this unbending rivalry with the Incomparable One, who is the Giver of all goods. This one is watchful on behalf of our deeper human vocation.

Religion of some sort is as native to the human condition as digestion or sex. It is common to the fallen human situation always to be prone to adore some object of worship, whether genuine or spurious. Of all the idolatries we are prone to create, the most subtly nuanced is religion itself.

---

[77]Worldly happiness is constituted by all those forms of fleeting, proximate happiness that rest anxiously in or are prone to idolatries. B 1:253, 624–26, 636–37; 3:97–98, 105–13, 234–36; 4:123–26, 206–7.

[78]"The Unity of the Divine Being," B 4:63–65, secs. 9–11.

[79]"Spiritual Idolatry," B 3:103–5; J VI:435–44.

[80]"Sermon on the Mount, 8," B 1:612–32; J V:361–77.

[81]FA, pt. 2, B 11:228–34, J VIII:161–64, sec. 2.16–20.

[82]This would become Kierkegaard's theme in *Sickness unto Death*; cf. *NDM*, vol. 1.

False religion only moves us further away from real happiness. It may appear as *dead conventional religion of opinions* or "*of barely outward worship*," which has the form but not the power of godliness.[83] One who talks a good God game may fail entirely to receive the grace and embody the love of the revealing God. In speaking sometimes harshly of dead orthodoxy, Wesley was not opposing classic Christian orthodoxy, except as its true teachings have been falsely reduced to dead opinions without behavioral consequence.[84]

False religion may appear as *a servile religion of works righteousness* in which we hold ourselves up before God, pretending, "Look, Lord, how wonderful," expecting to be received on the basis of our good deeds or services rendered or merits achieved. We conjecture that our own moral acts or religious works are the final good that we offer to God, and we turn our backs on trusting in God's incomparably good work.[85]

Finally, false religion may appear as an arid *practical atheism* that nonetheless continues to unconsciously adore some finite object of worship. Wesley was less interested in theoretical atheism than practical atheism, by which people actually live as though God does not exist.[86]

b. True Religion as Grateful Benevolence

True religion has two interconnected dimensions, like two halves of a whole: gratitude toward God and benevolence toward humanity. In contrast to all idolatries, true religion is expressed as a life of *gratitude for God's good gifts and benevolence toward the needy neighbor in response to God's gifts.*[87] True religion lives daily out of praise for the gifts of God in creation and redemption, grateful for life and finite freedom, and when freedom falls, the restoration of freedom to its deeper grounding in God.[88]

True religion reaches out to the wounded neighbor with goodwill in response to the good willing of God toward our wounded humanity. We are called to share the mercy of God with those who hunger for mercy, the goodness of God with the dispossessed, the love of God with the homeless.[89]

Those who try to develop a religious sensibility that has nothing in it of the neighbor's good have missed at least half of religion: benevolence toward others. Those who try to reduce religion to humanistic ethics lose the other half: the personal self-giving of God who invites and enables unfettered responsiveness to the neighbor.[90]

---

[83]"The Unity of the Divine Being," B 4:66, J VII:264–73, sec. 15, italics added

[84]Letter to Charles Wesley Jr., May 2, 1784, *LJW* 7:216–17, concerning Samuel Wesley who had "changed his religion" and become a Roman Catholic.

[85]"The Righteousness of Faith," B 1:204–9, sec. 1.

[86]"The Unity of the Divine Being," B 4:66, sec. 15; "On Living without God," J VII:351, sec. 7.

[87]"The Unity of the Divine Being," B 4:67, secs. 16–17.

[88]B 2:548–49.

[89]"The Unity of the Divine Being," B 4:66–68, secs. 16–18.

[90]"The Unity of the Divine Being," B 4:67, secs. 16–17.

The Father is revealed through the Son as love. "The love of God is shed abroad in our hearts by the Holy Spirit" (Rom. 5:5). The full response of faith and love to this one God is the ground of true human happiness and true religion. Such religion is all too rare in a history drenched with sin but is not beyond the reach of grace.

The one who is most deeply freed to love the neighbor is the one who has no other gods before him than the one who is "eternal, omnipresent, all-perfect Spirit, is the Alpha and Omega, the first and the last. Not his Creator only, but his Sustainer, his Preserver, his Governor; yea, his Father, his Savior, Sanctifier, and Comforter. This God is his God, and his all, in time and eternity."[91]

Wesley explicitly identified the threat to religion that comes from the great Enlightenment apostate "triumvirate, Rousseau, Voltaire, and David Hume,"[92] who extolled "humanity ... as the very essence of religion ... sparing no pains to establish a religion which should stand on its own foundation, independent of any revelation whatever." Even when fashionable, it is "neither better nor worse than Atheism," putting asunder what God has joined together — love of God and neighbor. Wesley may have smelled the approach of Nietzsche, Marx, and Freud in his critique of William Wollaston's *The Religion of Nature Delineated*, of Jean-Jacques Burlamaqui's *Principles of Natural Law*, and especially of Francis Hutcheson's *Conduct of the Passions*. Hutcheson "quite shuts God out" of moral reflection by regarding it as *"inconsistent with* virtue ... if in doing a beneficent action you expect God to reward it.... It is then not a virtuous but a selfish action."[93] The beast of modernity was already slouching toward Bethlehem, where the center would not hold.

Wesley gathered together all the divine attributes when he spoke of the wisdom of God.

8. The Wisdom of God's Counsels

The text of "The Wisdom of God's Counsels" is Romans 11:33: "O the depth of the riches both of the wisdom and knowledge of God!" [Homily #68 (1784), B 2:551–66; J #68, VI:325–37].

Divine wisdom and power work together to revitalize freedom when it falls, to redeem it from its follies.[94] God's providence encompasses means as well as ends, shaping consequences as well as antecedents of human choosing. Faith views all things as so adapted by divine wisdom to the ends for which they were designed, that taken together, creation is even yet seen as *very good*. The wisdom of God's counsels saturates the human story despite all transitory recalcitrance.[95]

---

[91]"The Unity of the Divine Being," B 4:71, sec. 24.
[92]"The Unity of the Divine Being," B 4:68, sec. 18. For Wesley's references to Hume, see B 11:460; *JJW* 5:458, 491, 523; on Rousseau, see B 4:60, 69; *JJW* 5:352–53; 6:23; on Voltaire, see *JJW* 4:45, 157; 6:211; 7:13; *LJW* 5:199; 6:123, 332, 338.
[93]"The Unity of the Divine Being, B 4:68, sec. 18, italics added.
[94]"The Wisdom of God's Counsels," B 2:552, J VI:325–37, sec. 2.
[95]*LJW* 3:380; 2:540–41, 552–53; 4:62, 523.

a. God's Wisdom Works Differently in Nature Than Human Freedom

God's guiding hand is present in the realm of the human spirit in a different way than amid physics. In nature, the creation is ordered by an unbending physical causality.[96] In the moral order, freedom itself shapes causality. Natural causality is reliable, but within the dependable chains of natural causality, there appears a history shaped by self-determined willing. This freedom that flows within causal determinants is itself a codeterminant.

If in nature there is no freedom, hence no opposition to God's will, in actual history there is constant opposition. God's wisdom therefore is more conspicuous in the arena in which evil must be counteracted without violating the nature of freedom.[97]

But why would an all-wise God make a vulnerable finite freedom that could stand in defiance of him? Here the mystery of God's wisdom is profound. God enables human freedom, drawing it by grace constantly toward the good, but when freedom falls, as it so often does, God's redemptive grace is constantly working to raise it up again.[98]

b. God's Wisdom in Providence Has a History

God's redemptive activity has a history converging on God's own covenant with a special people, Israel. That history comes to a new beginning, like a seed that is planted grows. Its ultimate revelation is found in the events surrounding the resurrection of Jesus and the gift of the Spirit at Pentecost. After Pentecost, the community of the resurrection grew through hazardous and challenging circumstances, persecutions, defections and apostasies, and violent attempts to resist faith.[99]

The accurate, descriptive beholding of the history of the faithful is itself an exercise in witnessing the unfolding of God's providence in history. Wesley knew well the history of the worshiping community. He realized that it was not simply a sentimental fabrication but a real history of men and women of faith willing to risk their lives for their witness to the truth. The seeds of martyrs did not grow without trial or peril. Scripture and church history evidence almost every imaginable kind of hardship in successive periods of the church's struggle.[100]

Wesley reflected on providence especially within the frame of reference of the evangelical revival in which he himself had been intensely engaged. In no period of church history is the Christian community fully responsive to the work of the Spirit, though in some periods, such as the apostolic, the ante-Nicene, and the early Reformation and the evangelical revival, the community was much more responsive.

96"The Wisdom of God's Counsels," B 2:552, sec. 3.
97JWO 450–51.
98"The Wisdom of God's Counsels," B 2:553, J VI:325–37, sec. 4.
99"The Wisdom of God's Counsels," B 2:553–54, sec. 5. For references to heresy, see LJW 3:182, 200; 7:4–16, 21; B 2:555–56; 3:62–63; 409–10; 4:394–95.
100"The Wisdom of God's Counsels," B 2:555–57, secs. 8–11.

However apostate, the church by grace survived. "The gates of hell did never totally prevail against it. God always preserved a seed for himself, a few that worshipped him in spirit and in truth." These few are not adequately represented by sunshine soldiers who "will always have number as well as power on their side." These few will sometimes be stigmatized as "heretics. Perhaps it was chiefly by this artifice of the devil ... that the good which was in them being evil spoken of, they were prevented from being so extensively used as otherwise they might have been. Nay, I have doubted whether that arch-heretic, Montanus, was not one of the holiest men in the second century." Wesley spoke of Pelagius as the "arch heretic of the fifth century." Wesley opposed Pelagianism, but on the question of the grace enabling human freedom, he conceded that Pelagius was not as bad as made out by Augustine, who was "a wonderful saint" but at times full of pride, passion, bitterness, and censoriousness.[101]

c. God's Wisdom in the Revival of Religion

Wesley was not one to idealize church history. He thought it had gone through long periods of disgusting alienation, as in medieval scholasticism. Just at the point at which the church became almost overcome with iniquity, "the Lord lifted up a standard against it."[102] Wesley saw Luther as a decisive renewer of evangelical faith. Yet he thought that too few fruits and many ambiguities had been produced by Luther's preaching. Wesley reminded his flock that "to be friends with the world means to be at enmity with God" (James 4:4 TCNT).[103]

In his own time, Wesley was convinced that there was a significant revival of religion occurring, beyond the magisterial Reformation, in which God's special providences were being manifested.[104] He thought that God's providence was working in the revival, mending what had become broken, repairing God's creation where fallen, filling the earth with the knowledge of the glory of God.[105]

Wesley marked the beginning of this evangelical reawakening in Britain as 1627 with the flowering of Puritan revivalism.[106] The seeds of the eighteenth-century Evangelical Revival were sewn with the teachings of John Owen, Jeremy Taylor, and William Law. They were marked especially by a recovery of the resolution to become radically responsive to the Spirit, and they were seen also in the revival led by Jonathan Edwards in North America.[107]

---

[101]"The Wisdom of God's Counsels," B 2:555 – 56, sec. 9; cf. letters to Alexander Coates, July 7, 1761, and John Fletcher, August 18, 1775. Wesley thought that the real reason Pelagius offended some was "neither more nor less than this, the holding that Christians may by the grace of God (not without it; that I take to be a mere slander), 'go on to Perfection.'"

[102]"The Wisdom of God's Counsels," B 2:556, sec. 10.

[103]"The Wisdom of God's Counsels," B 2:556 – 62, J VI:325 – 37, secs. 10 – 17.

[104]"The Signs of the Times," B 2:521 – 33.

[105]"The General Spread of the Gospel," B 2:490 – 99, secs. 13 – 27.

[106]"The Wisdom of God's Counsels," B 2:557n, sec. 11; cf. John Gillies, *Historical Collections of the Success of the Gospel* (Glasgow, 1754). Puritan revivals were regarded by Wesley as the forerunner of key reforming movements before the eighteenth-century evangelical revival.

[107]"The Wisdom of God's Counsels," B 2:558, sec. 12.

God chose to use in these revivals ordinary persons, even ignorant and unlettered minds, to confound the wisdom of the world and make his strength known through human weakness. This is the wisdom of God. These providences call the faithful to set aside inordinate worldly securities and freely seek the treasures of the coming reign of God.[108]

God endows many with the Spirit only to see them fall by the wayside, by neglect or temptation. Even amid the worst apostasies, God does not cease to pour out his Spirit to call humanity to repentance and full responsiveness to grace. If at first few fruits are born, and if the danger of laying up treasure on earth arises anew in each generation, God always supplies new witnesses as the old fall away.[109] Young persons are especially crucial instruments of God. When older witnesses "die in the Lord, or lose the spiritual life which God had given them, he will supply ... others that are alive to God, and desire only to spend and be spent for him."[110] "Nothing is impossible with God" (Luke 1:37). All can return if they choose.[111] Temptations can be rejected. Earnest prayer can protect from temptation.

9. The First Article of the Articles of Religion: On God

a. Classic Attributes Summarized

Everything necessary for confessing the Christian teaching of God was for Wesley concisely summarized in the Anglican First Article of Religion, which retained the sixteenth-century language of the Reformers: "There is but one living and true God, everlasting, without body or parts, of infinite power, wisdom, and goodness; the maker and preserver of all things both visible and invisible. And in unity of this Godhead there are three persons, of one substance, power, and eternity—the Father, the Son, and the Holy Ghost."

No appraisal of Wesley's teaching of God is complete without examining this same first article of the Twenty-Four Articles of Religion Wesley commended to the Christmas Conference of American Methodists in 1784.

Article 1 is the definitive teaching on God consensually held by those in the Wesleyan connection of Churches (United Methodists, British Methodists, AME, AME Zion, Nazarene, and many Wesley-based church bodies). It encompasses in briefest form the essential features of biblical teaching on God. This language has been incorporated into the constitutions of many in Wesleyan-tradition churches as that doctrine of God handed down from the apostolic faith through ancient conciliar, Reformation, and Anglican traditions to all who would choose to stand doctrinally in Wesley's connection of spiritual formation.[112] It corresponds completely with ancient consensual ecumenical tradition.

108"The Wisdom of God's Counsels," B 2:558 – 59, sec. 13; cf. B 1:496 – 97, 637 – 38, 697.
109"The Wisdom of God's Counsels," B 2:559 – 61, J VI:325 – 37, secs. 14 – 16.
110"The Wisdom of God's Counsels," B 2:563, sec. 19.
111"The Wisdom of God's Counsels," B 2:564 – 66, secs. 21 – 24.
112Cf. LJW 4:25, 60, 115, 131, 149, 295.

b. Key Terms of Article 1 Explained

That God is "without body or parts" means that God is incorporeal, hence not to be investigated as empirical objects are. If something can be reduced to empirical investigation, we know right away that this is not God. That is what is meant by the "negative way" (*via negativa*) to God. It points to the being of God by first setting aside all those things that are *not God*. Those who view the world as God's body run counter to the teaching that God is without body. The idea that God can be divided into components or phases or periods of development runs counter to classic Christian teaching that God is one, hence indivisible.[113] Rejected by this article are all pantheisms, all limitations of divine power excepting self-limitation, all views that imply that fate controls history — all of which are wearisome but familiar follies of more recent popular cultures.

The negative attributes of God (those typically beginning with *in-* or *im-*) imply absence or denial and thus assume an apophatic (*apophasis*, denial) or negative argument concerning the existence of God: God is *not* finite, *not* deficient in power, *not* lacking in justice or wisdom, *not* visible as an object.[114] In this way the *via negativa*, the negative way of reasoning about God, is written centrally into the Wesleyan tradition of the teaching of God.

If some ingenious new idea of God might be asserted as if it were Wesley's distinctive contribution to the doctrine of God, he would be first to deny it. He was a receiving conveyor of the apostolic witness. He affirmed the well-established Hebraic and apostolic recollection of God's action in history. It was far from his intention to invent an improved doctrine of God's power or love. He confidently appealed to sacred Scripture, and as an expression of Scripture, to the three creeds (Apostles', Nicene-Constantinopolitan, and *Quicunque* [i.e., "Athanasian"]) as reliable confessions of scriptural teaching.[115]

c. Confessing the True God

Those under Wesley's spiritual guidance confessed faith in one God, Creator, Sovereign, and Preserver of all things visible and invisible. The divine attributes — unity, aliveness, truth, and eternality — are expressed in the divine actions of creating, governing, and preserving all things. The one who is infinite in power, wisdom, justice, goodness, and love rules with gracious regard for the well-being of humanity. God's power, wisdom, and love provide a plan and a means for the salvation of humanity. God is incomparably capable of accomplishing the divine purpose, consummately powerful, knowing, and good.

For those who stand in the presence of one who is unsurpassably just, it is inconceivable to Christian confessors that God would act unjustly.[116] When God is alleged to have acted unjustly, he has been misunderstood by finite minds.

---

[113]As in the classic ecumenical rejection of modalism and Sabellianism.
[114]B 4:45.
[115]*JJW* 4:424; 8:332.
[116]*LJW* 3:382.

God is infinite in love, overflowing with goodness. We learn of divine love precisely through the palpable history of God's actual self-disclosure, especially on the cross. The same one revealed on the cross is Creator, the provider of all things, who exercises providential guidance and cares for all that happens in creation. One God is Father, Son, and Spirit, Creator and Redeemer of what is fallen in creation, who awakens in our hearts a response to his love, mercy, and grace.[117]

God has infinite power, knowledge, and goodness beyond that which any finite mind can conceive. The one living and true God is maker and preserver of all, providing for the continuity and sustenance of all that is.[118] God is not only the source and ground of all things that we can see and empirically investigate, but also of spiritual, incorporeal creatures. Everything that exists has been created by this one living, true God whom no finite mind can know exhaustively, yet the just, loving, and merciful character of God has been sufficiently disclosed in the history of revelation to allow trust and belief.[119]

What does it mean to say that if "your heart is as my heart, give me your hand"? Embedded in the crucial homily "The Catholic Spirit" is a series of personal questions assumed to be affirmatively answered by anyone whose life is hid in Christ: "Is thy heart right with God? Dost thou believe his being, and his perfections? His eternity, immensity, wisdom, power; his justice, mercy, and truth?"[120] How could our hearts be right with God if we distrust God's eternity, wisdom, and goodness?

Further Reading on God

Bryant, Barry Edward. *John Wesley on the Origins of Evil.* Derbyshire, UK: Moorley's Bible and Bookshop, 1992.

Burtner, Robert W., and Robert E. Chiles. *A Compend of Wesley's Theology.* Nashville: Abingdon, 1954.

Collins, Kenneth. *A Faithful Witness: John Wesley's Homiletical Theology,* 15–34. Wilmore, KY: Wesleyan Heritage, 1993.

Kirkpatrick, Dow, ed. *The Living God.* Nashville: Abingdon, 1971.

Miley, John. *Systematic Theology.* Reprint, Peabody, MA: Hendrickson, 1989.

Oord, Thomas Jay. "Prevenient Grace and Nonsensory Perception of God in a Postmodern Wesleyan Philosophy." In *Between Nature and Grace: Mapping the Interface of Wesleyan Theology and Psychology,* edited by Bryan P. Stone and Thomas Jay Oord. San Diego: Point Loma, 2000.

———. "A Process Wesleyan Theodicy: Freedom, Embodiment, and the Almighty God." In *Thy Name and Nature Is Love: Wesleyan and Process Theologies in Dialogue,* edited by Bryan P. Stone and Thomas Jay Oord, 193–216. Nashville: Kingswood, 2001.

---

[117]*LJW* 4:321; 5:213, 294.
[118]B 1:580–81, 690.
[119]Letter to William Law, January 6, 1756, *LJW* 3:343–49.
[120]"The Catholic Spirit," B 2:88, sec. 14.

Pope, William Burt. *A Compendium of Christian Theology.* 3 vols. London: Wesleyan Methodist Book-Room, 1880.

Ralston, Thomas N. *Elements of Divinity.* New York: Abingdon, 1924.

Reddish, Robert O. *John Wesley: His Way of Knowing God.* Evergreen, CO: Rorge, 1972.

Summers, Thomas O. *Systematic Theology.* 2 vols. Edited by J. J. Tigert.

Nashville: Methodist Publishing House South, 1888.

Truesdale, Albert. "Theism: The Eternal, Personal, Creative God." In *A Contemporary Wesleyan Theology,* edited by Charles W. Carter, 103 – 43. Grand Rapids: Zondervan, 1983.

Watson, Richard. *Theological Institutes.* 2 vols. New York: Mason and Lane, 1836, 1840; edited by John M'Clintock. New York: Carlton & Porter, 1850.

B. God the Father, God the Son, God the Spirit

1. On the Trinity

The text of "On the Trinity" is 1 John 5:7: "There are three that bear record in heaven, the Father, the Word, and the Holy Ghost" [Homily #55 (1775), B 2:373 – 86; J #55, VI:199 – 206].

a. The Triune Root of All Vital Religion

One cannot read the New Testament, Wesley thought, without constantly hearing of the sending of the Son by the Father and the Spirit's enabling and fulfilling of the mission of the Son. Triune teaching is a classic way of bringing together the witness of the apostles in a cohesive and comprehensive pattern.

Wesley's view was orthodox: God is one as Father, Son, and Spirit, not three gods, but one God in three persons. The Father is God, the Son is God, and the Spirit is God. Yet the Father is distinguishable from the Son, and the Son is distinguishable from the Spirit. The Son is sent by the Father; the Spirit fulfills and consummates the mission of the Son. These three are one in being, one in power, eternally God.[121] There is a community of discourse within the Godhead of persons who are equally the one God, coeternal and distinguishable as Father, Son, and Spirit. The persons of the Trinity can be distinguished but not separated as if one might consider the mission of the Son apart from the mission of the Spirit.[122] This is the baptism into which we have been baptized.

Since the ancient ecumenical Christian tradition so firmly assents to triune teaching as to make it definitive of orthodoxy, the triunity of God cannot be a point of indifference.[123] Wesley was a traditional Anglican in trinitarian belief and prac-

---

[121] Arts. 1 – 2.

[122] "On the Trinity," B 2:374 – 76, J VI:199 – 206, secs. 1 – 3.

[123] In a letter to Mary Bishop, April 17, 1776, Wesley commended William Jones's *The Catholic Doctrine of the Trinity,* 1756, as "more clear and more strong than any I ever saw.... If anything is wanting, it is the application ... but this is abundantly supplied by my brother's Hymns." *LJW* 6:213.

tice. He prayed daily with the prayer book to God the Son and God the Spirit who are together with the Father the one eternal God. Triune teaching is the heart of classic Christian teaching, "the root of all vital religion."[124]

b. The Triune Fact and Triune Language

Triunity is a mystery beyond human understanding. It is to be joyfully received and celebrated rather than explained using empirical judgments alone. Should anyone propose to exhaustively decipher the triune mystery, discount the pretended explanation. We can know *that* God is triune, not *how* or *why.* The central point of Wesley's homily "On the Trinity" is the modest conviction that God's triune life is hidden from rational-empirical inspection.

Wesley spoke of the Trinity as *a fact,* but not one that can yield to laboratory analysis. He did not attempt to render any definitive account of the triune mystery. The *manner* in which God is three in one can be left to honest, humble adoration and celebration as a mystery of faith.[125] *That* God is Father, God is Son, and God is Holy Spirit stands unassailably as the central feature of orthodox Christian teaching of God.[126]

The history of exegesis is strewn with numerous opinions as to how best to express the central *fact* of the triune mystery. The New Testament text merely reveals the triune God; it does not explain the Trinity or theorize about it or provide a language for construing it.[127] Wesley did not think it obligatory to side with "this or that explication" of the texts attesting the triune mystery, but rather only to celebrate "the direct words, unexplained, just as they lie in the text."[128]

c. Three Bear Record in Heaven: The Debate over 1 John 5:7

The first letter of John insists throughout that Jesus Christ is truly God without ceasing to be truly human, and truly human without ceasing to be truly God. The writer was showing that this God-man was baptized and died. Jesus was the Son of God not only at his baptism but at his death. If he had died as if one with a human nature only, his sacrificial death would not have been sufficient to reconcile the guilt of the whole history of human sin. It is the Holy Spirit who testifies that Jesus is the Son of God the Father by descending on him at his baptism, remaining with him through his death, and empowering his resurrection.[129]

The main text Wesley chose to attest the triune mystery remains replete with textual difficulties. The Authorized King James translation with which Wesley's

---

[124]"On the Trinity," B 2:384, sec. 17.

[125]According to Bishop Peter Browne, "The mystery does not lie in the fact 'These Three are One,' but in the manner, the accounting how they are one. But with this I have nothing to do. I believe the fact. As to the manner (wherein the whole mystery lies) I believe nothing about it," i.e., not in the sense of disbelieving the mystery, but not trying to assign specific language to it. Letter to Miss March, August 3, 1771, *LJW* 5:270; Peter Browne, *Procedure, Extent, and Limits of the Human Understanding* (1728).

[126]"On the Trinity," B 2:376, J VI:199–206, secs. 1–2; "On the Discoveries of Faith," B 1:220; 4:27–38.

[127]"On the Trinity," B 2:376–78, secs. 3–4.

[128]"On the Trinity," B 2:378, sec. 5.

[129]Ibid.

societies were familiar reads, "There are three that bear record in heaven, the Father, the Word, and the Holy Ghost: and these three are one" (1 John 5:7). The same text in the NRSV reads, "There are three that testify: the Spirit and the water and the blood, and these three agree," with the accompanying footnote on manuscript variants: "A few other authorities read (with variations) 'There are three that testify in heaven, the Father, the Word, and the Holy Spirit, and these three are one.'" Wesley was pondering the text in its original Greek, as with all his homilies.

Wesley offered an explicit argument for why this text is present in some manuscripts but absent in others, though he did not want to press his theory of manuscript variations on others. His suspicion was that the post-Constantine Arian theorists wanted to omit or redact Trinitarian texts held by the earliest apostles. He hypothesized that Arian transcribers so disliked the triune text that they amended or omitted it. Acknowledging that the text is missing in some early manuscripts, Wesley countered by this reasoning:

> (1) That though it is wanting in many ancient copies, yet it is found in more, abundantly more, and those copies of the greatest authority. (2) That it is cited by a whole train of ancient writers from the time of St. John to that of Constantine.... (3) That we can easily account for its being after that time wanting in many copies when we remember that Constantine's successor was a zealous Arian, who used every means to promote his bad cause ... in particular the erasing this text out of as many copies as fell into his hands.[130]

Although this hypothesis may to modern critics appear doubtful, it offers an intriguing glimpse into Wesley as textual critic. We learn from Wesley not to be afraid of rigorous historical textual criticism to search out which received text was the earliest. Even if his hypothesis is questionable, it signals that he was inviting leaders and laity in his spiritual connection to honestly enter into responsible textual critical inquiry, asking what is to be made of the differences among available manuscripts. Those who disagree with his technical conclusion can hardly disagree with his intent.

d. Classic Triune Language Affirmed and Limited

Wesley affirmed the specific triune language of the three most ancient creeds — Apostles', Nicene, and Athanasian — but did not wish to promote a particular interpretation of them. He refused to be locked into any specific language or post-apostolic terms considered necessary for their exposition The best traditional explication of the Trinity was in Wesley's view the Athanasian Creed (*Quicunque vult*), though he confessed to being uneasy with its prologue, which holds that those who do not assent to it "shall without doubt perish everlastingly."

Wesley admitted that he himself had "for some time scrupled subscribing to that creed, till I considered, (1), that these sentences only relate to *willful*, not involuntary unbelievers — to those who, having all the means of knowing the truth, nevertheless

---

[130]"On the Trinity," B 2:377, sec. 3, amended with numerals; cf. *LJW* 4:125.

obstinately reject it; (2), that they relate only to the *substance* of the doctrine there delivered, not the philosophical *illustrations* of it."[131] On these grounds he came to accept the Athanasian Creed as the best classic statement of triune teaching. But he was aware that any explication takes place in the context of some philosophical worldview, which he was not willing to allow to dominate over the wonder of the triune mystery.

Given the importance to Wesley of the triune teaching of the Athanasian Creed, it seems fitting that we quote it directly:

> We worship one God in Trinity, and trinity in Unity; Neither confounding the Persons; nor dividing the Substance. For there is one Person of the Father, another of the Son, and another of the Holy Ghost. But the Godhead of the Father, of the Son and of the Holy Ghost, is all one: the Glory equal, the Majesty co-eternal. Such as the Father is, such is the Son: and such is the Holy Ghost. The Father uncreate, the Son uncreate: and the Holy Ghost uncreate. The Father incomprehensible, the Son incomprehensible: and the Holy Ghost incomprehensible. The Father eternal, the Son eternal: and the Holy Ghost eternal. And yet they are not three eternals: but one eternal. As also there are not three incomprehensibles, nor three uncreated, but one uncreated, and one incomprehensible. So likewise, the Father is Almighty, the Son is Almighty: and the Holy Ghost Almighty. And yet they are not three Almighties: but one Almighty.[132]

Wesley urged newborn believers not to make belabored inquiries regarding particular words in the classic formulations, such as *ousia* and *hypostasis*. However authoritative the Athanasian Creed, it does not in itself provide a definitive explanation of the mystery of the Trinity. Some tender minds may even be made unbelievers by some particular explication of it, or by having a conjectural language imposed on it. Wesley did not want sincere questioners or doubters to be unnecessarily troubled or disabled or cast out of the circle of faith by excessive fondness for some specific nonconsensual reading of the New Testament text.

Though Wesley reserved room for different interpretations of the triune mystery, it was not his intention either to commend obscurantism or to welcome a wildly latitudinarian accommodation to any and all conceivable interpretations. He echoed Augustine's view that we do not speak of the Trinity because we can speak of it adequately, but because we must not be silent.[133]

Wesley urged neither silence nor detailed explication, but simple affirmation of the biblical texts and the ecumenical creeds.[134] What remains sufficient is the apostolic testimony itself, not subsequent accretions of interpretations that have been added in different cultures with various philosophical languages over diverse centuries.[135]

---

[131]"On the Trinity," B 2:377.
[132]This version quoted from the BCP.
[133]Augustine, *On the Trinity*, 1; Wesley, "On the Trinity," B 2:378, sec. 5.
[134]On the ecumenical spirit of Wesley, see JWO 90–91, 498–99.
[135]"On the Trinity," B 2:378, sec. 5.

e. Living within Mystery

When we stand within this mystery of the triune God, we do well to avoid either being immobilized by skepticism or imagining ourselves as set free to assert anything we wish.

We remain a mystery to ourselves. The deeper we probe the body-soul interface, the more we are humbled by its complexity and resistance to penetration. We still live as a body-soul composite even when we do not fully understand that interface in real time. So it is with the Trinity. We have the benefit of the sacred text of 1 John 5:7. We can receive and celebrate it, even while not pretending once for all to definitively grasp its mystery.

To those who make the counterclaim that we cannot believe what we cannot comprehend, and therefore should omit the triune confession altogether, Wesley rejoined that there are many things we practically believe in that we do not fully comprehend: We do not understand the energy of the sun yet live in its warmth. We walk by light and breathe without understanding light and respiration. We live within gravitational fields but do not fully comprehend their causes. We stand upon the earth, but our standing does not depend on our understanding of it.[136]

By similar reasoning, Wesley stated, "I believe this fact … that God is three and one…. I believe just so much as God has revealed, and no more. But this, the manner, he has not revealed."[137] Yet "I do not see how it is possible for any to have vital religion who denies that these three are one."[138]

Those who truly believe and confess the ancient triune teaching find their lives transformed by it. This stands as a credible pragmatic argument for its truth. The Christian community has in many historical situations relied on a gloriously mysterious teaching that has repeatedly brought it life and energy. The tenacious life of this community under persecution is historically unthinkable without the triune teaching.[139]

In commending Jonathan Swift's sermon "On the Trinity," Wesley approved the view that the Trinity is a mystery so far exceeding reason as to be altogether above rational explanation, in contrast to others who argued that the Trinity is rationally demonstrable.[140] Wesley did not pretend to make any original contribution to the interpretation of the Trinity.[141] There is a gentle spirit of toleration and patient trust that is at work here, yet without losing the central energy and substance of classic Christian triune thinking.

That Wesley earnestly confessed the triune teaching is clear from the first four of the essential Articles of Religion he commended to his connection: "There is but one living and true God," and "in the unity of this Godhead there are three persons

---

[136]"On the Trinity," B 2:379–83, secs. 6–13.
[137]"On the Trinity," B 2:384, sec. 15.
[138]"On the Trinity," B 2:386, sec. 18.
[139]"On the Trinity," B 2:384–86, secs. 15–18.
[140]Cf. J. Trapp, On the Trinity, 1730; Wesley, "On the Trinity," B 2:377, sec. 3.
[141]B 1:220; 2:101, 373–86; 4:31–32, 37.

of one substance, power and eternity—the Father, the Son, and the Holy Ghost." The Son is "the Word of the Father, begotten from everlasting of the Father, the very and eternal God, of one substance with the Father." The Holy Spirit, "proceeding from the Father and the Son, is of one substance, majesty, and glory with the Father and the Son, very and eternal God." All this is standard ancient ecumenical teaching.

f. Triune Baptism in the Spirit

No one is rightly baptized only in the name of the Father, or only in the name of the Son, but in the name of the triune God—Father, Son, and Spirit.

Triune reflection is simply a way of ordering the whole gospel of God into an arrangement or exegetical economy consistent with the apostolic testimony and baptismal faith. This is the baptism into which we are baptized, as the ancient councils never tired of repeating. Historically, all the ecumenically received expressions of the rule of faith (as expressed liturgically in the three creeds) emerged as baptismal formulae and confessional statements made at baptism, which seek to declare what is happening in baptism.

A creed is thus a summary way of talking of all that is crucial to the Christian faith. There is no topic of belief that does not fit into that pattern in some way. It is the Spirit who awakens our attentiveness to this Word spoken in baptism and Holy Communion.

This homily "On the Trinity" must be held in close connection with another homily that followed five years later, "Spiritual Worship." Both deal with aspects of the same text: 1 John 5:20.

2. Spiritual Worship—On Triune Spirituality

The text of "Spiritual Worship" is 1 John 5:20: "This is the true God, and eternal life" [Homily #78 (1780), B 3:88–102; J #77, VI:424–35].

a. On Personal Communion with the Triune God

In John's first epistle, the author focused on "the foundation of all, the happy and holy communion which the faithful have with God the Father, Son, and Holy Ghost."[142] The very structure of John's letters forms around communion with the Father (1 John 1), communion with the Son (1 John 2 and 3), and communion with the Spirit (1 John 4). The recapitulation of the whole argument is found in 1 John 5:18–20 and includes the guiding text of Homily #77, "Spiritual Worship," 1 John 5:20: this triune one "is the true God, and eternal life."[143]

To commune with the triune God, the true God, is to know him as one God over all, Father, Son, and Spirit.[144] In the Son we meet the Father.[145] The Son was

---

[142]"Spiritual Worship," B 3:89–90, J VI:424–35, proem 2.

[143]"Spiritual Worship," B 3:89–90, proem 1.

[144]In a letter to Hester Ann Roe, February 11, 1777, Wesley recounted the ecstatic experience of triune spirituality reported by Charles Perronet, LJW 6:253; cf. Letter to Lady Maxwell, July 4, 1787, LJW 7:392.

[145]B 1:578–79, 692.

with God from the beginning and was God. Wesley wrote to Mrs. Cock, November 3, 1789, "Do you still find deep and uninterrupted communion with God, with the Three-One God, with the Father and the Son through the Spirit?"[146]

b. Creator, Supporter, Preserver, Author, Redeemer, Governor, Consummator of All

The triune God is "the only Cause, the sole *Creator* of all things," and as true God "the *Supporter* of all the things that he hath made," sustaining all created things by the word of his power, "by the same powerful word which brought them out of nothing. As this was absolutely necessary for the beginning of their existence, it is equally so for the continuance of it: were his almighty influence withdrawn they could not subsist a moment longer. Hold up a stone in the air; the moment you withdraw your hand it naturally falls to the ground. In like manner, were he to withdraw his hand for a moment, the creation would fall into nothing."[147]

As *Preserver* of all, God "preserves them in that degree of well-being which is suitable to their several natures. He preserves them in their several relations, connections, and dependencies, so as to compose one system of beings, to form one entire universe."[148] "By and in him are all things compacted into one system."[149]

Whatever moves, moves by a mover. As primal *Author* of all motion in the universe, the true God has given to free spiritual creatures (angels and human beings) "a small degree of self-moving power, but not to [inorganic] matter. All matter ... is totally inert ... and whenever any part of it seems to move, it is in reality moved by something else."[150] When Isaac Newton spoke of the stars moving or attracting each other in proportion to the quantity of matter they contain, Wesley wanted to clarify the more fundamental premise that "they are continually *impelled* toward each other. Impelled, by what? 'By the subtle matter, the ether, or electric fire,'" but even this remains inert matter, consequently "as inert in itself as either sand or marble. It cannot therefore move itself; but probably it is the first material mover, the main spring whereby the Creator and Preserver of all things is pleased to move the universe."[151]

As *Redeemer* of all humanity, the incarnate God "tasted death for every man" (Heb. 2:9) that "he might make a full and sufficient sacrifice, oblation, and satisfaction for the sins of the whole world."[152] It is this triune God who is *Governor* of all, "Lord and Disposer of the whole creation," who presides "over each creature as if it were the universe, and over the universe as over each individual creature," yet caring especially for those most responsive to his revealed grace, who are the apple of his eye, whom he hides under the shadow of his wings.[153] Christianity celebrates the

---

[146]*LJW* 8:183.
[147]"Spiritual Worship," B 3:91, secs. 1.2, 3, italics added.
[148]"Spiritual Worship," B 3:91, J VI:424–35, sec. 1.4.
[149]Wesley's translation of Col. 1:17.
[150]"Spiritual Worship," B 3:92, sec. 1.5.
[151]"Spiritual Worship," B 3:92–93, sec. 1.6, italics added.
[152]BCP eucharistic prayer of consecration.
[153]"Spiritual Worship," B 3:93–94, sec. 1.8.

triune God as *Consummator* of all things: "Of him [as Creator], and through him [as Sustainer], and to him [as End], are all things" (Rom. 11:36).[154]

Triune teaching confirms and concisely draws together the major Christian doctrines of God as Creator, Supporter, Preserver, Author, Redeemer, Governor, and Consummator of all.

c. Eternal Life Is Life in the Son, Beginning Now with Faith

In all these ways the Son is truly God, with the Father and the Spirit. But how is this one God the Giver of eternal life? The triune God, who created us as finite bodies with self-transcending souls, invites to eternal life all who are ready to receive saving grace.

Those faithful unto death *will receive* the crown of life purchased by God the Son. Eternal life is far more than a future life. It is communion with what God the Son "is now." This triune God, made incarnate in the Son, is "now the life of everything that lives in any kind or degree," whether of *vegetable* life, "the lowest species of life ... as being the source of all the motion on which vegetation depends," or of *animal* life, the power by which the animal heart beats, or of *rational* life, the source of all that moves and all that is enabled to move itself according to its intelligence.[155]

Whoever has the Son has life eternal. This is the testimony that God has given us, "not only a title to but the real beginning of 'eternal life,'"[156] commencing when the Son is revealed in our hearts, enabling us to call him Lord and live by faith in him.[157]

d. The Happiness of Experienced Triune Spirituality

The fullest happiness is eternal life. It begins with faith in the love of God shed abroad in our hearts, "instantly producing love to all mankind: general, pure benevolence, together with its genuine fruits, lowliness, meekness, patience, contentedness in every state; an entire, clear, full acquiescence in the whole will of God."[158] We are happy when God takes "full possession of our heart; when he reigns therein without a rival, the Lord of every motion there," which is what is meant by the kingdom of God,[159] wherein we are made "complete in him" (Col. 2:10).

As the triune God is one, so there is one ultimate happiness for all. Our hearts cannot rest until they rest in God.[160] The vigor of youth may seem a kind of happiness, when "our blood dances in our veins; while the world smiles upon us and we have all the conveniences, yea, and superfluities of life," but in time it "flies away like a shadow."[161] "Give a man everything that this world can give," and still, as Horace

---

[154]"Spiritual Worship," B 3:94–95, sec. 1.19.
[155]"Spiritual Worship," 3:95, sec. 2.1–3.
[156]"Spiritual Worship," B 3:96, sec. 2.4.
[157]"On the Discoveries of Faith," B 4:31–32, J VII:233, sec. 7.
[158]"Spiritual Worship," B 3:96, J VI:424–35, sec. 2.5.
[159]"Spiritual Worship," B 3:96, sec. 2.6.
[160]"Spiritual Worship," B 3:97, sec. 3.1; from Augustine, *Confessions* 1.1; see "Awake, Thou That Sleepest," sec. 2.5.
[161]"Spiritual Worship," B 3:97, sec. 3.1.

knew, "something is always lacking to make one's fortune incomplete. . . . That *something* is neither more nor less than the knowledge and love of God without which no spirit can be happy."[162]

Wesley recalled his own experience as a child. Although "a stranger to pain and sickness, and particularly to lowness of spirits (which I do not remember to have felt one quarter of an hour since I was born), having plenty of all things . . . still I was not happy!" He lacked the knowledge and love of God.[163]

"This happy knowledge of the true God is only another name for *religion*; I mean *Christian religion*," which consists not in outward actions or duties or concepts, but more directly "in the knowledge and love of God, as manifested in the Son of his love, through the eternal Spirit."[164] No one who has turned aside from this grace is happy, even if surrounded with every possible aesthetic delight, as was Solomon, who teaches us plainly what happiness is not, more than what happiness is: it is "not to be found in natural knowledge, in power, or in the pleasures of sense or imagination."[165]

Further Reading on the Triune Teaching

Cannon, William R. *Theology of John Wesley: With Special Reference to the Doctrine of Justification*, 204 – 14. New York: Abingdon, 1946.

Collins, Kenneth. *A Faithful Witness: John Wesley's Homiletical Theology*, 58 – 62. Wilmore, KY: Wesleyan Heritage, 1993.

Mickey, Paul. *Essentials of Wesleyan Theology*, 29 – 44. Grand Rapids: Zondervan, 1980.

Miley, John. *Systematic Theology*. Reprint, Peabody, MA: Hendrickson, 1989.

Pope, William Burt. *A Compendium of Christian Theology*. 3 vols. London:

Wesleyan Methodist Book-Room, 1880.

Ralston, Thomas N. *Elements of Divinity*. New York: Abingdon, 1924.

Summers, Thomas O. *Systematic Theology*. 2 vols. Edited by J. J. Tigert. Nashville: Methodist Publishing House South, 1888.

Watson, Richard. *Theological Institutes*. 2 vols. New York: Mason and Lane, 1836, 1840; edited by John M'Clintock. New York: Carlton & Porter, 1850.

Williams, Colin W. *John Wesley's Theology Today*, 93 – 97. Nashville: Abingdon, 1960.

---

[162]"Spiritual Worship," B 3:97 – 98, sec. 3.1; Horace, *Odes* 3.24.64.

[163]"Spiritual Worship," B 3:98, sec. 3.2. Here Wesley anticipated Kierkegaard's aesthetic pseudonyms: "Look forward on any distant prospect: how beautiful does it appear! Come up to it; and the beauty vanishes away. . . . Just so is life!"

[164]"Spiritual Worship," B 3:99, J VI:424 – 35, sec. 3.4.

[165]"Spiritual Worship," B 3:99 – 100, sec. 3.5; cf. Matthew Prior, "An English Padlock" (n.p.: Jacob Tonson, 1705).

CHAPTER 2

The Primacy of Scripture

A. The Authority of Scripture

1. The Primacy and Normative Authority of the Plain Sense of Scripture

Wesley's primary appeal was to Scripture in all cases of Christian truth. This is why it is necessary to establish the authority of Scripture at the outset of the study of Wesley's teaching.

Three ancillary forms of authority are necessary in order to fully understand how God speaks to us decisively in Scripture. They are (1) Scripture confirmed by the apostolic *tradition*, (2) *reason* enabled by grace, and (3) the personal *experience* of the Spirit in grasping the Word of God proclaimed in Scripture. To understand how these three confirming elements work together is to grasp Wesley's theological method, a term theologians use today to point to how a thinker approaches the discernment of revealed truth.

a. A Man of One Book

As early as 1730, Wesley stated his firm determination to become "'a man of one book', regarding none, comparatively, but the Bible."[1]

Wesley had a lifelong habit of rising early in the morning for prayer and Bible study. He offered a poignant account of his intent in his preface to the *Sermons*:

> [As] a creature of a day, passing through life as an arrow through the air ... just hovering over the great gulf, till a few moments hence I am no more seen — I drop into an unchangeable eternity! I want to know one thing, the way to heaven — how to land safe on that happy shore. God himself has condescended to teach the way: for this very end he came from heaven. He hath written it down in a book. O give me that book! At any price give me the Book of God! I have it. Here is knowledge enough for me. Let me be *homo unius libri*.[2]

If anything appears confusing in the sacred text, it is always possible to pray for grace to the one who said, "'If any be willing to do thy will, he shall know'. I am

---

[1] *PACP*, 10, J XI:373.
[2] *SOSS*, pref. 5; B 1:104 – 5.

willing to do, let me know, thy will. I then search after and consider parallel passages of Scripture, comparing spiritual things with spiritual."[3] Comparison of text with text employs the classic Christian method of analogy, often called the analogy of faith. Faith thinks analogically by allowing all scriptural texts to illuminate each one, and each one to provide an angle of vision upon the whole.

Faith prays for grace to behold God's will. "If any of you lacks wisdom, you should ask God, who gives generously to all without finding fault, and it will be given to you" (James 1:5 NIV).

In describing himself as *homo unius libri*,[4] a man of one book,[5] Wesley did not imply that there were no other books to be usefully read. He himself was a voracious reader. Rather, he implied that all other books are best read in relation to this most revealing book — most revealing of God's being and purpose.[6]

To those who propose to read only the Bible, Wesley retorted, "If you need no book but the Bible, you are not above St. Paul. He called others to 'Bring the books,' says he, 'but especially the parchments.'"[7] The parchments were primary texts available to Paul that may have contained writings of the apostles that later would be received worldwide as sacred Scripture.

Wesley himself was editor of some four hundred books. He was also a lifelong avid reader for whom horseback was a moving library.[8] He was a publisher of books on many subjects as well, including physics, language learning, history, and social change.

b. The Written Word of Scripture as the Norm for Christian Teaching

It is "the faith of Protestants" to "believe neither more nor less than what is manifestly contained in, and provable by, the Holy Scriptures." "The written word is the whole and sole rule of their faith, as well as practice."[9] "We believe the Scripture to be of God."[10] We are asked to "*be not wise above what is written*. Enjoin nothing that the Bible does not clearly enjoin. Forbid nothing that it does not clearly forbid."[11] "I allow no other rule, whether of faith or practice, than the Holy Scriptures."[12] Because of the plenary extent of scriptural inspiration, there is no hidden or screened canon within the canon.[13]

Wesley did not deny that there were forms of human agency in the writing,

---

[3]*SOSS*, pref. 5, John 7:17; B 1:105.

[4]*LJW* 6:30, 130.

[5]*SOSS*, pref. 5; B 1:105.

[6]*LJW* 5:215, 221; 8:192; B 1:57, 71; 4:93.

[7]"Minutes of Several Conversations," Q33, J VIII:315.

[8]*LJW* 1:20, 65.

[9]"On Faith," Heb. 11:6, B 3:4, sec. 1.8; cf. "Justification by Faith," sec. 2. Wesley repeatedly held "the written word of God to be the only and sufficient rule both of Christian faith and practice"; see "The Character of a Methodist," J VIII:340, sec. 1.

[10]EA 13, B 11:19.

[11]Letter to John Dickins, December 26, 1789, *LJW* 8:191 – 92; cf. "The Witness of Our Own Spirit," B 1:303, sec. 6, italics added.

[12]Letter to James Hervey, March 20, 1739, *LJW* 1:285; cf. B 9:33 – 34, 527.

[13]"I make the Word of God the rule of all my actions," Wesley wrote to the bishop of London, Edmund Gibson, and "no more follow any *secret impulse* instead thereof than I follow Mahomet or Confucius." LLBL 4 – 5, B 11:337.

transmission, and hearing of Scripture, for "as God has made men the immediate instruments of all those revelations, so evangelical faith must be partly founded on human testimony."[14] Otherwise, Paul's idiomatic language would not differ from John's and Luke's, which it does.

c. Seeking Scripture's Literal Sense in Its Context

Wesley held to the *plain or literal sense unless irrational or unworthy of God's moral character.*[15] The seeker is called to look for Scripture's plain, literal, historical sense (*sensus literalis*) unless it has a metaphorical level or intent. Even in that case we must consider the metaphor in its plainest sense. The worshiping community reads Scripture for its straightforward, unadorned sense, without pretentious speculations on hidden or allegorical meanings. We are "never to depart from the plain, literal sense, unless it implies an absurdity."[16]

To quote text against context is to fail to see the way in which the Holy Spirit intends its use. Wesley urged his followers to "depart ever so little from ... *the plain, literal meaning of any text, taken in connection with that context.*"[17] Text and context belong together. Each requires the other.

Any text of Scripture can be warped for purposes of private interest. "Any passage is easily perverted, by being recited singly, without any of the preceding or following verses. By this means it may often seem to have one sense, when it will be plain, by observing what goes before and what follows after, that it really has the direct contrary."[18]

Scripture is composed of sentences. Each text seeks to constantly connect with our experience in whatever specific cultural or historical setting we find ourselves. We have this book originally written in Hebrew and Greek. If we are to come into credible contact with the text, we must study.[19]

Those who come seriously to the service of the Word do well to learn the original language of the text. Wesley was willing to engage in textual analysis and to search among the available manuscripts for the most reliable text. He offered numerous corrections to the Authorized Version in his *Explanatory Notes upon the New Testament.*

2. The Analogy of Faith

a. Each Part of Scripture Viewed in Relation to the Whole

Each particular text of Scripture is best read by analogy with other correlated passages of Scripture and the whole course of scriptural teaching, and in relation

---

[14]*Compendium on Natural Philosophy* B 11:447; J XIII:482–87.

[15]*ENOT*, pref.; cf. J XIV:266.

[16]"Of the Church," B 3:50, sec. 12.

[17]*PACP*, Q33, J XI:429, italics added; cf. "Cautions and Directions Given to the Greatest Professors in Methodist Societies," 1762; see also JWO 1:473n; R. Larry Shelton, "Wesley's Approach to Scripture in Historical Perspective," *WTJ* 16 (1981): 23–50.

[18]"On Corrupting the Word of God," B 7:470.

[19]B 3:192–93.

to the history of its consensual interpretation by the great teachers of Scripture. By this means we allow the *clear texts to illuminate obscure texts*.

This is the principle of the analogy of faith (*analogia fidei*), which in accord with classic Christian exegesis, Wesley constantly sought to employ. Scripture is the best interpreter of Scripture.[20] We begin to accumulate through the lifetime study of Scripture a sense of the wholeness of faith as one text illuminates another.

"The literal sense of every text is to be taken, if it be not contrary to some other texts; but in that case the obscure text is to be interpreted by those which speak more plainly."[21] Scriptural wisdom comes out of a broadly based dialogue with the *general sense of the whole* of Scripture, not a single set of selected texts. In the worshiping community, we bring previous memories of Scripture's prior address to each subsequent reading.

Wesley stated his intent in *Explanatory Notes upon the Old Testament*:

> To give the direct, literal meaning, of every verse, of every sentence, and so far as I am able, of every word in the oracles of God. I design only, like the hand of a dial, to point every man to this: not to take up his mind with something else, how excellent soever: but to keep his eye fixt upon the naked Bible, that he may read and hear it with understanding.... It is not my design to write a book, which a man may read separate from the Bible: but barely to assist those who fear God, in hearing and reading the Bible itself, by shewing the natural sense of every part, in as few and plain words as I can.[22]

b. Why Christians Study the Old Testament

Wesley rejected the temptation of Marcion to discard the Old Testament. The New Testament depends on the Old. The Old Testament looks toward its fulfillment in the New. The New Testament fulfills the promises of the Old. The interpretation of the Old Testament is assisted by the analogy of faith, where all Scripture texts illumine each. When Christians read the Old Testament, they read it in the light of its being fulfilled in the New.

Long before modern hermeneutics, Wesley made clear that "the Church is to be judged by the Scripture, not the Scripture by the Church." The Scriptures of both the Old and New Testaments guide the judgments of the church. Wesley added, "And Scripture is the best expounder of Scripture. The best way, therefore, to understand it, is carefully to compare Scripture with Scripture, and thereby learn the true meaning of it."[23] "Scripture interprets Scripture; one part fixing the sense of another."[24]

This enables the Christian reader of the Old Testament to view the moral commands as covered promises. Christians earnestly study the Hebrew Bible in relation to its having been fulfilled in Jesus Christ.[25]

---

[20]B 1:58 – 59, 106; 2:102 – 3; 4:5 – 6; 9:201, 353; 11:169, 504.
[21]Letter to Samuel Furly, May 10, 1755, *LJW* 111:129.
[22]*ENOT*, pref. 15, viii.
[23]"Popery Calmly Considered," J X:142, sec. 1.6.
[24]"Address to the Clergy," J X:482, sec. 1.l.
[25]B 1:381 – 82, 386 – 87, 394 – 95; 2:514.

Wesley's exegesis focused on the practical application of Scripture in walking in the way of holiness.[26] Christian experience becomes a confirming exercise, not a determining force, in wise and balanced forms of scriptural interpretation. Scripture, when experienced, acts as a corrective to rash and imbalanced interpretations.[27] Reason and experience in this way become servants, not masters, of the believer's understanding of revelation history.[28]

3. Spirit and Scripture

a. Scripture Judges All Other Alleged Revelations

God's Spirit accompanies every step of the thoughtful reading of Scripture:

> Whosoever giveth his mind to Holy Scriptures with diligent study and burning desire, it cannot be that he should be left without help. For either God will send him some godly doctor to teach him or God himself from above will give light unto his mind and teach him those things which are necessary for him. Man's human and worldly wisdom or science is not needful to the understanding of Scripture but the revelation of the Holy Ghost who inspireth the true meaning unto them that with humility and diligence search.[29]

"The Scriptures are the touchstone whereby Christians examine all, real or supposed, revelations."[30] Scriptures are not to be pitted against the Spirit. Scripture can be understood only through the same Spirit whereby it is given.[31] The Scriptures, inspired by the Spirit, form the written rule by which the Spirit thereafter leads us into all truth.[32] *"The historical experience of the church, though fallible, is the better judge overall of Scripture's meanings than later interpreters."*[33]

b. Mining the Textuary

To attest the work of the Spirit, we do well to mine the textuary of the Spirit's work and dig those jewels of instruction out of the hard rock of the written Word.[34] "Every good textuary is a good divine," and "none can be a good divine who is not a good textuary." Interpretation at times may be handicapped "without knowledge of the original tongues."[35]

If God the Spirit is the one who calls forth Scripture, then believers have good reason to assume that God will be present in their reading of Scripture. Scripture

---

[26]MOB, 89 – 96.

[27]B 4:246 – 47; 9:378 – 79; 11:509.

[28]B 3:16, 200 – 201; 4:198 – 99, 219.

[29]Preface to the Reader, DSF, JWO 123; B 1:381 – 82, 386 – 87, 394 – 95; 2:514. This work is Wesley's amended edition of the Elizabethan Homilies, which for Anglicans constitute a worthy guide to scriptural faith.

[30]Letter to Thomas Whitehead, February 10, 1748, *LJW* 11:117.

[31]MOB, 97.

[32]*LJW* 2:117; cf. B 3:496.

[33]Albert C. Outler on Wesley, in JWO, 1:58 – 59.

[34]*CH* 7:185 – 87, 474 – 75.

[35]"Address to the Clergy," J X:482, sec. 1.2.

is a means of grace by which God the Spirit leads sinners back to the love of the Father manifested in the Son.[36] The received canon is sufficient for faith and fully adequate to teach the truth.[37]

"Though the Spirit is our principal leader, yet He is not our rule at all; the Scriptures are the rule whereby He [the Holy Spirit] leads us into all truth." A *rule* implies "something used by an intelligent being" so as to make everything "plain and clear."[38] The Holy Spirit is far more than a rule. He is the Guide to make the rule of Scripture plain within the heart.

4. Scripture, Conscience, and General Revelation

a. The Heavens Declare God's Glory

The history of God's disclosure illumines all other forms of knowing. Special revelation does not on the whole run counter to general revelation but elucidates it.[39] God is present in the entire book of nature and history, for that is what Scripture itself teaches: "The heavens declare the glory of God; the skies proclaim the work of his hands. Day after day they pour forth speech" (Ps. 19:1–2 NIV).

Those who try to understand the ways of God in history and the love of God for fallen humanity do well to diligently study the history of divine self-disclosure both in nature and human history.[40] It is in human history through events that God has made known his holy, self-giving love, particularly in Jesus Christ.[41]

Scripture does not override the private sphere of conscience but points to it. Conscience is the internal witness testifying to moral awareness present within every human being. "Every man has a right to judge for himself, particularly in matters of religion, because every man must give an account of himself to God."[42]

b. Adequacy, Clarity, and Sufficiency of Scripture

Holy Scripture is "that 'word of God which remaineth for ever'; of which, though 'heaven and earth pass away, one jot or tittle shall not pass away.' The Scripture, therefore, of the Old and New Testament, is a most solid and precious system of divine truth. Every part thereof is worthy of God; and all together are one entire body, wherein is no defect, no excess. It is the fountain of heavenly wisdom, which they who are able to taste prefer to all writings of men, however wise or learned or holy."[43]

Wesley said, "I try every church and every doctrine by the Bible."[44] "The Scripture, therefore, being delivered by men divinely inspired, is a rule sufficient of itself.

---

[36]"The Means of Grace," B 1:386–88; J V:92–94.
[37]"On Corrupting the Word of God," B 7:470–71.
[38]Letter [to Thomas Whitehead?], February 10, 1748, *LJW* 2:117; B 1:302–3; 9:114–15, 198.
[39]"On Working Out Our Own Salvation," B 3:199–200, proem 1, 2.
[40]B 2:536; 1:420–21; 2:54–55, 588, 591–92; 3:4, 504.
[41]B 4:18.
[42]"Address to the Reader," 1771 edition of collected works, quoted in Preface to the Third Edition, 1:4.
[43]*ENNT*, pref. 10.
[44]*LJW* 111:172.

So it neither needs, nor is capable of, any further addition."[45] "If there be any mistakes in the Bible, there may as well be a thousand. If there be one falsehood in that book, it did not come from the God of truth."[46] If any way "be contrary to Scripture, it is not good, and the longer we are in it so much the worse."[47] In classic Christian reasoning, supposed "mistakes" in the Bible are misreadings, errors of the reader, assuming that text and context have been taken into proper account as applied by comparing Scripture with Scripture and the whole with the part.

Said Wesley, "The language of [God's] messengers, also, is exact in the highest degree: for the words which were given them accurately answered the impression made upon their minds; and hence Luther says, 'Divinity is nothing but a grammar of the language of the Holy Ghost.' To understand this thoroughly, we should observe the emphasis which lies on every word; the holy affections expressed thereby, and the tempers shown by every writer."[48] Wesley followed Luther and Calvin in their method of reading Scripture texts: understand each word, text in context, preferably in the original language, grasped analogically in relation to the whole testimony of Scripture.

c. Practical Guide to Reading the Sacred Text

In the preface to *Explanatory Notes upon the Old Testament*, Wesley set forth five practical steps to enable serious meditative Scripture study:

1. Set apart a specified daily time for Scripture study.
2. Read the Hebrew Bible in conjunction with the New Testament, reading both "with a single eye to know the whole will of God, and a fixed resolution to do it."
3. "Have a constant eye to the *analogy of faith*, the connection and harmony there is between those grand, fundamental doctrines, original sin, justification by faith, the new birth, inward and outward holiness."
4. Let your reading be surrounded by earnest prayer, "seeing 'Scripture can only be understood through the same Spirit whereby it was given.'"
5. Pause frequently for honest personal self-examination.[49]

B. The Inspiration of Holy Scripture

The Spirit works not only in the mind of the sacred writer but within the heart of the attentive reader: "All Scripture is inspired of God — the Spirit of God not only once inspired those who wrote it, but continually inspires, supernaturally assists, those that read it with earnest prayer."[50]

---

[45]"Popery Calmly Considered," J X:141, sec. 1.3.
[46]*JJW* 6:117.
[47]Letter to James Lowther, October 28, 1754, *LJW* 111:122. "I build upon no authority, ancient or modern, but the Scripture. If this supports any doctrine, it will stand; if not, the sooner it falls the better." Cf. MOB 113–14.
[48]*ENNT*, pref. 12.
[49]*ENOT*, pref. 18, I; ix; cf. B 1:58–59, 106; 2:102–3; 4:5–6, 246–47; 9:201, 353, 378–79; 11:169, 504, 509.
[50]*ENNT* 794, 2 Tim. 3:16.

Wesley's teaching on the inspiration of Scripture has its beginning and end in God's purpose to reveal divine grace to human persons. In a concise essay on the inspiration of sacred Scripture,[51] Wesley showed how the revelation of God in Scripture is accompanied by the Spirit's work to awaken the mind of the seeker.

1. A Clear and Concise Demonstration of the Divine Inspiration of Holy Scripture

a. Four Arguments from Miracles, Prophecies, Goodness, and Character

Wesley's brief essay "Four Arguments from Miracles, Prophecies, Goodness, and Character" is hardly intended to elaborate a complete doctrine of scriptural interpretation, but it does offer a striking glimpse into the heart of Wesley's view of Scripture. It is deceptively short. The first time we read it through we might think, *This is theology? Too simple.* The second time we begin to ponder whether something might be hidden there but wonder just what. Later a light begins to dawn. Following is the line of reasoning.

There are four grand and powerful inductive arguments that strongly induce us to believe that the Bible is from God:

1. the arguments from miracles experienced,
2. the argument from prophecy fulfilled,
3. the argument from the intrinsic moral goodness of scriptural teaching taken as a whole, and
4. the argument from the moral character of those who wrote it.[52]

Each argument has both inductive and deductive features. Wesley first looked inductively at empirical evidence of the inspiration of Scripture.

b. Inductive Arguments for the Inspiration of Scripture

Where miracles are attested, they must be true or false. If truly attested, they must flow from God's own power. Miracle requires the premise of one incomparably powerful and wise — namely, God. There can be no miracle without one capable of transcending normal human expectations. Later when we consider providence, I will speak of the relation of divine causality and the natural causality of physics.

Where prophecies are attested, they will be proven in history to be either true or false. If truly attested, it will be evident to any reasonable viewer of history that they are fulfilled. If in the process of being fulfilled, they can be seen as being precise, based on previous evidences made known in history. If prophecies are proven fulfilled, they must flow from God's unbounded knowing. Prophecy requires the premise of the wisdom of God. We cannot have fulfilled prophecy without positing God's eternal wisdom being revealed in time. There can be no fulfilled prophecy

---

[51]CCD, J XI:484.
[52]CCD, J XI:484.

without an eternally wise one capable of seeing past and future. That one the worshiping community calls God.[53]

The teachings of Scripture must be either morally good or evil. If the doctrines of Scripture are good, they of necessity flow out of the goodness of God. If they are incomparably good, compared to all natural and historical knowing, they must come from one who is incomparably good. The demonstrated goodness of the teaching requires the premise of the beneficence of God.

If the moral character of the authors of Scripture corresponds with their teaching, even under persecution and torture, a reasonable observer will take note of that correspondence. It is implausible that the martyrs of classic Christian faith were misinformed about the credibility of the resurrection and the promise of eternal life. Their very actions showed their moral character. Stephen is the model for all subsequent witnesses who are willing to die for their faith. The truth of their teaching is demonstrated in the testimony of their moral character. Their moral character must presuppose some source and ground of moral character. The holiness of lives lived out in relation to the events attested in Scripture points to the holiness of God.[54] There can be no reliable Christian teaching without positing one capable of living out the truth of Christian teaching under adverse circumstances, as Christ did on the cross and as Stephen did in his innocent death.[55]

These four arguments can be pictured in summary:

The Ground of Scripture's Authority Hinges on:	The attributes of God:
Miracles attested	Power of God
Fulfilled prophecy attested	Wisdom of God
Moral goodness attested	Goodness of God
Moral character of human authors of Scripture	Holiness of God

Thus, inductively, out of the personally experienced and attested evidences of miracles occurring, prophecies being fulfilled, moral goodness being taught, and the saints and martyrs living out that testimony even to death, the conclusion is that the sacred Scripture is a reliable source of knowing the only one who can be worshiped as having incomparable power, wisdom, goodness, and holiness. The infinite power, omniscience, incomparable moral excellence, and righteousness of God must be posited as the ground of these visible consequences of scriptural testimony to miracle, prophecy, moral teaching, and holy lives lived.[56]

These are all experiential and inductive arguments — that is, arguments based on observation of personal and historical human experiences. They can be tested by opening our eyes to the evidence.

---

[53]CCD, J XI:484 – 85.
[54]JWO 89 – 90, 181 – 82, 225 – 26, 375 – 76.
[55]CCD, J XI:484 – 86.
[56]LJW 2:62, 69, 90, 104.

Wesley turned then to the arguments for the veracity of Scripture based on deductive reasoning, including those that derive their conclusions logically from commonsense reason. These arguments may go by so quickly that many readers may not "get" them. As with the ontological argument for the existence of God, readers may have to ponder them repeatedly to grasp their consequence.

c. Deductive Arguments for the Inspiration of Scripture

Wesley was trying to demonstrate how the inspiration of Scripture is not an unreasonable judgment of unreasonable people. It is a reasonable operating premise that may be seen working in generations of good and thoughtful people.

Concisely he sought to demonstrate that the Bible must be the creation of either

> good human beings
> or angels
> or bad human beings
> or devils
> or God.

These are exhaustive alternatives.[57] After these five, there is no sixth.

First, he showed that the Bible could not have been written merely by good persons, because good persons would have been lying when they wrote, "Thus saith the Lord"; for if it were not the Lord but actually only the finite person speaking, just his or her own psychology or history or reason, that person would be lying. No good person (and the same argument applies to good angels) would write or attest such a statement unless it was the Lord who called it forth. So we can be sure that Scripture is not inspired by the good human beings, or even good angels, for they would not lie.[58]

But could the Bible have been written by deceivers, by evil persons or fallen angels? We can be sure that Scripture is not inspired by evil persons, because a bad person or bad angel could not have invented such good doctrine. Evildoers could not have invented a set of writings so wholly contrary to their own character.

Having thus eliminated all of the alternatives: inspiration by good humans, good angels, bad humans, and bad angels, as authors of Scripture, there is no other conclusion to draw than that it can only be breathed out as God's own Word. God's speech to us, of course, is written and addressed through human persons with human language within different historical contexts, but its author and inspirer is God.[59] We can then take it for granted in reading the testimony of the prophets and the apostles that this is God's own self-communication[60] to be taken with utter seriousness as reliable divine address.[61]

---

[57]"A Clear and Concise Demonstration of the Divine Inspiration of Holy Scripture," J XI:484.
[58]Ibid.; cf. B 2:310–11.
[59]*LJW* 2:62–69, 90, 100, 104; 5:245.
[60]*LJW* 2:148; 3:127; B 11:291, 504.
[61]"A Clear and Concise Demonstration of the Divine Inspiration of Holy Scripture," J XI:484.

That is it. You have just read it. If you missed its deductive logic, read it again.

In this short essay, Wesley showed himself to be a master of concise argument. In fact, this was his most important concise argument on the authority of Scripture.

Most of Wesley's readers were laypersons. He did not think that this argument required any extensive knowledge of philosophy. He thought that ordinary laypersons could understand and rely on this simple commonsense reasoning.

2. Wesley as Commentator on Scripture

These arguments on the inspiration of sacred Scripture may be extensively seen at work in Wesley's own commentaries and homilies on Scripture.

a. Notes upon the New Testament

Wesley's arguments are especially evident in his *Explanatory Notes upon the New Testament*. There Wesley's purpose was to make Scripture available in accessible format to Christian laity, especially in his own connection of spiritual formation, who had neither the means nor the time to read through highly technical treatises or commentaries. The relative cost of books was enormous in his day. So all of Wesley's publishing was designed for the thrifty buyer. He was producing these commentaries at an extremely marginal cost. His *Notes* were meant to guide daily Bible study for ordinary people who didn't have the resources to buy expensive books. He knew that most people were so hardworking that he had to deliver these insights plainly — without speculation, posturing, or deceit.

In his *Notes*, Wesley focused especially on application of spiritual truth to ordinary living.[62] He sought to adapt the wisest commentators of his day for a general reading audience. He gratefully acknowledged that he worked freely out of Matthew Henry[63] and William Poole[64] in his Old Testament *Notes*, and from John A. Bengel, John Heylyn's *Theological Lectures*,[65] John Guyse's *Practical Expositor*,[66] and Philip Doddridge's *The Family Expositor*.[67] Wesley often let Bengel speak for himself, especially in the commentary on Revelation: "All I can do is partly to translate, partly abridge the most necessary of his observations; allowing myself the liberty to alter some of them, and to add a few notes where he is not full."[68]

The *Notes* "were not principally designed for men of learning, who are provided with many other helps; and much less for men of long and deeper experience in the ways and Word of God. I desire to sit at their feet and learn from them. But I write chiefly for plain, unlettered men, who understand only their mother tongue, and yet reverence and love the Word of God, and have a desire to save their souls."[69]

---

[62]*LJW* 4:93, 125, 8:67.

[63]*Exposition of the Old and New Testament*, used especially in Genesis.

[64]*Annotations on the Holy Bible.*

[65]John Heylyn, *Theological Lectures*, 2 vols. (London: Westminster Abbey, 1749–61).

[66]John Guyse, *Practical Expositor*, 3 vols. (London, 1739–52).

[67]*ENNT*, pref. 8.

[68]*ENNT* 932.

[69]*ENNT*, pref. 3, 6; *JJW* 4:91–92, 361; 7:345.

Wesley commented, "I have endeavored to make the notes as short as possible, that the comment may not obscure or swallow up the text; and as plain as possible, in pursuance of my main design, to assist the unlearned reader. For this reason I have studiously avoided, not only all curious and critical inquiries, and all use of the learned languages, but all such methods of reasoning and modes of expression as people in common life are unacquainted with."[70]

b. Notes upon the Old Testament

The *Explanatory Notes upon the Old Testament*[71] were planned to be "delivered weekly to subscribers" in 60 installments, beginning April 25, 1765. Actually they extended to 110 numbers, priced at sixpence each, with the final manuscript dated December 24, 1766. All of these were later bound in three hefty folio volumes.[72] Regarding the Old Testament *Notes*, Wesley modestly recommended that each society subscribe, allowing "two, four, or six might join together for a copy, and bring the money to their leader weekly."[73] This ambitious reading program was designed for ordinary folks.

Wesley's distinctive, simple, personal style shows through even amid heavy editing. The *Notes* are "an artful blending of the best of other scholars' work into the stream of his own theological perspectives."[74] He took liberty in refining and adopting edifying words of others to fit his own ministry of witness.

Despite his best intentions to honor the sacred text as God's own Word, Wesley was fully aware that good Scripture might fall into bad hands. How are those who corrupt the Word different from those who allow the Word to speak?

3. On Corrupting the Word of God

The text of "On Corrupting the Word of God" is 2 Corinthians 2:17: "We are not as many, which corrupt the word of God" [Homily #137 (1727), B 4:243 – 51; J #136, VII:468 – 73].

Those who corrupt the Word of God are contrasted with those who read it plainly as God's own Word.

Today we have critical minds investigating the sacred text who come at it with what is called a "hermeneutic of suspicion," an approach that seeks to test the truth of Scripture against rigorous modern "historical-empirical methods," against the shared consensus of many modern writers who do not read Scripture as divine revelation. Some of these critics may try to be fair to give Scripture an opportunity to speak on its own terms, while others may impose on Scripture terms alien to its intent.

---

[70]*ENNT*, pref. 6, 7.
[71]*JJW* 5:112, 115.
[72]Bristol, UK: William Pine, 1765 – 66; reprint, Salem, OH: Schmul, 1975.
[73]*LJW* 4:312.
[74]Editor's Preface, *John Wesley's Commentary on the Bible*, ed. G. Roger Schoenhals (Grand Rapids: Zondervan, 1990), 7.

Wesley had some choice words for those in his day who had similar tendencies. He thought that an obsessive hermeneutic of suspicion[75] reflected poorly on its practitioners: "The honester any man is, the less apt is he to suspect another.... Would not any man be tempted to suspect his integrity who, without proof, suspected the want of it in another?"[76] To avoid corrupting the Word, the reader must let it speak for itself.

a. Three Marks of Corrupters of the Word

Three "marks of distinction" betray those prone to corrupt the Word of God. First, the corrupters are predisposed to *blend Scripture with political interests, economic motives, or various human admixtures,* diluting the divine Word with the errors of others or the fancies of their own brains, usually without any awareness of their own self-deception.[77]

A second type of corrupter perverts the sense of a passage of Scripture, *taking it out of context,* "repeating the words wrong," or "putting a wrong sense upon them ... foreign to the writer's intention" or even contrary to it. "Any passage is easily perverted" by neglecting its context.[78]

Third, others corrupt the Word not by adding to but *subtracting from it.* They "take either of the spirit or substance of it away, while they study to prophesy only smooth things, and therefore palliate and colour what they preach, to reconcile it to the taste of their hearers," washing their hands of "those stubborn texts that will not bend to their purpose."[79]

These three marks or tendencies distinguish the corruptors of the Word from those who are sincere in both their listening to and speaking of the written Word of God.

b. Sincerity in Hearing and Speaking the Word

Sincere hearers of the Word of God attest it "genuine and unmixed," without unnatural or artificial interpretations. They do not take away from the Word. They dare to say neither more nor less than that which the Word addresses to that audience. They preach the whole counsel of God. They are willing to discuss honestly the real resistances of hearers. They speak "with plainness and boldness," not softening the challenge of the Word.[80] Those who preach with sincerity and find only rejection need not fret, for they have done their duty as watchmen (Ezek. 33:1 – 9).[81]

Such sincerity is absolutely essential to effective preaching. It enables the hearer

---

[75] A hermeneutic of suspicion is a defensive assumption in relation to the text or the hearer that would begin ad hominem by questioning the arguer's motives or social location as determinative of its content. This sort of critique was later developed explicitly by the tradition of Marx, Freud, and Jacques Derrida, and more judiciously by Paul Ricoeur.

[76] "On Corrupting the Word of God," B 4:246, J VII:469 – 71, pref. 2, 3.

[77] "On Friendship with the World," B 3:126 – 40.

[78] "On Corrupting the Word of God," B 4:247, J VII:470, sec. 1.2.

[79] "On Corrupting the Word of God," B 4:247 – 48, J VII:470, sec. 1.3.

[80] "On Corrupting the Word of God," B 4:248, J VII:470, sec. 1.3; cf. *LJW* 6:276.

[81] "On Corrupting the Word of God," B 4:250, J VII:473, sec. 3.1.

to trust that the preacher has no end in view but the clear and accurate address of the Word.[82] When it comes from the heart, sincere communication has a capacity to "strangely insinuate into the hearts of others."[83] Its central concern: "Let the hearers accommodate themselves to the Word," not the Word to the hearers.[84] As Paul declared, "Unlike so many, we do not peddle the word of God for profit. On the contrary, in Christ we speak before God with sincerity, as those sent from God" (2 Cor. 2:17 NIV).

Further Reading on Wesley's Scriptural Teaching

Arnett, William M. "John Wesley and the Bible." *WTJ* 3 (1968): 3–9.

———. "John Wesley: Man of One Book." PhD diss., Drew University, 1954.

Artingstall, George. *A Man of One Book.* London: Epworth, 1953.

Bullen, Donald A. *A Man of One Book? John Wesley's Interpretation and Use of the Bible.* Waynesboro, GA: Paternoster, 2007.

Clemons, James T. "John Wesley —Biblical Literalist." *RL* 46 (1977): 332–42.

Dayton, Donald W. "The Use of Scripture in the Wesleyan Tradition." In *The Use of the Bible in Theology,* edited by Robert K. Johnston, 121–36. Atlanta: John Knox, 1985.

Ferguson, Duncan S. "John Wesley on Scripture: The Hermeneutics of Pietism." *MH* 22, no. 4 (1984): 234–45.

Green, Joel B. *Reading Scripture as Wesleyans.* Nashville: Abingdon, 2010.

Greenway, Jeffrey, and Joel B. Green. *Grace and Holiness in a Changing World: A Wesleyan Proposal for Postmodern Ministry.* Nashville: Abingdon, 2007.

Hilderbrandt, Franz. *Christianity according to the Wesleys,* 9–27. London: Epworth, 1956.

Jones, Scott J. *John Wesley's Conception and Use of Scripture.* Nashville: Kingswood, 1995.

Källstad, Thorvald. *John Wesley and the Bible: A Psychological Study.* Stockholm: Nya Bokforlags, 1974.

Kimbrough, S. T., Jr., ed. *Orthodox and Wesleyan Scriptural Understanding and Practice.* Crestwood, NY: St. Vladimir's Seminary Press, 2005.

Lawson, John. *The Wesley Hymns: As a Guide to Scriptural Teachings.* Grand Rapids: Zondervan, 1988.

McCown, Wayne G. "Wesley's Suggestions for Study of the Bible." In *A Contemporary Wesleyan Theology,* edited by Charles W. Carter. Grand Rapids: Zondervan, 1983.

Mullen, Wilbur H. "John Wesley's Method of Biblical Interpretation." *RL* 47 (1978): 99–108.

Oswalt, John N. "Wesley's Use of the Old Testament." *WTJ* 12 (1977): 39–53.

Pellowe, William C. S. "John Wesley's Use of the Bible." *MR* 106 (1923): 353–74.

---

[82]B 1:281, 683–84; 4:365.
[83]"On Corrupting the Word of God," B 4:245, J VII:469, pref. 2.
[84]"On Corrupting the Word of God," B 4:250, J VII:472, sec. 2.4.

Scoggs, Robin. "John Wesley as Biblical Scholar." *JBR* 38 (1960): 415–22.

Shelton, R. Larry. "Wesley's Approach to Scripture in Historical Perspective." *WTJ* 16 (1981): 23–50.

Smith, Timothy L. "John Wesley and the Wholeness of Scripture." *Int* 39 (1985): 246–62.

Turner, George Allen. "John Wesley as an Interpreter of Scripture." In *Inspiration and Interpretation*, edited by John F. Walvoord, 156–78. Grand Rapids: Eerdmans, 1957.

Yates, Arthur S. "Wesley and His Bible." *MR* (1960): 8.

Wesley's Sources

Bengel, Johann A. *Gnomon of the New Testament*. Grand Rapids: Baker, 1983.

Guyse, John. *Practical Exposition of the Four Gospels*. London, 1739.

Henry, Matthew. *A Commentary on the Holy Bible*. 6 vols. New York: Revell, 1935.

Heylyn, John. *An Interpretation of the New Testament*. London, 1749, 1761.

Wesley's Explanatory Notes

Arnett, William M. "A Study in John Wesley's *Explanatory Notes upon the Old Testament*." *WTJ* 8 (1973): 14–32.

Earle, Ralph. "John Wesley's New Testament." *AS* 14, no. 1 (1960): 61–67.

Laws, C. H. "Wesley's Notes on the New Testament." *PWHS* 18 (1931): 37–39.

Schoenhals, G. Roger, ed. *John Wesley's Notes on the Bible*. Grand Rapids: Zondervan, 1987.

Simon, John S. "Mr. Wesley's *Notes upon the New Testament*." *PWHS* 9 (1914): 97–105.

Smith, Timothy L. "Notes on the Exegesis of John Wesley's *Explanatory Notes upon the NT*." *WTJ* 16, no. 1 (1981): 107–13.

God's Particular Method of Working

In the homily on "The Promise of Understanding," Wesley wrote, "It is the Divine Spirit 'who worketh in us both to will and to do of his good pleasure,' of this, experience, and reason, and Scripture convince every sincere inquirer," which is God's "particular method of working."[1]

This lucid sentence brings us to what theologians today call "theological method." Wesley preferred to speak more plainly of "God's particular method of working."

Wesley taught the authority of Scripture in a way that honors those who have appropriated it faithfully and consensually over the centuries. Neither tradition nor reason nor experience is a criteria separable from the source of Christian truth: the narrative of God's revelation of the meaning of universal history that culminates in Jesus Christ.

Wesley's theological method may be cautiously summarized as "the authority of Scripture understood in the light of tradition, reason, and experience." This formulation is quite different from making tradition, reason, and experience equal partners in authority to God's revealed Word.

The Quadrilateral Method

The so-called quadrilateral method (the authority of Scripture understood in the light of tradition, reason, and experience) was spelled out or implied in several locations in Wesley's writings: (1) in the early part of *The Doctrine of Original Sin*, (2) in the *Appeals*, and (3) most explicitly in the homily "On Sin in Believers."[2]

The metaphor of quadrilateral historically has referred to four walls or bulwarks. It is a defensive military metaphor. It has sometimes been wrongly interpreted as the "four permissions," or four open doors, rather than the four bulwarks of defense. The problem with the metaphor is that Scripture is the fundamental premise of the other three. They stand as cooperative, not judging, partners to Scripture.

---

[1]"The Promise of Understanding," B 4:284, sec. 1.3.

[2]"On Sin in Believers," B 1:318–19, J V:144–56, sec. 1.5. Alternatively, Wesley listed Scripture, reason, and experience as doctrinal norms, as in "The Repentance of Believers," sec. 1.2, and on other occasions "Scripture, reason, and Christian antiquity," as in his preface to his collected works, vol. 1 (1771). This method, as defined more fully by Albert C. Outler, Donald Thorsen, and Charles Yrigoyen, appears in some form in all United Methodist Disciplines written after 1968 and revised in 1988.

Those who wish to carefully examine Wesley's systematic theological method are well advised to also investigate the homilies on "The Catholic Spirit," "A Caution against Bigotry," "The Case of Reason Impartially Considered," "The Promise of Understanding," "The Imperfection of Human Knowledge," "A Clear and Concise Demonstration of the Divine Inspiration of Holy Scripture," and the argument of the "Appeals" ("An Earnest Appeal to Men of Reason and Religion" and "A Farther Appeal to Men of Reason and Religion").[3]

[3]Albert C. Outler, "John Wesley's Heritage and the Future of Systematic Theology," in *Wesleyan Theology Today*, ed. Theodore H. Runyon (Nashville: Kingswood, 1985), 38 – 46; Albert C. Outler, "John Wesley's Interests in the Early Fathers of the Church," in *WTH*, 97 – 110.

CHAPTER 3

Tradition

The task at hand is to review Wesley's teaching on the three supportive voices that confirm and reasonably illumine the Word of God in sacred Scripture. The first of these voices is often called simply "tradition." It deals with the role of the apostolic tradition in transmitting the gospel in history. It is followed by the role of grace-enabled reason and the role of personal experience as shaped inwardly by the Holy Spirit.

A. Tradition as the Consensual Reception of the Apostolic Teaching

1. The Unchanging Apostolic Tradition of Scripture Teaching through Changing History

a. Christian Antiquity: The Special Place of the Ancient Christian Writers

In the preface of his collected works, Wesley sought to present thoughts "agreeable, I hope, to Scripture, reason and Christian antiquity."[1] In this preface it is clear that the element of experience is correlated with each of these modes of knowing. The term *antiquity*, as Wesley used it, referred to "the religion of the primitive church, of the whole church in the purest ages," with special reference to "Clemens Romanus, Ignatius, and Polycarp ... Tertullian, Origen, Clemens Alexandrinus,[2] and Cyprian[3] ... Chrysostom,[4] Basil,[5] Ephrem Syrus,[6] and Macarius."[8] Wesley grew up in the Anglican tradition. Honoring ancient Christian writers and ecumenical

---

[1]Wesley's preface to the 1771 edition of his works, quoted by Jackson in his Preface to the Third Edition, March 1771, I:4, sec. 4,; cf. "On Sin in Believers," sec. 3.1–10.

[2]For other references to Clement of Alexandria, see *LJW* 2:327–28, 342, 387; 5:43; 6:129; cf. B 3:586; 4:402; 9:31; *JJW* 5:197.

[3]For Wesley's extensive references to Cyprian, see B 2:461–62; 3:196–97, 450–51, 458–59, 469–70; *LJW* 1:277, 323; 2:320, 333–37, 361, 373, 387; B 1:437; JWO 42, 126, 195, 264, 309, 328; *JJW* 1:416; 2:263; 4:97.

[4]For further references to John Chrysostom, see FA, B 11:156–62, 175; B 1:155–59, 381–453; 2:113; 3:586; 4:402; JWO 131–32, 264, 328; see also K. Steve McCormick, "John Chrysostom and JohnWesley" (PhD diss., Drew University, 1983), for a comparative study of John Chrysostom and John Wesley.

[5]*LJW* 4:176; 11.8.

[6]*JJW* 1:276, 279, 284–85, 294–95; 3:284; 4:457–59.

[7]For notes on the identity and view of "Macarius the Egyptian," see JWO ix, 9, 31, 119, 252, 274–75; *JJW* 1:254; *LJW* 2:387.

[8]"On Laying the Foundation of the New Chapel," 1777, B 3:586, sec. 2.3; *LJW* 11:387.

documents of the first five centuries was highly valued by classic Anglican scholars (Cranmer, Hooker, Pearson, and many others). Wesley was steeped in this tradition.

Wesley wrote, "We prove the doctrines we preach by Scripture and reason, and if need be, by antiquity."[9] This practice does not pit Scripture against the tradition of antiquity. Rather, it views the original apostolic preaching of the New Testament as awakening an ongoing tradition of accurate and reliable recollection of the events of salvation surrounding the history of Jesus of Nazareth. This recollection was most vital and purest in its earliest periods, the earliest Christian centuries. Then the price of witnessing was often persecution and all too frequently death. The third-century tradition did not come without a high cost.

b. The Early Church Fathers

Wesley took very seriously the early Christian writers. In his Christian Library, he featured the ante-Nicene fathers and many writers who held closely to classic Christology and deep-going spiritual formation. No thinking person, wrote Wesley, will easily dismiss and certainly never "condemn the Fathers of the Church," whose views are "indispensably necessary" for the practice of ministry. There is no excuse for "one who has the opportunity, and makes no use of it," to fail to read the best patristic texts—the writings of the early church fathers. There is no warrant for any "person who has had a University education" to bypass or ignore the wisdom of the ancient Christian writers.[10]

Wesley remembered how his own father had early provided him with the fervent living model of "reverence to the ancient church."[11] This family training would prepare Wesley later to debate in detail with learned patristic interpreters like Richard Smalbroke and Conyers Middleton on specific patristic references and translation nuances of the works of Irenaeus,[12] Minucius Felix,[13] Origen,[14] Didymus of Alexandria,[15] Eusebius,[16] Athanasius,[17] Epiphanius,[18] Gregory of Nyssa,[19] Gregory Nazianzen,[20] Augustine,[21] Jerome,[22] Pachomius,[23] Theophylact,[24] Pseudo-Dionysius,[25] John of Damascus,[26] and others.[27]

---

[9]FA, pt. 3, B 11:310, sec. 3.28.

[10]"Address to the Clergy," J X:484, sec. 1.2.

[11]Thirty years prior to his writing to William Dodd, March 12, 1756 (LJW 111:172), hence probably around 1726.

[12]For further references to Irenaeus, see LJW 2:319, 332, 387; JJW 1:356.

[13]LJW 2:332, 348.

[14]For further references to Origen in Wesley, see LJW 2:91–92, 100, 105, 324, 332, 353, 362, 387; 3:137; 4:176; B 4:33n.

[15]Didymus Alexandrinus (the blind), JWO 129.

[16]LJW 2:331.

[17]FA, B 11:162–63, 175; LJW 1:367; B 2:397.

[18]LJW 2:360.

[19]B 1:75, 188n; JWO 9–10, 31, 119.

[20]JWO 130.

[21]The bulk of Wesley's references to Augustine (St. Austin) are to be found in the letters, LJW 1:45;

c. Three Creeds: How Ancient Orthodoxy Formed Methodist Doctrine

Wesley argued that the Methodist Societies from the beginning had been *"orthodox* in every point." The criterion he had in mind for orthodoxy was equally clear: "firmly believing ... the Three Creeds."[28] "Firmly believing" for Wesley meant believing "from the heart" without deception or uncertainty. Confessing the creeds with reservations or qualifiers was not what Wesley had in mind.

"Were you to recite the whole catalogue of *heresies* enumerated by Bishop Pearson, it might be asked, 'Who can lay any one of these to their [the Methodists'] charge?' "[29] This catalogue included the ancient deceptions of grace-disabled Pelagianism, incarnation-denying Arianism, and Marcionitic rejection of the Old Testament, with its consequent tendency to anti-Semitism. It applied to both their original and recurrent forms.

d. The Ancient Christian Writers as Scriptural Exegetes

The Fathers are "the most authentic commentators on Scripture, as being both nearest the fountain, and eminently endued with the Spirit by whom all Scripture was given," wrote Wesley. "I speak chiefly of those who wrote before the Council of Nice [Nicaea, AD 325]. But who would not likewise desire to have some acquaintance with those that followed them? with St. Chrysostom, Basil, Jerome, Austin [Augustine]; and above all, the man of a broken heart, Ephraim Syrus?"[30]

Typical of the church fathers' reliance on Scripture was Cyril of Jerusalem, who wrote in his Fifth Catechetical Lecture: "It behoveth us not to deliver, no not so much as the least thing of the holy mysteries of faith without the holy Scripture."[31] Do not try to teach Christianity without constant reference to canonical Scripture.

Wesley was quick to concede that the ancient Christian writers made many occasional "mistakes, many weak suppositions, and many ill-drawn conclusions." Nonetheless, "I exceedingly reverence them as well as their writings ... because they describe true, genuine Christianity."[32] He was thinking of great exegetes like Origen when he wrote, "Some of these Fathers, being afraid of too literal a way of

---

2:60, 70; 3:171; 4:176; 6:175; 7:58, 333; see also B 2:548, 566; 11:236, 492; JWO 124–26, 131–32, 409; *JJW* 5:118.

[22]*LJW* 2:353; B 2:113; 3:62n; FA, B 11:156, 159.

[23]B 9:354.

[24]B 4:6.

[25]*JJW* 2:365.

[26]B 11:189n.

[27]FA, pt. 1, B 11:155–63, sec. 5.16–22.

[28]Nicene, Athanasian (*Quicunque*), and Apostles' Creeds; "On Laying the Foundation of the New Chapel," B 3:582, sec. 1.3, italics added. For various comments on orthodoxy, see B 1:220, 694; 2:415–16; 3:582, 587; 4:50, 57, 146, 175, 398; 11:22, 39, 477–78; *LJW* 3:183, 203; 4:347, 364.

[29]FA, pt. 2, B 11:277, sec. 1.9.

[30]"Address to the Clergy," J X:484, sec. 1.2; cf. Dailie's treatise on patristic writers noted, *JJW* 3:390.

[31]"A Roman Catechism, with a Reply," J X:91, sec. 1.Q8; cf. "Popery Calmly Considered," J X:141, sec. 1.

[32]LCM 3.11–12, *LJW* 11:387. For Wesley's somewhat idiosyncratic views on Montanus, Augustine, and Pelagius, see "The Wisdom of God's Counsels," B 2:556, J VI:325–37, sec. 9.

expounding the Scriptures, leaned sometimes to the other extreme. Yet nothing can be more unjust than to infer from hence 'that the age in which they lived could not relish or endure any but senseless, extravagant, enthusiastic, ridiculous comments on sacred writ.'"[33]

The serious reading of the church fathers[34] is especially helpful at two decisive points: "the *explication* of a doctrine that is not sufficiently explained, or for *confirmation* of a doctrine generally received.[35] When Wesley appealed alternatively to "reason, Scripture, or authority," the "authority" of which he was speaking was the authority of the early ecumenical tradition: the ancient ecumenical creeds and councils and the most widely sensually received consensual classical Christian writings.[36]

On the relation of Scripture and tradition, Wesley observed: "The Scriptures are a complete rule of faith and practice; and they are clear in all necessary points. And yet their clearness does not prove that they need not be explained; nor their completeness, that they need not be enforced.... The esteeming the writings of the first three centuries, not equally with, but next to, the Scriptures, never carried any man yet into dangerous errors, nor probably ever will."[37] Although these most widely received ancient Christian writers were fallible, their authority can be relied on more confidently than that of any or all later or modern interpreters.[38]

2. Wesley as Editor of Classic Christian Writings

a. The Wide Range of Wesley's Work as Editor

Wesley wrote grammars in seven of the eight foreign languages he knew (Hebrew, Greek, Latin, French, German, Dutch, Spanish, and Italian).[39] His lifelong fascination with the learning of languages rightly should put to rest the caricature of Wesley as an uneducated, nonscholarly, Bible-thumping "enthusiast." He read comfortably in more languages than Luther, Calvin, Jonathan Edwards, Joseph Butler, or Immanuel Kant. He also published a general history of Christianity, a history of England, a library of Christian classics, a system of natural philosophy, a general commentary on Scripture, a compendium of logic, and considerable poetry and hymnody, some in his own translation from the original Latin or Greek.

The wide range of Wesley's work as an editor of the Christian tradition of spiri-

---

[33]LCM, *LJW* 11:362, quoting Middleton's *A Free Inquiry into the Miraculous Powers Which Are Supposed to Have Subsisted in the Christian Church, Etc.*, 1748.

[34]JWO 62, 119, 182, 195, 307, 336, 365, 375; see also "Manners of the Ancient Christians."

[35]"A Roman Catechism, with a Reply," J X:87, pref., italics added; cf. *JJW* 1:367.

[36]FA, pt. 1, B 11:176, sec. 5.31.

[37]LCM, J X:14.

[38]For Wesley's implicit use of the Vincentian canon, see Outler's introduction, B 1:58–59; cf. 1:324n, 550n.

[39]In addition to an English grammar, Wesley wrote grammars in Hebrew, Greek, Latin, French, and Dutch. He also studied German in some detail, translated German poetry, and compiled a dictionary and grammar of German (*JJW* 1:110–12, 133–34, 209–10, 278, 295, 300); compiled a Spanish grammar (*JJW* 1:237–38, 299); and for a time studied Italian (*JJW* 1:354). He showed himself in debate to be far more accomplished in Greek and Latin than many who had reputations of being highly proficient.

tuality is seen in the prefaces of the various works he edited, abridged, and published, found in *Prefaces to Works Revised and Abridged from Various Authors*[40] in volume XIV of the Jackson edition of *Wesley's Works*. The 118 works listed show Wesley's tireless enterprise in making available to the common reader, and especially his societies, the best literature of spiritual formation over the ages, in plain language and thrifty format for common use.

Wesley was particularly interested in presenting personal histories and testimonies to the holy life. In addition to editing hagiographies like Foxe's *Acts and Monuments of the Christian Martyrs*, Wesley added his own recensions of more recent Protestant hagiography,[41] along with collected letters of Joseph Alleine and Samuel Rutherford.

In some cases, Wesley presented controversial materials with which he partly disagreed, yet in which he found sufficient merit to publish nonetheless due to other benefits. This was the case in *An Extract from the Life of Mr. Thomas Firmin*, who was a "pious man" even if his "notions of the Trinity were quite erroneous."[42] Wesley also published *An Extract of the Life of Madam Guion* [sic] (1766), who "was actually deceived in many instances; the more frequently, because she imagined herself to be infallible,"[43] who resisted being "guided by the written word," and who exaggerated the efficacy of suffering for spiritual formation. Yet even with these limitations, Wesley found in Madame Guyon's writings an admirable "pattern of true holiness."[44]

Wesley's special interest in the biographies of holy women is seen in his editions of the letters of Jane Cooper and in the lives and spiritual journals of Mary Gilbert (1769), Elizabeth Harper (1772), and many others.

He found in *An Extract of Mr. Richard Baxter's Aphorisms of Justification* (1745) a "powerful antidote against the spreading poison of Antinomianism."[45] Most volumes of the *Arminian Magazine* (1778–91) contained accounts and letters of pious persons, sacred poetry, lives of saints, and classic essays defending the universal offer of free grace.[46]

That Wesley was interested in what today is called the practice of holistic medicine and the analysis of the body-soul interface is evident from his popular series of advisories on health matters: *Advice with Respect to Health* (1769, based on a work by Dr. Tissot), *An Extract from Dr. Cadogan's Dissertation on the Gout, and All Chronic Diseases* (1774), and his much reprinted *Primitive Physic: Or, an Easy and Natural Method of Curing Most Diseases* (23rd edition, 1791), containing "safe, cheap, and easy medicines."[47] As to works on the natural sciences, in addition to his

---

[40] J XIV:199–318.
[41] As in *An Extract of the Life and Death of Mr. Thomas Haliburton* (1741), *Thomas Haliburton*, (1741), and *David Brainerd, Missionary to the Indians* (1768).
[42] J XIV:293.
[43] J XIV:176.
[44] J XIV:278.
[45] J XIV:216.
[46] J XIV:280.
[47] J XIV:312.

five-volume *Compendium of Natural Philosophy: A Survey of the Wisdom of God in the Creation* (1784), Wesley wrote *The Desideratum: Or, Electricity Made Plain and Useful* (1759).[48]

Wesley's fascination with history[49] and its importance in spiritual formation is seen in his editions of *A Short Roman History* (1773), *A Concise History of England* (1776), *An Account of the Conduct of the War in the Middle Colonies* (1780), and *A Concise Ecclesiastical History* in four volumes (1781).[50]

b. A Christian Library

Wesley published the fifty volumes of a series of books called A Christian Library between 1749 and 1755. Its subtitle is *Extracts from, and Abridgments of, the Choicest Pieces of Practical Divinity Which Have Been Published in the English Tongue.*[51] His intent was to edit and publish at low cost for his circle of spiritual formation "such a collection of English divinity, as (I believe) is all true, all agreeable to the oracles of God; as is all practical, unmixed with controversy of any kind, and all intelligible to plain men; such as is not superficial, but going down to the depth, and describing the height, of Christianity; and yet not mystical, not obscure to any of those who are experienced in the ways of God."[52]

Wesley's hope was that the whole series would "conspire together to make 'the man of God perfect, thoroughly furnished unto every good word and work.'" He felt himself "at full liberty" not only to abridge the content but to add his own comments and corrections.[53] He was aware that one could spend one's whole life reading the classical Christian writers and still "not read all." "This very plenty creates a difficulty," an information overload. So his editorial purpose was to make a fit selection, avoiding those that focused unnecessarily on controversy, that would more "tend to promote vain jangling, than holiness."

He largely avoided writings so mystical that they found "hidden meanings in everything," seeking "mysteries in the plainest truths, and mak[ing] them such by their explications." He shunned writers who made things unintelligible. This was "a fault which is not easy for men of learning to avoid."[54] He remained convinced that "the genuine religion of Jesus Christ has been one and the same from the beginning."[55]

c. Highlighting the Earliest Apostolic Fathers

Wesley began his Christian Library with a "Preface to the Epistles of the Apostolical Fathers" of the earliest Christian years. He presented and commended the

---

[48]*LJW* 4:123, 166; 5:176, 342; *JJW* 3:320; 4:190; 5:247.
[49]*JJW* 3:499; 6:96; B 2:451; 3:108.
[50]Redacted from the M'Laine translation of the work of J. L. von Mosheim.
[51]*JJW* 1:425; 3:391 – 92; 4:91, 94.
[52]CL, pref., J XIV:222.
[53]Ibid.
[54]CL, pref., J XIV:221.
[55]CL, pref., J XIV:223.

writings of Clement of Rome,[56] Ignatius,[57] and Polycarp[58] as those who delivered "the pure doctrine of the Gospel; what Christ and his Apostles taught, and what these holy men had themselves received from their own mouths."[59]

The early apologists had "the advantage of living in the apostolic times, of hearing the holy Apostles and conversing with them." They had been chosen by them for leadership in the nascent church. So we "cannot with any reason doubt of what they deliver ... but ought to receive it, though not with equal veneration, yet with only little less regard than we do the sacred writings of those who were their masters and instructors" and "as worthy of a much greater respect than any composures which have been made since."[60]

Polycarp knew John personally; Irenaeus knew Polycarp personally. Irenaeus took the gospel to southern France. This closeness to the original apostles is what made these earliest writers worthy of the highest respect.

As "persons of consummate piety; adorned with all those Christian virtues which they so affectionately recommend to us," these writers were "in all the necessary parts of it ... so assisted by the Holy Ghost, as to be scarce capable of mistaking."[61] It is not because of their cleverness or intellectuality that the earliest postapostolic writers command our attention. Rather, they were living so close to God that they breathed in the same Spirit as did the apostles.[62]

Further Reading on Wesley's Historical Sources

The Christian Library

Dodge, Reginald J. *John Wesley's Christian Library.* London: Epworth, 1938.

"Wesley's Christian Library." *WMM* 50 (1827): 310–16.

The Freedom to Learn from Tradition

Harkness, Georgia. "The Roots of Methodist Theology." In *The Methodist Church in Social Thought and Action.* Nashville: Abingdon, 1964.

Shelton, R. Larry. "Wesley on Maintaining a Catholic Spirit." *PM* 53, no. 4 (1978): 12, 13.

Southgate, Wyndham M. *John Jewel and the Problem of Doctrinal Authority.* Cambridge: Harvard University Press, 1962.

Wesley and Christian Antiquity

Benz, Ernst. *Die Protestantische Thebais: Zur Nachwirkung Makarios des Agypters im Protestantismus der 17. and 18. Jahrhunderts in Europa und*

---

[56]See also *LJW* 2:330; 3:137; B 3:586.

[57]For further references to Ignatius, see *LJW* 2:327–28, 387; 3:137; B 1:36, 437; 3:5; *JJW* 2:467–68; 3:65.

[58]*LJW* 2:327–30, 362, 387; 3:137.

[59]CL, J XIV:223.

[60]CL, J XIV:223–25.

[61]CL, J XIV:224–25.

[62]Some remarks of Mr. Hill's "Review of All the Doctrines Taught by Mr. John Wesley," J X:387.

Amerika. Wiesbaden: Verlag der Academie der Wissenschaften und der Literatur in Mainz, 1963.

Campbell, Ted A. *John Wesley and Christian Antiquity: Religious Vision and Cultural Changes*. Nashville: Kingswood, 1991.

McCormick, K. Steve. "John Chrysostom and John Wesley." PhD diss., Drew University, 1983.

Orcibal, Jean. "The Theological Originality of John Wesley." In *A History of the Methodist Church in Great Britain*. London: Epworth, 1965.

Outler, Albert C. "John Wesley's Interests in the Early Fathers of the Church." In *The Wesleyan Theological Heritage: Essays of Albert C. Outler*, edited by Thomas C. Oden and Leicester R. Longden. Grand Rapids: Zondervan, 1991.

Petry, Ray C. "The Critical Temper and the Practice of Tradition." *Duke Divinity School Review* 30 (Spring 1965).

Stoeffler, F. Earnest. *The Rise of Evangelical Pietism*. Leiden: E. J. Brill, 1965.

Comparative Studies

Baker, Frank. *John Wesley and the Church of England*. Nashville: Abingdon, 1970.

———. "John Wesley and William Law." *PWHS* 37 (1970): 173–77.

Brantley, Richard E. *Locke, Wesley and the Method of English Romanticism*. Gainsville: University of Florida Press, 1984.

———. *Wordsworth's "Natural Methodism."* New Haven, CT: Yale University Press, 1975.

Brigdon, Thomas E. "Pascal and the Wesleys." *PWHS* 7 (1909): 60–63, 84–88.

Church, Leslie F. "Port Royal and John Wesley." *LQHR* 175 (1950): 291–93.

Cragg, Gerald R. *The Church and the Age of Reason*. Baltimore: Penguin, 1966.

Glasson, T. Francis. "Jeremy Taylor's Place in John Wesley's Life." *PWHS* 36 (1968): 105–7.

Green, J. B. *John Wesley and William Law*. London, 1945.

Hooper, Henry T. "Wesley and St. Francis." *WMM* 143 (1920): 527–28.

Howard, Ivan. "Wesley versus Phoebe Palmer." *WTJ* 6 (1971): 31–40.

Hughes, H. Trevor. "Jeremy Taylor and John Wesley." *LQHR* 174 (1949): 296–404.

Hutchinson, F. E. "John Wesley and George Herbert." *LQHR* 161 (1936): 439–55.

Leach, Elsie A. "Wesley's Use of Geo. Herbert." *Huntington Library Quarterly* 16 (1953): 183–202.

Lloyd, A. K. "Doddridge and Wesley." *PWHS* 28 (1951): 50–52.

Marriott, Thomas. "John Wesley and William Wilberforce." *WMM* 68 (1945): 364–65.

McDonald, Frederick W. "Bishop Butler and John Wesley." *MR* (1896): 142, 156, 172.

Moore, Sydney H. "Wesley and Fenelon." *LQHR* 169 (1944): 155–57.

Pask, A. H. "The Influence of Arminius on John Wesley." *LQHR* 185 (1960): 258–63.

"Pusey and Puseyism: Wesley and Methodism." *MR* (1882).

Reist, Irwin W. "John Wesley and George Whitefield: The Integrity of Two Theories of Grace." *EQ* 47, no. 1 (1975): 26–40.

Simon, John S. *Wesley or Voltaire*. London: C. H. Kelly, 1904.

Taylor, A. E. "St. John of the Cross and John Wesley." *JTS* 46 (1945): 30–38.

Thomas, Gilbert. "George Fox and John Wesley." *MR* (1924): 11.

Tyson, John R. "John Wesley and William Law: A Reappraisal." *WTJ* 17, no. 2 (1982): 58–78.

Watchhurst, Percy L. "Francis of Assisi and John Wesley." *WMM* 128 (1905): 484–86.

Weaver, Sampson. "Wesley and Wordsworth." *WMM* 127 (1904): 835–37.

Wiseman, Frederick Luke. "Herbert and Wesley." *MR* (1933): 14.

Assessments of Wesley's Place in History

Baker, Frank. "Unfolding John Wesley: A Survey of Twenty Years' Studies in Wesley's Thought." *QR*, no. 1 (1980).

Heitzenrater, Richard P. "The Present State of Wesley Studies." *MH* 22 (1984): 221–31.

———. "Wesley Studies in the Church and the Academy." *Perkins Journal* 37, no. 3 (1984): 1–6.

Langford, Thomas. *Practical Divinity: Theology in the Wesleyan Tradition.* Nashville: Abingdon, 1982.

Meeks, Douglas M., ed. *The Future of the Methodist Theological Traditions.* Nashville: Abingdon, 1985.

Minus, Paul. *Methodism's Destiny in an Ecumenical Age.* New York: Abingdon, 1969.

Outler, Albert C. "Methodism's Theological Heritage." In *The Wesleyan Theological Heritage: Essays of Albert C. Outler*, edited by Thomas C. Oden and Leicester R. Longden, 189–211. Grand Rapids: Zondervan, 1991.

Rack, Henry D. *The Future of John Wesley's Methodism.* London: Lutterworth, 1965.

Rowe, Gilbert T. *The Meaning of Methodism.* Nashville: Cokesbury, 1926.

Rowe, Kenneth, ed. *The Place of Wesley in the Christian Tradition.* Metuchen, NJ: Scarecrow, 1976.

Urlin, R. D. *John Wesley's Place in Church History.* London: Rivington, 1879.

Wilson, Woodrow. *John Wesley's Place in History.* New York: Abingdon, 1915.

CHAPTER 4

Reason

Of the four bulwarks of the quadrilateral method, we have discussed two — sacred Scripture and sacred tradition, with Scripture always taking the primary place. Now we will sort out Wesley's view of reason and experience, thus completing the account of his theological method.

A. On Reason

1. Reason as God's Gift

Wesley urged his connection not to "despise or lightly esteem reason, knowledge, or human learning."[1] "To renounce reason is to renounce religion," for "all irrational religion is false religion."[2] Religion is hobbled when reason is neglected: "It is impossible, without reasoning, either to prove or disprove anything."[3]

Reason is God's gift: "In all the duties of common life, God has given us our reason for a guide. And it is only by acting up to the dictates of it, by using all the understanding which God hath given us, that we can have a conscience void of offence towards God and towards man."[4]

In his letter to Dr. Rutherforth of Cambridge, Wesley rejected the view that "human learning is an impediment to a divine." "I do not depreciate learning of any kind," he said. He defended his traveling preachers as "not ignorant men," who though they did not profess to know languages and philosophy, yet "some of them [understood] them well ... better than a great part of my pupils at the university did."[5]

2. Reasoning Out of Scripture

Reason and Scripture, far from being pitted against each other, are linked intimately in the attempt to find "the plain scriptural rational way."[6] Wesley said, "Passion and prejudice govern the world, only under the name of reason. It is our part,

---

[1]*PACP*, J X:429, sec. 25.
[2]Letter to Dr. Rutherforth, March 28, 1768, *LJW* 5:364.
[3]"A Dialogue between an Antinomian and His Friend," J X:267.
[4]"The Case of Reason Impartially Considered," B 2:592, sec. 2.10.
[5]"A Letter to the Rev. Dr. Rutherforth," B 9:376–80, sec. 2.1–9.
[6]"The Nature of Enthusiasm," B 2:55, sec. 26.

by religion and reason joined, to counteract them all we can."[7] "You cannot but allow that the religion which we preach and live to be agreeable to the highest reason."[8]

Wesley's main dissatisfaction with "mystic divines" was their tendency to "utterly decry the use of reason."[9] He knew of "no method of bringing any to the knowledge of the truth, except the methods of reason and persuasion."[10] True religion is not irrational: "Christianity requires our assent to nothing but what is plain and intelligible in every proposition. Let every man first have a full conviction of the truth of each proposition in the gospel, as far only as it is plain and intelligible, and let him believe as far as he understands."[11]

In his "Earnest Appeal," Wesley wrote, "So far as he departs from true genuine reason, so far he departs from Christianity."[12]

Yet reason alone cannot pass easily "from things natural to spiritual.... A gulf is here!"[13] "Let reason do all that reason can; employ it as far as it will go," realizing that it is "utterly incapable of giving either faith, or hope, or love; and consequently of producing either real virtue, or substantial happiness."[14]

Further Reading on Books and Culture

Wesley on Editing, Education, Books, Scholarship, and Culture

Herbert, T. W. *John Wesley as Editor and Author.* Princeton, NJ: Princeton University Press, 1940.

Jackson, F. M. "A Bibliographical Catalogue of Books Mentioned in John Wesley's Journals." *PWHS* 4 (1902–4): 17, 47, 74, 107, 134, 173, 203, 232.

Joy, James R. "Wesley: A Man of a Thousand Books and a Book." *RL* 8 (1939): 71–84.

Lawton, George. *John Wesley's English: A Study of His Literary Style.* London: Allen and Unwin, 1962.

Lewis, Thomas H. "John Wesley as a Scholar." *MQR* 73 (1924): 648–58.

Mathews, Horace F. *Methodism and the Education of the People, 1791–1851.* London: Epworth, 1949.

Rogal, Samuel J. "A Journal and Diary Checklist of John Wesley's Reading." *Serif* 11, no. 1 (1974): 11–33.

Wesley on Science and Medicine

Collier, Frank. *John Wesley among the Scientists.* New York: Abingdon, 1928.

Hill, A. Wesley. *John Wesley among the Physicians: A Study of 18th Century Medicine.* London: Epworth, 1958.

Hunter, Richard A. "A Brief Review of the Use of Electricity in Psychiatry with Special Reference to John Wesley." *British Journal of Physical Medicine* 20, no. 5 (1957): 98–100.

---

[7]Letter to Joseph Benson, October 5, 1779, *LJW* 5:203.
[8]EA, B 11:53, sec. 22.
[9]EA, B 11:55, sec. 30.
[10]"On Laying the Foundation of the New Chapel," B 3:588, sec. 2.11.
[11]"Compendium of Natural Philosophy," J II:448–49.
[12]EA, B 11:55, sec. 27.
[13]EA, B 11:57, sec. 35.
[14]"The Case of Reason Impartially Considered," B 2:600, sec. 2.10.

Oord, Thomas Jay. "Prevenient Grace and Nonsensory Perception of God in a Postmodern Wesleyan Philosophy." In *Between Nature and Grace: Mapping the Interface of Wesleyan Theology and Psychology*, edited by Bryan P. Stone and Thomas Jay Oord. San Diego: Point Loma, 2000.

———. "A Process Wesleyan Theodicy: Freedom, Embodiment, and the Almighty God." In *Thy Name and Nature Is Love: Wesleyan and Process Theologies in Dialogue*, edited by Bryan P. Stone and Thomas Jay Oord, 193–216. Nashville: Kingswood, 2001.

Pellowe, William C. S. "John Wesley's Use of Science." *MR* 110 (1927): 394–403.

Rogal, Samuel J. "Pills for the Poor: Wesley's Primitive Physick." *Yale Journal of Biology and Medicine* 51 (1978): 81–90.

Stewart, David. "John Wesley, the Physician." *WTJ* 4 (1969): 27–38.

Stillings, Dennis. "John Wesley: Philosopher of Electricity." *Medical Instrumentation* 7 (1973): 307.

Sweet, W. W. "John Wesley and Scientific Discovery." *ChrCent* 40 (1923): 591–92.

Turrell, W. J. "Three Electrotherapists of the Eighteenth Century: John Wesley, Jean Paul Marat and James Graham." *Annals of Medical History* 3 (1921): 361–67.

3. The Case of Reason Impartially Considered

The text of "The Case of Reason Impartially Considered" is 1 Corinthians 14:20: "Brethren, be not children in understanding: howbeit in malice be ye children, but in understanding be men" [Homily #70 (1781), B 2:587–600; J #70, VI:350–60].

Reason remains useful in its own proper sphere but apart from that sphere is often either overvalued or undervalued.

Reason must neither be exalted to presume to be an ultimate judge of revelation nor ignored as a balance to emotive excess.[15] The medium between these two extremes has been generally anticipated by "that great master of reason, Mr. Locke," but with inadequate applications.[16]

Wesley fought a twofold battle against both unreasonable charismatic enthusiasts who overstressed emotive spirituality and excessive rationalists who wanted to impose hyperskeptical criteria on the inquiry into Christian truth.

a. On Not Undervaluing Reason

Critics sometime consider religion as the enemy of reason. The religious are viewed by them as emotively charged enthusiasts who tend to substitute their own dreams and fantasies for rational analysis. Wesley warns against substituting our own imagination for the written Word, the reliable revelation of God. So "stop thinking like children. In regard to evil be infants, but in your thinking be adults" (1 Cor. 14:20 NIV).

Those who seek to find some deprecation of reason by Wesley must look hard.

---

[15]B 1:271–72; 2:591–95.
[16]"The Case of Reason Impartially Considered," B 2:587–88, J VI:350–60, pref. 1–5.

He was never attracted to anti-intellectual fideism. Though not a rationalist in the reductionist sense, he valued the place of reason in its own proper sphere.[17]

Faith is not to be pitted against reason. Growing faith searches for the best reasons available for its grounding in revelation. Faith invites the best arguments it can find to account for its own infinite depth.[18] It is pathetic stewardship not to use what God gives. What God gives to humans as distinguished from brute creation is our minds. Depending on our will to exercise reason and depending on our various stages of development, humans are distinguished by having some capacity for reasoning.[19]

b. On Not Overvaluing Reason

Others make the opposite mistake of overvaluing the omnicompetence of finite reasoning, admitting too few limits, imagining that reason can be trusted to analyze the truth with complete impartiality, forgetting the universality of sin. They lose track of reason's limitations, expecting reason to carry more than its poor powers allow. They mistake themselves as wholly objective observers. This opens the door for finite reason to overextend itself as a censor of divine revelation.[20]

Reason in this way becomes oppressive in its relation to the testimony of revelation. Sin-drenched reasoning mistakenly fantasizes itself as an omnicompetent, autonomous guide that needs neither the embrace of divine forgiveness nor the light of revelation. Thus, some rationalists have failed to be grasped by the mystery of God's self-disclosure in history. Having little patience with talk of revelation, and unable to get their minds around it, they want to reduce incarnation and resurrection to natural events and biblical history to flat causal explanations.[21]

Wesley searched for a right balance fitting to the real but limited competencies of reasoning. He sought a middle ground that would neither over- nor underestimate reason's abilities.

He pursued the middle way by first defending reason in two aspects: when modestly viewed either as *argument* or *understanding*, reason has a significant role in the nurture of true religion.

c. On Reason as Argument

Wesley viewed reason first as the grace-enabled power of *argument*. Argument refers to that capacity of human intelligence to account for the route by which a person moves from premises to conclusions. Reason can serve logical and sequential argument. It can move from hypothesis to conclusion smoothly without a leap

---

[17]EA, J XIII:8 – 10, secs. 20 – 25.
[18]JWO 396 – 97.
[19]"The Case of Reason Impartially Considered," B 2:587 – 88, pref. 1 – 5.
[20]Letter to Dr. Robertson, September 24, 1753, *LJW* 3:104 – 10.
[21]In his letter to Joseph Benson, September 27, 1788, *LJW* 8:89 – 90, Wesley reported how he had been plunged into "unprofitable *reasonings*" by Isaac Watts's speculations on the glorified humanity of Christ.

in logic.[22] The function of self-constrained reason is to unpack assertions and show the layers of judgment that lie behind them.[23]

Wesley was an old hand at analyzing argument. He learned his logic at Oxford. This surfaces especially in his writings with a polemical edge.[24] With Isaiah, he invited his partners in dialogue to "Come now, let us reason together" (Isa. 1:18). He said, in effect, when you make statements, give me your reasons, and I will give you mine. Those in his connection of spiritual formation were expected to be prepared to give reasons for their conclusions. This is a duty owed to all with whom one enters into discourse. To shout is not to present a plausible argument. "If you denounce against me all the curses from Genesis to Revelation they will not amount to one argument."[25]

These days we distinguish between left-brain (linear) functions and right-brain (intuitive) functions.[26] Wesley anticipated this with his distinction between rational argument (left brain) and rational understanding (right brain) in "The Case of Reason Impartially Considered."

d. On Reason as Understanding

Reason has another deeper and more intuitively diffuse task: *as understanding*, reason is that faculty of human consciousness that has a capacity to apprehend, organize complex data, and name experiencing; to make judgments on the basis of evidence as to whether statements agree or disagree, distinguishing one judgment from another. Reasoning persons can discourse, dialogue, and interact with one another to seek to grasp the *truth* of various arguments.

Reason as understanding assumes the capacity to empathize with another sufficiently that we understand what that person is saying. On this ground, intelligible discourse is possible, where two minds have the possibility of being of one mind.

In these two complementary ways — by argument and understanding — reason remains an important resource for human interaction and the good life. The body of Christ embodies both forms of reasoning by means of navigating the hazards between premises and conclusions and by understanding the truth of assertions. The worshiping community is found reading Holy Writ, discerning its meaning, and living together meaningfully in a community. All of these require the rational function of understanding.[27]

---

[22] Wesley published a *Compendium of Logic* (1750; B 2:547), an adaptation of Dean Henry Aldrich's *Logic*, for use at the Kingswood School (*JJW* 3:459). He highly commended the learning of logic to all in leadership in his connection (*JJW* 3:391, 285).

[23] B 2:589 – 90; 4:21 – 22.

[24] When chided for his tendency to press logical points so as to "distinguish them away," Wesley retorted, "When men tack absurdities to the truth of God with which it hath nothing to do, I distinguish away those absurdities and let the truth remain." Letter to John Smith, March 25, 1747, *LJW* 2:90.

[25] FA, pt. 1, B 11:138, sec. 4.7.

[26] "The Case of Reason Impartially Considered," B 2:589 – 90, sec. 1.1; cf. B 1:59 – 60, 613 – 14.

[27] "The Case of Reason Impartially Considered," B 2:590, sec. 1.2.

4. What Reason Can and Cannot Do

a. What Reason Can Do

Some things reason does better than others. Wesley plainly set forth the competencies of reason in three spheres: physical, religious, and moral.

First, reason is singularly useful in ordering the physical world, searching for plausible evidences and explanations of causes of effects. Horticulture, music, seamanship, and the healing arts proceed by reason, as do all the sciences, mathematics, philosophy, grammar, logic, law, magistracy, and metaphysics.[28]

Reason uses sensory experience and logic to understand how the world works, how effects are caused.[29] Wesley had hardly a trace of antiscientific prejudice. He was keenly interested in experiment and often displayed an investigative attitude toward the world, as with his special interest in electricity and medicine. Original scientific inquiry — observing, testing, hypothesizing, analyzing, discovering — Wesley found appealing.[30] He was a practical scientist in the areas of organizational leadership, medical remedies for poor people, and motivation for social change. In all these arenas, he wanted to learn as much as he could firsthand by experimentation — something like Benjamin Franklin or Thomas Jefferson.

Second, reason has a key role to play in religion, both with regard to its foundation and its coherence. As to its foundation, reason is needed to achieve an intelligible *reception of revelation.* We use our rational capacity critically to understand what Scripture is saying, to analyze its language, its historical setting, and its moral consequences. The translation of meaning from one language to another requires rational capacities. This evangelical Oxford don was a practiced classic linguist who read Latin and Greek as quickly as he read English. He was at home in the Oxford world of reasoned debate, whether about God or the human condition.

In the sphere of religion, good reasoning offers useful help in providing a critique of religious conceptualities, organizing thinking, and seeking to clarify the basis of faith. It tries to tell the truth about its evidences and make proper distinctions. Reason seeks to provide order and cohesive structure to the teaching of the truth.[31] Reason helps organize disparate empirical data into cohesive reflections, especially concerning the meaning of history.[32] We cannot give counsel or attest intelligibly without rational reflection. What is said about human existence must correspond consistently with what is said about creation, the course of human history, the predicament of the will, and the future of humanity. Reason is in these ways a critical companion to the life of faith.[33]

Third, reason recognizes the moral consequences of ideas. It seeks to help each

---

[28]On mathematics, see *LJW* 3:104; on metaphysics, see B 3:108 – 9, 235.
[29]B 2:587 – 88, 599 – 600.
[30]"The Case of Reason Impartially Considered," B 2:590 – 91, sec. 1.3.
[31]*LJW* 5:357.
[32]In reference to Peter Browne, "On Human Understanding," see *JJW* 4:192; *LJW* 1:56 – 58; 6:113.
[33]EA, B 11:37 – 95; J VIII:1 – 45.

moral agent understand what conscience is inwardly saying. Conscience needs rational deliberation to clarify its practical alternatives. Conscience is the witness of moral self-awareness that either accuses or excuses us. We hear ourselves constantly assessing ourselves morally. Reason helps us discern that assessment accurately.[34]

b. What Reason Cannot Do

If these are services reason can render, what can reason not do? Reason is powerless to elicit faith or hope or love — all theological virtues – excellent behaviors enabled by God's grace.

First, reason cannot produce *saving faith.* That is enabled only by saving grace under the guidance of God the Spirit. Reason cannot of itself bring us to a firm conviction of that which is not seen. It cannot bring us to trust in God. We can put beliefs to the test of rational analysis, but we will never experience saving faith simply from a sequence of reasoning. For faith is a decision, a choice we make to trust Another. We may find reasons that will lead us toward an act of faith, but reason as such lacks the capacity to take the risk-laden step of saving faith so as to participate deeply in life in Christ.

It is difficult to engender trust without shifting into a narrative mode, without telling a story. We learn to trust in God by listening to a history of revelation. From this history, we learn that the Life-giver is personally trustworthy. We know this by sharing actively in God's own personal coming in the incarnate, crucified Lord.[35]

Second, reason is unable to elicit the fullness of *hope.* No matter how much evidence is piled layer upon layer, that does not of itself, without faith, elicit the fullness of hope.[36] What reason can do is analyze the conditions under which hope can be grasped. But hope emerges only out of faith's trust in God revealed in history. God is most fully revealed in the history of his incarnate Son, Jesus.

Third, above all, reason by itself cannot *love.* None of us loves because we have come to that conclusion on the basis of rational argument.[37]

So reason is inadequate at the most crucial points upon which human happiness hinges. Reason can define, think about, and conceptually order ideas of the virtues. It can describe and elicit to some extent actual behavioral excellences, such as wisdom, courage, temperance, and justice. But reason falls short in engendering faith, hope, and love, on which the blessed life depends.[38] This means that reason cannot make us happy unless it is rightly related to the ground of happiness, faith that loves all in God and God in all.[39]

The proper and modest use of reason does not pretend omnicompetence. Those who belittle reason may dishonor God because they fail to acknowledge God's own

---

[34]"The Case of Reason Impartially Considered," B 2:592, sec. 1.7.
[35]"The Case of Reason Impartially Considered," B 2:593, sec. 2.1.
[36]"The Case of Reason Impartially Considered," B 2:595 – 97, sec. 2.5 – 7.
[37]"The Case of Reason Impartially Considered," B 2:598, sec. 2.3, 8.
[38]Reason offers "dim light," B 2:172, for that which leads to enduring happiness; B 1:60, 258; 2:593 – 99.
[39]"The Case of Reason Impartially Considered," B 2:598 – 600, sec. 2.10.

gift of reasonable reflection. Those who fail to see the limits of reason compound reason's difficulties by imagining that reason itself can elicit faith, hope, and love.[40]

5. The Imperfection of Human Knowledge

The text of "The Imperfection of Human Knowledge," is 1 Corinthians 13:9, "We know in part" [Homily #69 (1784), B 2:567 – 86; J #69, V:337 – 50].

a. The Desire to Know

From this tiny window of time, we grasp only slivers, not the whole of reality. How little we know, mused Wesley. We see society and history and nature from our fleeting glimpse of this moment of time and space.

Nonetheless, the desire to know remains as immeasurable as time and space, and as universal as it is irrepressible. There is no circumference to our desire to know. But on every hand we find our knowledge limited. This suggests that human meaning is forever pointed toward some future state in which our knowledge shall be complete.[41] If reasoning about the fullness of time is implanted in our human consciousness, that fact points to some future reason why it is so implanted. Not knowing this reason does not eliminate its trajectory to some future knowing.

However limited and subject to distortion, the desire to know is intrinsic to human consciousness. It is difficult to imagine human beings without a hunger to know that which reaches beyond our grasp.[42] Although this desire has no bounds, our actual range of knowing does.[43] No matter how wise, we only "know in part" (1 Cor. 13:9), which is the lead text of Homily #69.[44]

b. Cosmology Reveals the Austere Limits of Human Knowing

Human knowing is experienced only within a vast cosmic scale of being. Within this incalculable scale, it is possible to some degree to know something of the things we see in the physical world, living things, and to some degree ourselves. But far less do we know fully the ground and giver of all knowing.[45] Even the wisest "know in part." Think about this: Who knows the extent of the universe, or the structure of light? How little we know of such elementary constituents as air, earth, fire, and water. How little we know about the depths of the sea, the dynamics, structure, and function of vegetable and animal life.[46]

When we trudge through the thought worlds of astronomy and physics asking about the extent of the universe and the nature of physical bodies, how little we know. Is light composed of waves or particles? Of what are chemical particles made

---

[40]Ibid. See Letter to Elizabeth Morgan, January 1, 1779, LJW 6:335.
[41]"The Imperfection of Human Knowledge," B 2:568, pref. 1.
[42]EA, J VIII:18 – 20.
[43]"The Imperfection of Human Knowledge," B 2:568 – 69, pref. 1 – 4.
[44]B 2:100 – 103, 568 – 86; 4:287 – 88.
[45]"The Imperfection of Human Knowledge," B 2:570 – 77, sec. 1.2 – 13.
[46]"The Imperfection of Human Knowledge," B 2:572 – 73, sec. 1.5 – 7.

up? In geology, what lies beneath the earth's surface?[47] In biology and botany, we are confronted constantly by the mysteries of microscopic organisms and plant life. Up and down the line of this protracted chain of being we often learn that the more we study the less we know.

From the study of creation, we can reason formally that God exists, but beyond that little is known, except by revelation, of the divine attributes. We can hypothesize divine characteristics such as justice, eternity, omnipresence, and the divine necessity from natural reasoning, but we cannot know them fully unless they are illumined by the revelation of God in history. These are amenable to some preliminary rational analysis, but always only with a heavy residue of mystery.[48]

We learn of God from his creation, but only indirectly, from within our fragile sensory apparatus. And even among believers, whatever is known of God's atoning grace within time tends to underscore our deeper ignorance of his eternal counsels before time.[49]

We may speak of creation as the beginning of time, but no speaker was there when it happened. We have a small aperture of vision in glimpsing finite, fleeting time.[50] This makes it all the more fitting for us "to adore the wisdom of God who has so exactly proportioned our knowledge to our state!"[51]

c. The Study of Providence and Suffering Yields Only Partial Knowledge of God

But there is much more: how little we know of ourselves, of providence, of God's design, of suffering. Profound mystery is present not only in God but also in ordinary history. We often do not know why we suffer. We all suffer. Suffering is one of the most pervasive of human experiences. Yet it is there that we find how intimately one human life is connected with others. My sin affects you. Your sin affects me. My grandparents' sin affects me, and I affect my grandchildren yet unborn. Suffering is wrapped in mystery.

Providence is God's provision for what humans with short vision cannot see or prepare for. It is that understanding that reaches out beyond the mystery and affirms that we are being held in the hands of God even if our outcomes are empirically unknowable. It remains beyond the comprehension even of the most faithful why one person may be given a long, slogging path, and another an easy one. One may find saving grace early, and another is left to struggle for a long time.[52] God knows. We do not.

---

[47]"The Imperfection of Human Knowledge," B 2:573–74, sec. 1.8–9.

[48]B 11:268–69.

[49]"The Imperfection of Human Knowledge," B 2:569–71, sec. 1.1–4.

[50]"The Imperfection of Human Knowledge," B 2:574–75, sec. 1.10–13. See also Wesley's conclusion to *Compendium of Natural Philosophy*, reprinted as *Remarks on the Limits of Human Knowledge*, J XIII:488–99.

[51]Conclusion to Wesley's *Compendium of Natural Philosophy*, reprinted as *Remarks on the Limits of Human Knowledge*, J XIII:498.

[52]"The Imperfection of Human Knowledge," B 2:578, sec. 2.2, 3.

Knowledge of our ignorance may teach us the first steps toward dealing with our suffering. Though we may know some of the psychological and social causes of our own suffering and of others, we never know them exhaustively. That belongs only to God, who sees the past and future clearly. The very recognition that we do not know the causes of our suffering brings us to a precipice in which we are ironically being freed to trust Another who does understand future times in a way we never will.[53]

Even if we may grasp the general outlines of God's providential ordering, how little we know of its particulars: why great nations are "now swept away," why so many in the "populous empire of Indostan" live in poverty, why Africans have been "continually driven to market and sold, like cattle, into the vilest bondage," why "American Indians, that is, the miserable remains of them" are slaughtered, and why myriads of Laplanders and Siberians must live under freezing conditions, and why "many, if not more ... are wandering up and down the deserts of Tartary."[54]

Why isn't the medicine of the gospel sent to every place where the contagion of sin is found? Why is there "little more mercy or truth to be found among Christians than among Pagans," and why are many who are "called Christian ... far worse than the Heathens?" Why does the antidote of Christianity at times become grievously adulterated and so mixed with poisonous ingredients that it retains little of its original virtue, and at times "adds tenfold malignity to the disease which it was designed to cure"?[55] We may speculate, but without certain and complete knowing. Meanwhile we confess that God knows the future, since God is present already to all future moments.

d. Even the Study of God's Grace Yields Only Limited Knowledge of the Wisdom of God's Counsels

The limits of human knowing apply to revealed religion as well as natural religion.[56] How can we explain why "a Hottentot, a New-Zealander, or an inhabitant of Nova-Zembla" does not have an equal chance at a decent education?[57] These questions are still being asked in our churches with regard to Bangladesh and Somalia.

The profundity of these mysteries tends to drive some beyond a suspension of theoretical judgment and toward the decisive choice between atheism and saving faith. The force of such enigmas is so strong that they cannot be avoided except "by resolving all into the unsearchable wisdom of God, together with a deep conviction of our own ignorance, and inability to fathom his counsels."[58]

"Even among us ... to whom are entrusted the oracles of God ... there are still many circumstances in his dispensations which are above our comprehension. We know not why he suffered us so long to go on in our own ways ... or why he made use

---

[53]"The Imperfection of Human Knowledge," B 2:578–79, sec. 3.4, 5.

[54]"The Imperfection of Human Knowledge," B 2:578–80, sec. 2.1–6.

[55]"The Imperfection of Human Knowledge," B 2:581, sec. 2.8.

[56]Cf. Wesley's remarks on Lord Karnes in "Morality and Natural Religion," JJW 6:21; B 3:493; B 4:151; JJW 6:21; B 3:493; B 4:151.

[57]"The Imperfection of Human Knowledge," B 2:582–83, sec. 3.1, 2; cf. B 3:348–49.

[58]"The Imperfection of Human Knowledge," B 2:583, sec. 3.2; cf. 7:247.

of this or the other instrument.... It is enough that God knoweth.... God undoubtedly has reasons; but those reasons are generally hid from the children of men."[59] Since we remain in time even when receiving the revelation provided in Scripture, the knowledge of believers is less than God's own knowledge. Scripture reveals what is necessary for salvation. We see this revelation with dim eyes. We know in part.

e. What We Learn from Our Own Ignorance

The greatest lesson we learn from the study of human consciousness is of our own ignorance. Each penitent believer is being taught humility, trust, and resignation precisely by these limits. The very shallowness of our knowing elicits

- *Humility.* The knowledge of our imperfection teaches us to be a little less proud and assertive about how inclusive is our knowing.
- *Trust.* To learn most profoundly from our ignorance is to learn to trust God's incomparably adequate knowing of us so as to awaken faith. The abysmal nature of our ignorance moves us ever closer to the personal decision to trust in God. "A full conviction of our own ignorance may teach us a full trust in his wisdom."[60]
- *Resignation.* To learn from our ignorance is to develop a yielding spirit, as Jesus expressed in Gethsemene.[61] Our limits as human beings are finally brought to deepest awareness in the reality and fact of death. There we come absolutely to terms with our finitude. There we are given the most complete opportunity to learn to say, "Yet not my will, but yours" (Luke 22:42 NIV).[62]

"As thinking is the act of an embodied spirit, playing upon a set of material keys, it is not strange that the soul can make but ill music when her instrument is out of tune." Aware that "finite cannot measure infinite ... there always will be something incomprehensible, something like Himself, in all his dispensations. We must therefore be content to be ignorant, until eternity opens our understanding."[63] Participation in Christ elicits faith that in the future we will know what we do not know now.

B. Natural Philosophy

1. Whether There Is Gradual Improvement in Natural Philosophy

a. Survey of the Wisdom of God in the Creation, or a Compendium of Natural Philosophy

In his introduction to the *Compendium of Natural Philosophy*[64] (later published under the title *Of the Gradual Improvement of Natural Philosophy*), Wesley

---

[59]"The Imperfection of Human Knowledge," B 2:583–84, sec. 3.3–5.

[60]"The Imperfection of Human Knowledge," B 2:585, sec. 4; CH 7:96–97.

[61]"The Imperfection of Human Knowledge," B 2:584–86, sec. 4.

[62]"The Imperfection of Human Knowledge," B 2:585–86, sec. 4.2, 3.

[63]Letter to Mrs. Elizabeth Bennis, October 28, 1771, LJW 5:284.

[64]1777, following the work of Charles Bonnet of Geneva, 3rd American ed.; notes by B. Mayo, 2 vols. (New York: N. Bangs and T. Mason, 1823); cf. B 1:60, 90–91; 3:108, 272; B 1:91–92; 2:362–65, 394, 571–76.

distinguished two phases of natural philosophy: "Speculative philosophy ascends from man to God; practical descends" from God to creatures. The mind tries to reach up to God while God is reaching down for humanity. The issues of natural philosophy "ascend from the consideration of man through all the order of things, as they are farther and farther removed from us, to God the center of all knowledge."[65]

Wesley consistently challenged the prejudice that assumed all significant scientific discoveries are recent and that the ancients had little knowledge of the natural world. The arts of genetics, chemistry, and glassmaking were studied and "in some measure known long ago. But ... cultivated in our age, with far greater accuracy." The microscope is not a recent invention; rather, it should be regarded as a reinvention. The empirical evidence Wesley presented for this is a tiny fifteen-hundred-year-old seal of France, "which to the naked eye presents only a confused group, but under a microscope, distinctly exhibits trees, a river, a boat, and sixteen or seventeen persons."[66] Many other forms of evidence show that the ancients were vastly more intelligent that our prejudices imagine. "It is commonly supposed that our age has a vast advantage over antiquity" in the study of the human body. "But this will bear a dispute. For ... the chief of our hypotheses are not new, but known long ago," and in truth the modern studies often "terminate in mere conjectures."[67]

This is seen in the two leading ancient traditions of inquiry — Hebrew and Greek. The Hebraic mind views the visible world in relation to its Creator. The Greek intellectual tradition seeks to discover "the material causes of natural things."[68] Among Greek schools, the subject of divinity became the special preoccupation of the Platonists, logic of the Paripatetics, morality of the Stoics, and sensuality of the Epicureans. Most of the major questions had been well framed by the third century BC. The medieval scholastics neglected what was commendable in Aristotle and tended "to obscure and pollute all philosophy with abstract, idle, vain speculation. Yet some of them, after the Arabians had introduced the knowledge of chemistry into Europe, were wise above the age they lived in," notably the thirteenth-century Franciscan Roger Bacon and the Dominican Albertus Magnus.[69]

b. The Scientific Enterprise Since Francis Bacon

Later, Francis Bacon (1561 – 1626) grasped "the defects of the school philosophy, incited all lovers of natural philosophy to a diligent search into natural history ... by many experiments and observations."[70] From this followed William Harvey's seventeenth-century discovery of the circulation of the blood, John Pecquet's study of the thoracic duct, and other experiments in genetics and blood transfusion. Wesley was well versed in these discoveries. Physicians have made such discoveries

---

[65]"Of the Gradual Improvement of Natural Philosophy," J XIII:482, sec. 1.
[66]"Of the Gradual Improvement of Natural Philosophy," J XIII:485 – 86, secs. 11 – 19.
[67]"Of the Gradual Improvement of Natural Philosophy," J XIII:487, sec. 23.
[68]"Of the Gradual Improvement of Natural Philosophy," J XIII:482, secs. 2, 3.
[69]"Of the Gradual Improvement of Natural Philosophy," J XIII:483, secs. 4, 5.
[70]"Of the Gradual Improvement of Natural Philosophy," J XIII:483, sec. 6; cf. *JJW* 7:162; *LJW* 3:5n.

concerning the human body so as to provide a providential reason to a theodicy even for diseases: "In diseases themselves, the wonderful wisdom of the Author of nature appears; and by means of them many hidden recesses of the human frame are unexpectedly discovered."[71] This insight into the meaning of disease has largely been forgotten or ignored in our society, whose science is unprepared to grasp it.

The divisions of natural inquiry may be conveniently sorted out in relation to the four ancient elements: (1) *air* (as in the discovery of the barometer, thermometer, and air pump); (2) *earth* (geology; telescopy; the study of sunspots, planet motions, and the Milky Way; and various cosmic theories, from Ptolemaic to post-Copernican); (3) *fire* (as in the discovery of gunpowder and phosphorus); and (4) *water* (as in the diving bell and submarine, and attempts to convert saltwater into freshwater uses).[72] Wesley was intrigued with the history of science.

In the attempted ascent of philosophical reflection from humanity to spiritual creatures (angels) and finally to God, "we can neither depend upon reason nor experiment" but do well ultimately to turn to the wisdom of Scripture. "Here, therefore, we are to look for no new improvements; but to stand in the good old paths; to content ourselves with what God has been pleased to reveal."[73]

2. On Human Understanding

In 1781 Wesley wrote an illuminating critical essay titled "Remarks upon Mr. Locke's Essay on Human Understanding." "For some days I have employed myself on the road in reading Mr. Locke's *Essay*," a "solid, weighty treatise" that shows evidence of a "deep fear of God." When compared to "the glittering trifle of Montesquieu," Locke is like gold.[74]

From Locke, the notion "that all our ideas come from sensation or reflection is fully proved."[75] Here we see the intellectual power of Wesley's mind going head-to-head with the achievements and limitations of one of the eighteenth century's leading minds.

a. Wesley's Critique of Locke

The following mistakes of Locke, on which the remarks focus, Wesley thought to be compensated by his many useful reflections.[76] Note the rich breadth and depth of the knowledge base Wesley was articulating.

First, Wesley thought that Aristotle's simpler threefold division of the mind into apprehension, judgment, and discourse is a more accurate account than Locke's

---

[71]"Of the Gradual Improvement of Natural Philosophy," J XIII:484, sec. 11.

[72]"Of the Gradual Improvement of Natural Philosophy," J XIII:486, secs. 18 – 21.

[73]"Of the Gradual Improvement of Natural Philosophy," J XIII:487, sec. 24.

[74]"Remarks upon Mr. Locke's Essay on Human Understanding," J XIII:455 – 56; cf. Richard E. Brantley, *Locke, Wesley, and the Method of English Romanticism* (Gainesville: University of Florida Press, 1984). For more of Wesley's reflections on Locke, see *JJW* 3:179; 4:192; B 2:571n, 589n; 3:361 – 62; *LJW* 1:136; 2:314; 7:228.

[75]"Remarks upon Mr. Locke's Essay on Human Understanding," J XIII:455 – 56.

[76]"Remarks upon Mr. Locke's Essay on Human Understanding," J XIII:455.

account of perception, judgment (which includes discerning, comparing, compounding, and abstracting), and memory. Pleasure determines the will as often as pain. Desire must be distinguished both from the enjoyment of pleasure and the avoidance of pain.

Second, Locke wrongly argued that a person's body undergoes dramatic changes within a lifetime that essentially obscure the person's continuing identity. Rather, it is the human soul that gives animation and unity to the body. "I call Cato the same person all his life, because he has the same soul. I call him the same man, because he has the same body too, which he brought into the world."[77] Wesley disagreed with Locke's inference that "Socrates asleep and Socrates awake is not the same person." Absurdly, "Mr. Locke thinks, 'consciousness makes personal identity'; that is, knowing I am the same person, makes me the same person.... Does knowing I exist make me exist? No; I am before I know I am."[78]

Third, Locke's "grand design was ... to drive Aristotle's logic out of the world, which he hated cordially, but never understood."[79] Wesley doubted that Locke ever read the fifteenth- and sixteenth-century "schoolmen" against whom he railed. He too readily abandoned the usefulness of logic, judging its use by its abuse. Rightly employed, logic is the best means "to prevent or cure the obscurity of language. To divide simple terms according to the logical rules of division, and then to define each member of the division according to the three rules of definition, does all that human art can do, in order to having a clear and distinct idea of every word we use."[80]

This essay shows how astutely Wesley was following the course of natural philosophy in his day, and how he was capable of intelligent critical assessment of it.

b. The Manners of the Present Times

In "An Estimate of the Manners of the Present Times," Wesley anticipated the spirit of modern narcissism by describing a world without God. "See here the grand cause (together with intemperance) of our innumerable nervous complaints!" "How many, even young, healthy men, are too lazy either to walk or ride!... They waste away in gentle activity." Our "luxury increases sloth, unfitting us for exercise either of body or mind.... And how many does a regular kind of luxury betray at last into gluttony and drunkenness; yea, and the lewdness too of every kind?"[81]

The best that the deism of Wesley's day could say about God in such a situation was that God

> "set this whirligig a-spinning," he left it, and everything therein, to spin on its own way. Whether this is right or no, it is almost the universal sentiment of the English nation.... They do not take God into their account; they can do their whole business without him.... They take it for granted, that the race is to the swift, and the battle to the strong ... [and] impute all to natural causes....

---

[77]"Remarks upon Mr. Locke's Essay on Human Understanding," J XIII:459.
[78]"Remarks upon Mr. Locke's Essay on Human Understanding," J XIII:458.
[79]"Remarks upon Mr. Locke's Essay on Human Understanding," J XIII:460.
[80]"Remarks upon Mr. Locke's Essay on Human Understanding," J XIII:462.
[81]"An Estimate of the Manners of the Present Times," J XI:156, sec. 1.

We talk indifferently on everything that comes in the way; on everything—but God. If any one were to name him in good company, with any degree of seriousness, suppose at a Gentleman or Nobleman's table, would not they all stand aghast? Would not a profound silence ensue, till someone started a more agreeable subject?[82]

c. Wesley's Critique of Montesquieu

In his "Thoughts upon Baron Montesquieu's Spirit of Laws," 1781, Wesley challenged Montesquieu's self-admiration, faddism, and rationalistic "air of infallibility, as though he were the Dictator not only of France, but of Europe."[83] Aesthetically, Montesquieu "touches none of the passions," "gives no pleasure ... to a thinking mind." "The more I study, the less I comprehend.... I verily believe he did not comprehend [his own words] himself." Worse, Wesley said, Montesquieu took "every opportunity to depreciate the inspired writers."[84] "Other talents he undoubtedly had; but two he wanted—religion and logic." Compared to Pascal, Malebranche, or Locke, Wesley considered Montesquieu infantile.[85]

Here we glimpse Wesley, after spending hours riding on horseback while reading Montesquieu, in a moment of perceptive commentary on the follies of his own culture. The avid reader of Wesley will find many such glimpses.

d. Natural History

Many of Wesley's critical thoughts on geological and natural history are found in his intriguing "Remarks on the Count de Buffon's 'Natural History,'" in *Arminian Magazine*, 1782.[86] Decades before Darwin's research, Wesley agreed with the Count that many parts of the earth were once covered with the sea for many ages, that strata were formed, and that stones were once a soft paste.[87]

Yet Wesley argued pithily against the hypotheses that there is no final cause or purpose in natural history; that in most beings there are fewer useful or necessary organs than those that are useless or redundant; that there is no essential difference between vegetables and animals; that the world existed from eternity; that the earth is "only a slice of the sun, cut off from it by the stroke of a comet"; that the inner core of the earth is glass; that the sea covered *the whole earth* for many ages ("I think this is highly improbable; though it has doubtless covered many parts of it for some time"); and that the world was created by chance. On these grounds Wesley ranked Count de Buffon "far beneath Voltaire, Rousseau, and Hume (all of whom acknowledge the being of a God) in religion as in understanding."[88] All this is concisely stated in this short article, easily read in a short time.

---

[82]"An Estimate of the Manners of the Present Times," J XI:160–61, secs. 13–16.
[83]"Thoughts upon Baron Montesquieu's Spirit of Laws," J XIII:415.
[84]Ibid.
[85]"Thoughts upon Baron Montesquieu's Spirit of Laws," J XIII:416.
[86]B 2:588n.
[87]"Remarks on the Count de Buffon's 'Natural History,'" J XIII:448–51 (*AM*, 1782, J V:546–48).
[88]"Remarks on the Count de Buffon's 'Natural History,'" J XIII:455.

e. Natural Religion: An Assessment of Hinduism

In his "Remarks on Mr. H.'s 'Account of the Gentoo Religion in Hindustan,'" 1774,[89] Wesley offered a critique of a romanticizing admirer of the Hindu religion in India. He was especially skeptical regarding the extreme antiquity claimed for Hinduism. It should be remembered that because of his Georgia mission with the American Indians, Wesley could plausibly have taken on the role of having some practical expertise in reporting on non-Christian religions.[90] Who else among his readers had dealt hands-on with the noble savage or an alternative civilization? He remarked, "Are these twelve articles of his creed 'the fundamental points of [natural] religion?' ... I never met with an American Indian who believed half of them."[91]

The points covered included the fantasy of metempsychosis,[92] the transmigration of souls through extensive ethereal spheres of purification, and the account of the creation (with the earth sitting on the head of a snake on the back of a tortoise).[93] For Wesley this was proof that "they that do not believe the Bible will believe anything."[94] The lack of external verification suggests that these claims are to be ranked with the fairy tales.[95] It is circular reasoning to argue that the antiquity of the writing is proved by the tradition that they were perpetuated in antiquity.

At this time of his life (1774), Wesley was having second thoughts about his previous romantic tendency to idealize some individualistic forms of mysticism, including those Protestants who had gone too far with them. Whereas once the Wesleys had held the "Mystic Divines ... in great veneration, as the best explainers of the gospel," now their tune had changed: "We are now convinced, that we therein greatly erred, not knowing the Scriptures, neither the power of God."[96]

Wesley was warning the Methodist Societies that the mystics would edify them by a "solitary religion," not troubling about outward works, but only "to work virtues in the will." "Directly opposite to this is the gospel of Christ. Solitary religion is not to be found there. 'Holy solitaries' is a phrase no more consistent with the gospel than holy adulterers. The gospel of Christ knows of no religion, but social; no holiness but social holiness."[97] This now famous comment on social holiness was pointedly made in a critique of the temptation of all forms of mysticism, such as the Eastern religions, to forget the social implications of the gospel.

---

[89]Cf. *LJW* 6:118; B 2:381n.

[90]*JJW* 1:156–62, 236–39, 248–50, 297–98, 346, 406–9; B 1:502; 3:449; 4:52; 5:226, 8:289, 317; *LJW* 1:201–3; 8:24.

[91]"Remarks on Mr. H.'s 'Account of the Gentoo Religion in Hindustan,'" J XIII:407.

[92]*LJW* 2:279.

[93]"Remarks on Mr. H.'s 'Account of the Gentoo Religion in Hindustan,'" J XIII:404.

[94]"Remarks on Mr. H.'s 'Account of the Gentoo Religion in Hindustan,'" J XIII:408.

[95]"Remarks on Mr. H.'s 'Account of the Gentoo Religion in Hindustan,'" J XIII:405.

[96]*HSP* (1739), pref. 1; J XIV:319; see also Wesley's "Thoughts upon Jacob Behmen (Boehme)" (1780), J IX:509–14; and "A Specimen of the Divinity and Philosophy of the Highly-Illuminated Jacob Behmen," J IX:514–19, on the limits of speculative mysticism; cf. *JJW* 3:17, 282; 4:411; 5:46, 521; *SS* 1:240; B 2:48n.

[97]*HSP* (1739), prefs. 4, 5; J XIV:321. For Wesley's ambivalent reflections on mysticism, see *LJW* 1:289, 243; on kinds of mysticism, see JWO 252; on Quietism, see *LJW* 1:276; on the poison of mysticism, see

Further Reading on Reason and Philosophy

Mystical Experience and the History of Religions

Brigden, Thomas E. "The Wesleys and Islam." *PWHS* 8 (1911): 91–95.

Turner, E. E. "John Wesley and Mysticism." *MR* 113 (1930): 16–31.

Van Valin, Howard F. "Mysticism in Wesley." *AS* 12, no. 2 (1958): 3–14.

Wilson, David D. "John Wesley and Mystical Prayer." *LQHR* 193 (1968): 61–69.

———. "John Wesley, Gregory Lopez and the Marquis de Renty." *PWHS* 35 (1966): 181–84.

———. "John Wesley's Break with Mysticism Reconsidered." *PWHS* 35 (1965): 65–67.

Reason and Authority

Cragg, Gerald R. *Reason and Authority in the Eighteenth Century.* Cambridge: Cambridge University Press, 1964.

Frost, Stanley B. *Authoritäteslehre in den Werken John Wesleys.* Munchen: Ernst Reinhardt, 1938.

Lacy, H. E. "Authority in John Wesley." *LQHR* 189 (1964): 114–19.

Stoeffler, F. Ernest. "The Wesleyan Concept of Religious Certainty—Its Prehistory and Significance." *LQHR* 33 (1964): 128–39.

"Wesley's Epistemology." *WTJ* 10 (1975): 53–55.

Wesley and Philosophical Wisdom

Barber, F. L. "Wesley's Philosophy." *Biblical World* 54 (1920): 142–49.

Cannon, William R. "Methodism in a Philosophy of History." *MH* 12, no. 4 (1974): 27–43.

Eayrs, George. *John Wesley: Christian Philosopher and Church Founder.* London: Epworth, 1926.

Eckhart, Ruth Alma. "Wesley and the Philosophers." *MR* 112 (1929): 330–45.

Fox, Harold G. "John Wesley and Natural Philosophy." *University of Dayton Review* 7, no. 1 (1970): 31–39.

Matthews, Rex D. "'Religion and Reason Joined': A Study in the Theology of John Wesley." ThD diss., Harvard University, 1986.

———. "'We Walk by Faith, Not by Sight': Religious Epistemology in the Later Sermons of John Wesley." Paper privately circulated.

Outler, Albert C. *Theology in the Wesleyan Spirit,* 1–23. Nashville: Tidings, 1975.

Shimizu, Mitsuo. "Epistemology in the Thought of John Wesley." PhD diss., Drew University, 1980 (revised for publication in Tokyo, 1993).

JJW 5:28; JWO 45–46, 63, 375–76, 394. On the French mystical writers, see comments on Madame Guyon, *JJW* 3:18; 5:382–83; 6:130; 7:319; *LJW* 5:341–42; 6:39, 42–44, 125, 233; 8:18; on Madame Antoinette Bourignon, see *LJW* 7:66, 126; *JJW* 1:170, 191–92; 2:15–16; 6:11; 8:277; and Marquis Gaston de Renty, see B 1:36, 61, 75, 344; 3:166–67, 627; *JJW* 1:414, 450; *LJW* 4:184, 264, 293, 321; 5:129, 268, 271; 7:127.

CHAPTER 5

Experience

A. On Experience

Through experience one may "observe a plain, rational sense of God's revealing himself to us, of the *inspiration* of the Holy Ghost, and of a believer's *feeling* in himself the mighty working of the Spirit of Christ."[1] The mighty work of the Spirit of Christ is able to be observed and felt by believers in themselves. Reason and experience work together inwardly to confirm saving faith. Wesley had witnessed this assurance in his own experience and seen it attested by thousands in the course of the revival. In this chapter, we will see how he explained what he and others have felt in their experience of divine grace.

1. The Necessity and Limits of Experience in Religion

In the homily on "The Witness of the Spirit," Wesley wrote:

> And here properly comes in, to confirm this scriptural doctrine, the experience of the children of God — the experience not of two or three, nor of a few, but of a great multitude which no man can number.... It is confirmed by *your* experience and *mine*. The Spirit itself bore witness to my spirit that I was a child of God, gave me an evidence hereof, and I immediately cried, "Abba, Father!" And this I did (and so did you) before I reflected on, or was conscious of, any fruit of the Spirit.[2]

Believers of all ages have felt this: The Spirit is bearing witness to God's saving work within, which enables the believer to so trust in God that it is effortless to call out to God in the most intimate way, "Abba, Father!" The Spirit is bearing witness within our spirits that we are children of God.

Experience confirms but does not override Scripture. Experience is not a private matter alone, but a matter that believers share in a community of memory. It is our experience together — yours and mine — that confirms the very sonship and daughterhood promised in Scripture.

Wesley was not talking just about human experience in general. He was talking

---

[1]FA, pt. 1; B 11:167, sec. 5.24, italics added.
[2]"The Witness of the Spirit," pt. 2, B 1:290, sec. 3.6.

about a particular experience that multitudes have had: the recognition that "I am a child of God." This occurs when the Spirit is bearing witness to that experience promised by the gospel. Wesley was like a reporter, reporting the evidence of the assurance of saving faith.

a. Personal Experience of Trust in Christ

Wesley had his own testimony to report. In the Aldersgate experience, Wesley wrote one of the most quoted of all his writings: "I felt my heart strangely warmed. I felt I did trust in Christ, Christ alone for salvation. And an assurance was given me, that he had taken away *my* sins, even mine, and saved me from the law of sin and death."[3]

The heart is "strangely warmed" when this awareness dawns. It is something felt. It provides assurance that our relation to God has been transformed. It is "our sins" that have been taken away. We know by this experience that our relation with God has been forever changed.

It is of this experience that Wesley was speaking, not just any experience in general, or some general category of consciousness called experience. It is not the idea of experience but of *my* experience. It is my personal awareness of my new relation with God as "Abba, Father." It is felt in the very core of a person whose heart has been softened by the Spirit and led to faith.

b. Enter Peter Böhler

In the events leading to the Aldersgate experience, Wesley's dialogue with the Moravian Peter Böhler focused on the close interconnection between "Scripture and experience." Böhler had argued that true faith would have "two fruits inseparably attending it, 'dominion over sin and constant peace from a sense of forgiveness.'" Wesley looked for evidence of these fruits of faith first in Scripture, where he found them abundantly attested. Yet he did not feel the evidence inwardly and personally.

Before his talks with Böhler, Wesley had not heard of this abiding peace from a sense of forgiveness plausibly attested. He had long waited "'till I found some living witnesses of it.' He [Böhler] replied he could show me such at any time; if I desired it, the next day. And accordingly the next day he came again with three others, all of whom testified, of their own personal experience, that a true living faith in Christ is inseparable from a sense of pardon," and that this faith was "the free gift of God; and that he would surely bestow it upon every soul who earnestly and perseveringly sought it."[4] Böhler brought him living witnesses to the experience of assurance.

c. The Experience of Assurance

The criterion of experience[5] pertains especially to the inner testimony of the assurance of salvation. No words "will adequately express what the children of God

---

[3]*JJW*, May 24, 1738, B 1:475, sec. 14.
[4]*JJW*, May 24, 1738, B 1:471–72, sec. 12.
[5]For further reference to Christian experience, see B 1:154, 293, 297, 323; JWO 79–80, 191–94, 209–19; 387–88, 392–93; *CH* 7:3.

experience ... an inward impression on the soul, whereby the Spirit of God directly witnesses to my spirit, that I am a child of God ... a consciousness of our having received, in and by the Spirit of adoption, the tempers mentioned in the word of God ... a consciousness that we are inwardly conformed, by the Spirit of God, to the image of his Son."[6] This consciousness is offered as a birthright for all believers.[7] Wesley would travel to Germany in 1736 to learn more from the Moravians and German pietists.[8]

Wesley witnessed in his own experience the truth that had been promised in Scripture: "I now am assured that these things are so: I *experience* them in my own breast. What Christianity (considered as a doctrine) promised is accomplished in my own soul."[9] This form of religious experience is more an *appropriation* of scriptural authority than the *source* of authority.[10] The appropriation of the promise of Scripture is received by the spiritual senses.

2. On Spiritual Senses

a. Natural and Spiritual Senses

Spiritual knowledge is discerned with spiritual senses.[11] Wesley agreed with Locke that "our ideas are not innate, but must all originally come from our senses." But unlike Locke, he distinguished between *two types of senses: natural senses and spiritual senses.*[12]

The spiritual senses make it possible

> to discern spiritual good and evil. It is necessary that you have the *hearing* ear and the *seeing* eye ... that you have a new class of senses opened in your soul, not depending on organs of flesh and blood, to be "the *evidence* of things not seen," as your bodily senses are of visible things, to be the avenues to the invisible world, to discern spiritual objects, and to furnish you with ideas of what the outward "eye hath not seen, neither the ear heard." And till you have these internal senses, till the eyes of your understanding are opened, you can have no apprehension of divine things, no idea of them at all.[13]

It is a diminution of our sensory capacity to view humans as only having senses that see and hear empirical evidence. We have latent abilities built into our created humanity that make it possible to behold spiritual evidence of "things not seen" (Hebrews 11:1).

Wesley offered this analogy: "As you cannot reason concerning colours if you

---

6"The Witness of the Spirit," pt. 1, B 1:273–74, sec. 1.6, 7.

7"Marks of the New Birth," B 1:423, sec. 2.3.

8For Wesley's visit to Halle to meet the son of August Herman Francke, "whose name is indeed as precious ointment, Oh may I follow him, as he did Christ," see *JJW* 2:58; 2:16–17; cf. *JJW* 1:116, 121, 124.

9LCM 2.12, *LJW* 11:383, italics added.

10*JWTT*, 33; cf. *LJW* 1:172; 3:137; 5:17; 6:129, 132, 136; SS 2:349.

11On Wesley's spiritual theory of perception, see JWO 190–91, 209–10, 293–95, 395–96; B 11:46–47.

12For Wesley's physical theory of perception, see JWO 284–85, 475–76, 487–88

13EA, B 11:57, sec. 32; cf. JWO 47; B 4:170–71; 1:145–46.

have no natural sight ... so you cannot reason concerning spiritual things if you have no spiritual sight."[14] Everyone has some capacity for spiritual sight, but the gospel releases these senses to an incomparable extent.

b. The Great Work of God

Wesley argued that "a great work of God" was under way in the revival on the basis of "common sense. I know it by the evidence of my own eyes and ears. I have seen a considerable part of it; and I have abundant testimony, such as excludes all possible doubt, for what I have not seen."[15]

Wesley said, "I do not undervalue traditional evidence.... And yet I cannot set it on a level with this"—the experience of the inner witness of the Spirit with our spirits that we are children of God. "Traditional evidence is of an extremely complicated nature, necessarily including so many and so various considerations that only men of strong and clear understanding can be sensible of its full force. On the contrary, how plain and simple is this! And how level to the lowest capacity! Is not this the sum? 'One thing I know: I was blind, but now I see.' An argument so plain that a peasant ... may feel its force."[16]

The great work of God occurring in the revival may be grasped by plain common sense: those who were blind now see. What do they see? God's forgiving love to them as sinners.

3. On Living without God—The Parable of the Tree Toad

The text of the homily "On Living without God" is Ephesians 2:12: "Without God in the world" [Homily #130 (1790), B 4:169–76; J #125, VII:349–54].

Wesley developed a curious, almost comic, metaphor of a creature receiving renewed capacity to see and hear the world: the plight of the person "without God in the world" is compared to the condition of a very large toad reportedly discovered alive inside the core of an ancient oak tree. When the tree was split open, the frog inside was found sightless. It had never had any sensory experience whatever of the visible world. Wesley took this reputed empirical report as a parable for experiential deprivation.

The sensory deprivation of the ungodly life is set forth by analogy with such a creature who indeed possesses eyes but has no sight and no exercised practice of seeing, who has senses such as hearing but has remained totally destitute of any actual sensations. Lacking sensation, there is no reflection, memory, or imagination.[17]

The parallel is between this sequestered creature and the person who is living "without God in the world," having no sense of God.[18] Like the toad who was "shut up from the sun, moon, and stars, and from the beautiful face of nature; indeed from the

---

[14]EA, B 11:55–56, sec. 32.

[15]Letter to the author of The Enthusiasm of Methodists and Papists Compar'd (Bishop George Lavington), sec. 32, LJW 11:374; cf. B 2:526–31; 3:452–53.

[16]LCM, LJW 11:383–84.

[17]"On Living without God," B 4:179, sec. 5.

[18]"On Living without God," B 4:170, secs. 5–7.

whole visible world, as much as if it had no being,"[19] such a person has no experience whatever of the invisible world on which to reflect, no memory or imagination concerning any spiritual reality. Such is the deprived condition of the sensory apparatus in which the spiritual senses have remained entirely undeveloped, as in the practical atheists who have "not the least sight of God, the intellectual Sun, nor any the least attraction toward him,"[20] who have never once had "God in all their thoughts."[21]

Like the tree toad, the atheist — without God in the world — lives as though the spiritual world has no being. "He has not the least perception of it; not the most distant idea."[22]

4. The New Birth of the Spiritual Senses

a. The Reviving of Spiritual Senses in the New Birth

New life in the Spirit is like receiving a new sensory capacity, so that we can see with newly opened eyes that we have "an Advocate with the Father" (1 John 2:1), can hear the voice of one who is the resurrection, *feel* the love of God "shed abroad in our hearts."[23]

The moment the Spirit strikes our hearts, God breaks the hardness, like the splitting of the oak tree. All things become new. The sun of righteousness appears, revealing "the light of the knowledge of God's glory displayed in the face of Christ" (2 Cor. 4:6 NIV).[24] Like being born, his eyes now see, his ears now hear. He is able to taste how gracious the Lord is, how "Jesus' love is far better than wine."[25] He is consumed with the ecstatic joy of enjoying and using his entire sensory apparatus to soak up knowledge and love of God through all available means: reason, nature, and above all the history of revelation.[26]

"This change from spiritual death to spiritual life is properly the new birth,"[27] which empowers a fundamental change of heart. It is not merely a conceptual shift of ideas. The entire sensory apparatus is awakened to a new way of living and sensing the reality at hand. The new birth and the filling of the Spirit are like the opening up of a new life, while the old, closed-down self is seen by analogy as the ensconced condition of the sinner, withdrawn from the exercise of all capacities of the spiritual senses.[28] To respond in faith to grace is to become a new creature in Christ.[29] We move from the spheres of natural appetite and tedious morality to new life in the Spirit, from natural to legal to evangelical life.[30]

---

[19]"On Living without God," B 4:170, sec. 3.
[20]"On Living without God," B 4:171, sec. 8.
[21]"On Living without God," B 4:171, sec. 7.
[22]"On Living without God," B 4:171, sec. 8; *LJW* 4:60; 7:263.
[23]"On Living without God," B 4:173, sec. 11; Rom. 5:5.
[24]"On Living without God," B 4:172, sec. 9.
[25]"On Living without God," B 4:172–73, secs. 9–11.
[26]Letter to Elizabeth Ritchie, January 17, 1775, *LJW* 6:136.
[27]"On Living without God," B 4:173, sec. 11.
[28]"On Living without God," B 4:172–73, secs. 9–11.
[29]"On Living without God," B 4:173–74, secs. 12, 13.
[30]"On Living without God," B 4:174–76, secs. 14–16.

b. Experiential Excesses in Baron Swedenborg

There are dangers in overemphasizing experience. This was made clear in "Thoughts on the Writings of Baron Swedenborg," in which Wesley directly disputed many idiosyncratic ideas of that popular writer that were troubling some in his societies: that God cannot be angry; that creation was not ex nihilo; that those who die go through three states before they enter either heaven or hell, providing instruction and discipline for reprobates; that angels were once human beings; that hell is merely symbolic; that there is still time for repentance in hell; that Scripture is full of blasphemy; that all who believe in the Trinity are possessed of the devil; that the Nicene Creed gave "birth to a faith which has entirely overturned the Christian church."[31] All false.

Swedenborg exemplifies the danger of exalting our own personal experience above the experience of the Christian community over the centuries. The grand error of Baron Swedenborg was in his rejection of the triune teaching in favor of his own private experience. All of this is best explained in relation to Swedenborg's own account that "in the year 1743 the Lord was pleased to manifest himself to me in a personal appearance ... to enable me to converse with spirits and angels; and this privilege I have enjoyed ever since."[32]

As if this were not enough, Wesley wryly added an account of the "very serious Swedish Clergyman," Mr. Mathesius, who reported an incident when Swedenborg became "totally delirious ... ran into the street stark naked, proclaimed himself the Messiah, and rolled himself in the mire. I suppose he dates from this time his admission into the society of angels."[33]

Modern Christianity, whether liberal or evangelical, has all too many examples of those who appeal to private experience exalted above the historical experience of believers whose lives have been transformed by the gospel.

B. On Enthusiasm

1. The Nature of Enthusiasm

The text of the homily "The Nature of Enthusiasm" is Acts 26:24: "Paul, thou art beside thyself" [Homily #37 (1750), B 2:44 – 60; J #37, V:467 – 79].

"A religion of form ... performed in a decent, regular manner" will not provoke others to say, as they said of Paul, "Much religion doth make thee mad." The religion of the heart where one is "alive to God, and dead to all things here below" may prompt others to pass the sentence: "Thou art beside thyself."[34]

Enthusiasm is a term sometimes used to refer either to a divine impulse that for

---

[31]"Thoughts on the Writings of Baron Swedenborg," J XIII:429.
[32]"Thoughts on the Writings of Baron Swedenborg," J XIII:425.
[33]"Thoughts on the Writings of Baron Swedenborg," J XIII:426.
[34]"The Nature of Enthusiasm," B 2:46, sec.1; Rom. 6:11; Acts 26:24.

the moment suspends reason and sense,[35] or to an uncommon ability in which the natural faculties are elevated to a higher degree than normal.[36]

In Wesley's day, enthusiasm was more popularly viewed as a disorder of the mind that shuts the eyes of understanding, greatly hindering the exercise of reason. It was regarded as a species of madness in which one draws right conclusions from wrong premises.[37]

While true religion manifests the spirit of a sound mind, *enthusiasm* was defined by Wesley as "a religious madness arising from some falsely imagined influence or inspiration of God; at least, from imputing something to God which ought not to be imputed to him, or expecting something from God which ought not to be expected from him."[38]

Enthusiasm talks loosely as if God were acting directly within the self without any correctives of scripturally informed reasoning.[39] Enthusiasts "undervalue the experience of almost every one in comparison" with their own.[40]

2. Types of Enthusiasm

Wesley provided examples of the dangers of enthusiasm. He spoke of those who imagine they have grace, which they have not, so as to result in pride, excessive sentimentality, and distance from the mind of Christ.

Wesley also cautioned those who imagine they are champions of faith but produce no fruits:[41] "Ah, poor self-deceivers! Christians ye are not. But you are enthusiasts in an high degree. Physicians, heal yourselves. But first know your disease: your whole life is enthusiasm, as being all suitable to your imagination."[42] He especially warned Thomas Maxfield against "overvaluing feelings and inward impressions ... and undervaluing reason, knowledge, and wisdom in general."[43]

Among other enthusiasts found in revival circles are "those who imagine they have such gifts from God as they have not" and feel they are "directed by the Spirit when they are not."

Some think they can defy laws of nature or prophesy the literal future, or they feel that God is dictating the very words they say when they are carrying out their own private interests.

Wesley said to beware of mediums, sorcerers, fortune-tellers, and spurious

---

[35]"The Nature of Enthusiasm," B 2:48, sec. 8.
[36]"The Nature of Enthusiasm," B 2:49, sec. 9.
[37]"The Nature of Enthusiasm," B 2:49, secs. 10 – 11; JJW 2:130; B 1:267 – 68; 1:269 – 70; 2:44 – 60; 2:587 – 88; FA, B 11:96 – 98; cf. 11:354 – 56, 361 – 74, 382 – 83; 468 – 81, 491 – 95; LJW 2:204 – 6; CH 7:199.
[38]"The Nature of Enthusiasm," B 2:50, sec. 12.
[39]Answer to Thomas Church, J VIII:405 – 13; LJW 2:204 – 11, 241 – 42.
[40]Letter to Mrs. Ryan, June 28, 1766, LJW 5:17 – 18. Cf. Wesley's comments on Montanus, B 1:76, 268; 2:461, 555; LJW 3:357, 360; 4:133, 327 – 29, 336.
[41]"The Nature of Enthusiasm," B 2:50 – 52, secs. 13 – 17.
[42]"The Nature of Enthusiasm," B 2:52, sec. 17.
[43]Letter to Thomas Maxfield, November 2, 1762, LJW 4:193.

teachers who imagine they are receiving particular directions from God even in the most trifling circumstances of life.

He also said to beware of those who neglect the means of grace in common worship. There are those enthusiasts "who think they attain the end without using the means, by the immediate power of God." Some imagine they can understand Scripture without studying it. They are often found speaking in public without any premeditation.[44]

Finally, Wesley warned those enthusiasts who treat natural effects as if they are acts of special providence. Such people often ignore the multilayered aspect of the Christian doctrine of general providence available to all.[45]

The remedy: God has given believers reason as a guide. Christians must never exclude the quiet assistance of the Holy Spirit to aid the understanding. They must pray for the Spirit to illumine their perception of the will of God by the power of the Spirit.[46]

a. The Bitter Fruits of Emotional Excess

Believers are called to examine their own lives for signs of excess.[47] Enthusiasm breeds pride and self-deception. It may block persons from the actual grace of God and from seeking the good counsel of faithful friends.

There is no need to hastily employ the volatile word *enthusiasm*. We do far better by simply studying carefully the temptations to self-deception.[48] "Think before you speak." Do not rashly label others unfairly as enthusiasts.[49]

Apply "the plain Scripture rule, with the help of experience and reason, and the ordinary assistance of the Spirit of God" to discern the will of God, using the "ordinary channels of his grace,"[50] expecting to grow daily in pure and holy religion, so as to be deserving of the charge of enthusiasm in a positive sense of faithful zeal, and avoiding the sort of enthusiasm that is "merely nominal Christianity."[51]

The "ordinary channels of grace" are praying, reading Scripture, and attending public worship, especially receiving Holy Communion. I will discuss these later in connection with the homily on "The Means of Grace."

b. Whether Inward Feelings Confirm Saving Faith according to Scripture

In "A Letter to Dr. [Thomas] Rutherforth," Regius Professor of Divinity at Cambridge, March 28, 1768 [B 9:373–88; J XIV:347–59; *LJW* 5:357–69], Wesley

---

[44]"The Nature of Enthusiasm," B 2:56, sec. 27; *PACP*, J X1:429–30.

[45]"The Nature of Enthusiasm," B 2:56, sec. 28.

[46]"The Nature of Enthusiasm," B 2:52–56, secs. 18–26.

[47]Letter to Bishop Warburton, *LJW* 4:358–59.

[48]Wesley himself had been charged with "enthusiasm"; see 39:114–21, 182–83, 196–213, 228–29, 304–6.

[49]"The Nature of Enthusiasm," B 2:59, sec. 39.

[50]"The Nature of Enthusiasm," B 2:59, secs. 38–39.

[51]"The Nature of Enthusiasm," B 2:60, sec. 39.

replied to Anglican charges that Methodists reject the aid of human learning and exaggerate inward feelings and divine assurances. Wesley argued that his sentiments on Christian experience during the "last thirty years" (1738–68) had been consistent, with "few, if any, *real* contradictions," though there may have been "some *seeming* contradictions, especially considering I was answering so many different objectors."[52]

This was Wesley's position: (1) "Few, but very few, Christians have an *assurance* from God of *everlasting salvation,*" or the "plerophory, or full assurance of hope." (2) "More have such an *assurance* of being *now in the favour of God* as excludes all doubt and fear." (3) "A *consciousness of being in the favour of God* ... is the common privilege of Christians." "Yet I do not affirm, there are no exceptions to this general rule. Possibly some may be in the favour of God, and yet go mourning."[53]

Wesley summarized for Dr. Rutherforth the position he had held consistently for "above these forty years" (at least since 1728) on the role of "*inward feelings*"[54] in religious knowledge: "(1). The fruit of [the Spirit's] *ordinary influences* are love, joy, peace, long-suffering, gentleness, meekness. (2). Whoever has these, *inwardly feels* them. And if he understands his Bible, he discerns from whence they come. Observe, what he inwardly feels is *these fruits themselves; whence they come* he learns from the Bible."[55] "By 'feeling' I mean being inwardly conscious of."[56] "I look upon some of these bodily symptoms [in reference to fits and tears] to have been preternatural or diabolical, and others to have been effects which in some circumstances naturally followed from the strong and sudden emotions of mind ... springing from gracious influences."[57]

Wesley appealed to article 17 of the Anglican Thirty-Nine Articles of Religion, which teaches that "godly persons *feel in themselves the working of the Spirit* of Christ, mortifying the works of the flesh ... and drawing up their mind to high and heavenly things."[58]

3. How Scripture Corrects Experience

The scriptural rule is not reversed by alleged private revelations. In Wesley's Letter to a Person Lately Joined with the People called Quakers,[59] 1748, he stated his objection to the teaching of the premier Quaker theologian Robert Barclay that private revelations "are not to be subjected to the examination of the Scriptures," and that "the Scriptures are not the principal ground of all truth," but are secondary

---

[52]Letter to Dr. Rutherforth, *LJW* 1.3, 9:375.
[53]Letter to Dr. Rutherforth, *LJW* 1.4, 9:375–76.
[54]Cf. B 11:399, 492; EA, B 11:35; *LJW* 4:359; 6:18.
[55]Letter to Dr. Rutherforth, *LJW* 9:381, sec. 3.1, italics added.
[56]FA, pt. 1, J V:2, B 11:139–40.
[57]Letter to Dr. Rutherforth, *LJW* 9:387, sec. 3.12.
[58]Art. 17, XXXIX; *DSWT* 117, italics added; cf. B 9:384.
[59]For further reference to Quakers, see *LJW* 2:116–28; 4:123; B 2:265; 3:257, 260, 589; FA, B 11:171–72, 254–60, 290.

and "subordinate to the Spirit."[60] Rather, "the Scriptures are the rule whereby [the Spirit] leads us into all truth. Therefore, only talk good English: call the *Spirit our guide*, which signifies an intelligent being, and the *Scriptures our rule*, which signifies something used by an intelligent being."[61] The Scriptures are the measuring rod for examining all, real or supposed, revelations.

The inordinate focus on private revelation may tempt toward "flat justification by works,"[62] toward antipathy toward reasoning, toward a form of worship that is reduced to quietism, toward neglect of the singing of psalms, toward the complete elimination of visible signs in baptism and the Lord's Supper, toward ordination without the laying on of hands, toward prohibitions against swearing before magistrates, and toward any form of kneeling or bowing. Those who have "an honest heart but a weak head" are called to abandon such trifles, and return to "spiritual, rational, scriptural religion."[63]

Further Reading on Experience

Bence, Clarence L. "Experimental Religion." *PM* 56, no. 1 (1980): 50–51.

Brown, Robert. *John Wesley's Theology: The Principle of Its Vitality and Its Progressive Stages of Development.* London: Jackson, Walford and Hodder, 1865.

Dieter, Melvin. "John Wesley and Creative Synthesis." *AS* 39, no. 3 (1984): 3–7.

Dreyer, Frederick. "Faith and Experience in the Thought of John Wesley." *AHR* 88, no. 1 (1983): 12–30.

Garrison, R. Benjamin. "Vital Interaction: Scripture and Experience." *RL* 25 (1956): 563–73.

Gunter, W. Steven. Chap. 1, "Enthusiasm"; chap. 5, "Quest for Certainty"; chap. 9, "John Wesley as Improper Enthusiast"; and chap. 10, "More Heat Than Light." In *The Limits*

of Divine Love: John Wesley's Response to Antinomianism and Enthusiasm. Nashville: Kingswood, Abingdon, 1989.

Langford, Thomas. *Practical Divinity: Theology in the Wesleyan Tradition.* Nashville: Abingdon, 1982.

Lindström, Harald. "Experience in Wesley's Theology." In *Wesley and Sanctification.* Nashville: Abingdon, 1946.

Monk, Robert C. "Experience." In *John Wesley: His Puritan Heritage,* 70ff. Nashville: Abingdon, 1966.

Starkey, Lycurgus. "Freedom of the Holy Spirit and Authority of Christian Faith." In *The Work of the Holy Spirit,* 140ff.; also 15ff. Nashville: Abingdon, 1962.

Williams, Colin. "Authority and Experience." In *John Wesley's Theology Today,* 23ff. Nashville: Abingdon, 1960.

---

[60] A Letter to a Person Lately Joined with the People called Quakers, J X:178, sec. 3.
[61] Ibid., italics added.
[62] A Letter to a Person Lately Joined with the People called Quakers, J X:179, sec. 7.
[63] A Letter to a Person Lately Joined with the People called Quakers, J X:187, sec. 15.

C. The Catholic Spirit

1. The Premise of Tolerance

Can Christians be of one heart even if they have differing opinions? Wesley preached a homily on "The Catholic Spirit" to answer this question.

a. A Right Heart

The text of the homily "The Catholic Spirit" is 2 Kings 10:15: "Is your heart right?" [Homily #39 (1749), B 2:79–96; J #34, V:492–504; JWO 91ff.].

The memorable text for the homily on the catholic spirit is "If your heart is as my heart, then give me your hand" (2 Kings 10:15, Wesley's paraphrase). The text refers to the meeting between the ruthless Jehu and the religious fanatic Jehonadab. Sensing that Jehonadab might be a valuable asset, Jehu asked, "Are you in accord with me, as I am with you?" When Jehonadab[64] answered, "I am," Jehu replied, "If so ... give me your hand" (2 Kings 10:15 NIV).

Wesley was concerned here not with Jehu's mixed motives but with the form of reconciliation of human estrangement that is due not to intellectual agreement but to goodwill. He called it a "right heart." The major thesis is that *we may be of one heart even though not of one opinion.*[65] Human barriers are overcome by the love of God and humanity, which reaches beyond human antipathies and cultural differences.

b. Honoring Legitimate Freedom to Hold Diverse Opinions

However dissimilar our cultural, moral, or religious opinions may be, persons of goodwill may become united by grace in trusting affection. Partisan disputation usually fails to grasp how hearts can be knit together despite conceptual, cultural, political, and economic differences. Persons holding divergent opinions and shaped by different generations of thinking and worship may still be joined in love, warmth, and mutual affection. Wesley's teaching on this text offers a decisive clue to the affectionate temperament of the Methodist movement.[66]

As inveterate sinners, we are forever prone to shortsightedness in the formation of our opinions. The knowing process is shaped by our social location, our way of looking at the world from a highly particular historical and class status. Thinking emerges always out of highly circumstantial and culture-specific contexts. This is endemic to the way all humans think: always out of a specific cultural location. Combine this viewpoint with our pride, and it results in egocentric and ethnocentric history. None of us can know with full adequacy just how much our social prejudices shape our present vision. Conceptual and social differences in religion are an unavoidable consequence of our finitude, dullness of human understanding, and lack of empathy.

---

[64]Jehonadab was the biblical type of one who had vowed to live always in tents away from a corrupt civilization, abstain from wine and strong drink, and struggle against idolatry. SS 1:128.
[65]JJW 3:178–80; B 9:31–34, 125–26, 254–55, 285–86; LJW 2:110.
[66]LJW 3:35, 180–83,

Wesley exhibited an unremitting resistance to petty prejudice and social bias. He was aware that Christian teaching is always expressed through changing, variable social memories.

By "opinions" Wesley meant ideas nonessential for Christian teaching. These ideas often focus on ancillary matters (*adiaphora*) neither commanded nor forbidden by Scripture that could be matters of free interpretation without straining the limits of genuine Christianity.[67] Disciplined believers honor the legitimate freedom of fellow Christians to hold diverse opinions.

From his mother, Wesley had inherited a Puritan sense of discipline. From his father, he had inherited an enduring Anglican loyalty to the ancient Christian consensus of faith. However deeply committed to classic Christian essentials,[68] John Wesley resisted the notion that they could be captured in a single unalterable form of language.

c. Love, the Core of True Religion

The essential core of true religion is "as I have loved you, so you must love one another" (John 13:34 NIV).[69] "This is love: not that we loved God, but that he loved us and sent his Son as an atoning sacrifice for our sins" (1 John 4:10 NIV).[70] "True religion is right tempers toward God and man. It is, in two words, gratitude and benevolence: gratitude to our Creator and supreme Benefactor, and benevolence to our fellow creatures. In other words, it is loving God with all our heart, and our neighbor as ourselves."[71]

There remain "grand, general hindrances" to the practice of such love: "We can't all think alike"; hence, we do not all walk alike.[72] "So long as 'we know' but 'in part,' all of us 'will not see things alike,'" as an "unavoidable consequence of the present weakness and shortness of human understanding."[73] It is a regrettable characteristic of human finitude that every ego "necessarily believes that every particular opinion which he holds is true (for to believe any opinion is not true is the same thing as not to hold it)."[74] Egotism intrudes into religion and into the relation of religious groups with others: "A difference in opinions or modes of worship may prevent an entire external union, yet need it prevent our union in affection?"[75]

Wesley's golden rule of tolerance states, "Every wise man therefore will allow

---

[67] WQ 161.

[68] Stated clearly in "The Way to the Kingdom," sec. 1.6; and his "A Letter to a Roman Catholic," 1749. For Wesley's distinction between opinion and essential (or fundamental) Christian teaching, see *LJW* 2:110; 4:297; 5:224; 7:216; 8:47; B 1:175, 508; 2:374–76; 3:588; 4:146; JWO 77–78, 99–100; *JJW* 3:178–80; B 9:31–34, 125–26, 254–55, 285–86.

[69] Wesley also spoke of true religion as having the mind of Christ (B 9:527) and, similarly, the restoration of the image of God in humanity (B 9:255).

[70] B 1:530; 3:389, 313, 448, 585–86; 4:57, 66–67; 9:502.

[71] "The Unity of the Divine Being," sec. 16; cf. EA sec. 1.11–45.

[72] "The Catholic Spirit," B 1:82, proem 3.

[73] "The Catholic Spirit," B 1:83, sec. 1.3.

[74] "The Catholic Spirit," B 1:83–84, sec. 1.4.

[75] "The Catholic Spirit," B 1:82, sec. 1.4.

others the same liberty of thinking which he desires they should allow him"[76] We do well to hold opinions in good conscience but not impose them unilaterally on one another as if to make every minor opinion a test case of religious principle.[77]

d. Respect for Conscience

Wesley was appealing to the freedom to hold opinions, even peculiar ones, that do not dislodge the heart of Christian teaching. It is possible to embrace another affectionately who has a different persuasion on matters not essential to saving faith. Amid the multiplicity of sentiments and inclinations, there remains room for the address of conscience, for each one finally must stand before God.[78]

No one should seek to rule the conscience of another. I must not impose on your conscience what my conscience is attesting to me. Better, rather, to seek inwardly a heart of sincerely penitent faith, leaving plenty of room for candid consultation, the free interplay of ideas, and a tolerance for alternative pathways. "Everyone must follow the dictates of his own conscience in simplicity and godly sincerity ... then act according to the best light he has."[79] "I dare not therefore presume to impose my mode of worship on any other. I believe it is truly primitive and apostolical. But my belief is no rule for another."[80]

From this there follows a spirit of proportional tolerance that has become deeply written into the Wesleyan evangelical ethos. On matters of opinion, "we think and let think."[81] This conviction helped establish and refine the Anglican tradition of toleration and the Reformation achievement of "the right of private judgment."[82] It took special form in the Evangelical Revival, where sincerity of the heart became just as highly valued as detailed confessional agreement. The bands and societies came together on the basis not of strict doctrinal concurrence but of active repentance.

2. Challenging Latitudinarianism

a. Think and Let Think Does Not Imply Indifference to Doctrine and Worship

The catholic spirit must not be confused either with latitudinarianism on the one hand or partisan bigotry on the other. Wesley was concerned about valid argument and defensible exegesis concerning classic consensual teaching, which he called the old catholic faith, but he was less intent upon specific doctrinal definition of minutiae that do not arise from the heart of faith.[83]

This does not imply that anything goes, or that doctrinal truth is diminished in

---

[76]"The Catholic Spirit," B 1:84, sec. 1.6.

[77]JJW 7:389.

[78]LA 11 – 19; J VIII:6 – 8, 124 – 20, 206   7.

[79]"The Catholic Spirit," B 1:85, sec. 1.9; 2 Cor. 1:2; cf. Letter to the Rev. Mr. Potter, November 4, 1758, J IX:88 – 89.

[80]"The Catholic Spirit," B 1:86, sec. 1.11.

[81]B 2:59, 341, 376; 4:145; JJW 7:389.

[82]"The Catholic Spirit" B 1:86, sec. 1.10; cf. J V:136.

[83]Letter to Adam Clarke, September 10, 1756, J XIII:213 – 15.

importance. Wesley strongly resisted the indifferentism that he termed "specula-tive latitudinarianism" — an indifference to all opinions.[84] He called it "the spawn of hell, not the offspring of heaven." It results in "being 'driven to and from, and tossed about with every wind of doctrine.'" That is "a great curse, not a blessing; an irrec-oncilable enemy, not a friend to true Catholicism. A man of a truly catholic spirit has not now his religion to *seek*. He is fixed as the sun in his judgment concerning the main branches of Christian doctrine," though "always ready to hear and weigh whatsoever can be offered against his principles." Wesley said those who think they have a catholic spirit may have only "a muddy understanding; because your mind is all in a mist; because you have no settled, consistent principles, but are for jumbling all opinions together.... Go first and learn the first elements of the gospel of Christ, and then shall you learn to be of a truly catholic spirit."[85]

Nor is the catholic spirit a practical latitudinarianism that would become indif-ferent to public worship and the observance of common prayer.[86]

The Anglican latitudinarians appealed to an age weary of religious controversy. While remaining in the Church of England, they attached minimal importance to distinct doctrinal definition, sacramental practice, and church discipline, appealing to reason and toleration, and promoting only irenic pluralism. They formulated Christian teaching always in ambiguous and minimalist terms, a view that Wesley sharply resisted.

b. How the Sincerity of the Catholic Heart Is Tested

There is a brilliant reversal of momentum in the homily "The Catholic Spirit" in section 1, subsections 12 – 18. In countering latitudinarianism, it is wise to test the sincerity of the catholic heart. Wesley proposed a series of questions asking whether one has become personally accountable to the core of Christian teaching.

Pivotal to the structure of the homily is this reversal. It consists of fifty-three questions to be put soberly not to the head but to the heart.

How do I assess whether "my heart is as your heart"? Instead of a confessional approach that would say, "Here are confessional definitions on which we must agree," Wesley calmly addressed the hearer with this powerful series of highly per-sonal questions, treating the uprighted heart as a matter of intense personal self-examination. This is a different approach to theological truth-telling than is typical in traditional confessionalism. Personal honesty is here paramount. What matters most is the state of the heart in the presence of God.

These self-examination questions have a triune structure and sequence: the first series of issues for self-appraisal deals with God the Father, the second with Christ the Savior, and the third with the work of the Holy Spirit. Questions are raised from one's own heart to one's own heart.

First, concerning God the Father, each person is to ask inwardly: Do I experience

---

[84]B 2:92 – 93; 4:312; JWO 101 – 2, 306.
[85]"The Catholic Spirit," B 1:83, sec. 3.1, italics added.
[86]"The Catholic Spirit," B 1:92, sec. 3.1.

God as eternal? Incomparably just? Merciful?[87] Have I personally appropriated the Christian teaching of the attributes of God?

Second, concerning God the Son, am I justified by faith in his atoning action on the cross, or do I expect my own works to justify me?[88]

Third, concerning God the Spirit, am I receptive to God's own working to bring justifying grace to a full personal expression of maturity?[89]

Having our hearts right before God is not simply an emotive matter that can brush aside scriptural doctrine, but it requires pressing these questions with inward intensity and honesty. Wesley was arguing for doctrinal purity manifested in "catholic love," not for doctrinal pluralism.[90]

It is by all persons answering inwardly a cascade of fifty-three profoundly doctrinal and personal questions that they come to discover whether their hearts are right with God and rightly prepared for the openness of faith active in love. Each question is asked in God's presence as attested by the inner court of conscience. Each asks whether a person's conscience attests a serious, probing self-appraisal.[91]

Some have taken Wesley's theme "If your heart is as my heart, then give me your hand," and his phrase "Think and let think,"[92] and turned them into an appeal for absolute tolerance. They do well to ponder one by one these fifty-three test questions for the catholic heart.

c. An Invitation to a True and Generous Catholicity

If your heart, as defined after this exercise in self-examination, is right with God, then extend to me your hand. This is an invitation to fellowship based not on moral rules or opinions but on inward self-examination of the rightness of one's heart in the presence of God.[93] If your heart is as my heart, we are invited by the Spirit to be joined together into a bonded society of persons whose lives are committed to radical accountability to God. Though some read the catholic spirit as if to imply that doctrinal standards[94] are minimized, or that there are few or no insignificant confessional boundaries in this life that we share with God in Christ, this is hardly the intention of Wesley's text.

By "Give me your hand," "I mean, first, love me" with a "very tender affection," as if "closer than a brother," because it comes from being a "companion in the kingdom." "Love me with the love that 'is not provoked' either at my follies or infirmities, or even at my acting (if it should sometimes so appear to thee) not according to the will of God. Love me so as to 'think no evil' of me." Love me with "the love that 'covereth all things,'" that "'believeth all things,' that is always willing to think the best,

---

[87]"The Catholic Spirit," B 1:87, sec. 1.12.
[88]"The Catholic Spirit," B 1:87, sec. 1.13.
[89]"The Catholic Spirit," B 1:88–89, sec. 1.14–18.
[90]"The Catholic Spirit," B 1:88–89, sec. 1.14–18; *Hymns and Spiritual Songs*, 21st ed., 1777, pref., J XIV:338–39.
[91]Minutes, May 13, 1746, J VIII:288–89.
[92]B 2:59, 341, 376; 4:145; JJW 7:389.
[93]"The Catholic Spirit," B 1:89, sec. 2.1.
[94]For a fuller discussion of Wesleyan doctrinal standards, see *DSWT*; cf. JJW 4:32; 8:70–71.

to put the fairest construction on all my words and actions," hoping "to the end that whatever is amiss will, by the grace of God, be corrected."[95]

Those whose hearts are in accord will show their care by interceding for each other, hoping that shortcomings may be amended to better fulfill God's will. By this means believers stir each other to good works, to acts of mercy, and to loving not in word only but in deed and truth.[96] Such is the catholic spirit, not a spirit that seeks first to get agreement on formal confessions, but under the rule of Scripture, seeks to reach out in dialogue,[97] honoring good conscience, faith, and fervent intercession for the partner in dialogue. "With open arms the world embrace, but cleave to those who cleave to thee."[98]

3. To a Roman Catholic—An Irenic Letter

In "A Letter to a Roman Catholic," Wesley gives us a model of what is meant by the catholic spirit. Wesley had often been accused of being a papist by those who inaccurately viewed his doctrine of sanctification as echoing certain phrases in the Council of Trent.[99]

He shared typical Anglican hesitations about Rome and anxieties about Roman abuses. Yet he became aware during his Irish visits of 1747 and following that Catholics showed up frequently in Methodist preaching services and were eager to hear him.

That was the context of this letter. Catholics and Protestants should not be "looking on the other as monsters."[100] He called for "allowing both sides to retain our own opinions" for "the softening [of] our hearts toward each other." "I do not suppose that all the bitterness is on your side. I know there is too much on our side also. So much that I fear many Protestants (so-called) will be angry at me, too, for writing to you," thinking you deserve no special treatment. "But I think you do ... deserve the tenderist regard I can show, were it only because ... the Son of God has bought you and me with his own blood."[101]

Catholics were welcomed into the preaching events of the evangelical revival in Ireland. "I am not persuading you to leave or change your religion, but to follow after that fear and love of God without which all religion is vain."[102] "A true Protestant believes in God" and "loves his neighbor (that is, every man, friend or enemy, good or bad) as himself, as he loves his own soul, as Christ loved us.... This, and this alone, is the old religion. This is true primitive Christianity. O when ... shall it be found both in us and you?"[103] "Then if we cannot as yet *think alike* in all things,

---

[95]"The Catholic Spirit," B 1:90–91, sec. 2.3, 4.
[96]"The Catholic Spirit," B 1:91, sec. 2.5–7.
[97]*LJW* 3:180.
[98]"Catholic Love," *PW* VI:71–72.
[99]Cf. *LJW* 4:140; 6:371; 7:7; *JJW* 2:469; 3:409.
[100]"A Letter to a Roman Catholic," J X:80, sec. 1, JWO 492.
[101]"A Letter to a Roman Catholic," JWO 493–94, secs. 3–4.
[102]"A Letter to a Roman Catholic," JWO 496, sec. 13.
[103]"A Letter to a Roman Catholic," JWO 498, sec. 14.

at least we may *love alike*.... Let us resolve, first, not to hurt one another...; secondly ... to speak nothing harsh or unkind of each other. The sure way to avoid this is to say all the good we can, both of and to one another...; thirdly, resolve to harbour no unkind thought, no unfriendly temper towards each other...; fourthly, endeavour to help each other on in whatever we are agreed leads to the Kingdom."[104]

D. A Caution against Bigotry

The text of the homily "A Caution against Bigotry" is Mark 9:38: "We saw one casting out devils in thy name" [Homily #38 (1750), B 2.61 – 78; J #38, V:479 – 92].

1. Why Bigotry Is an Offense against the Catholic Spirit

a. Demonic Divisions

Wesley vividly spoke of a demonic element in human divisions and tendencies to unnecessary social conflict. He wrote with unnerving realism about the embittered adversary's efforts to divide human beings into enemy camps.

Who but the Devil could so enjoy needling, segregating, disjoining, and alienating? The catholic spirit wants to reach out, mend, transcend difference, include, welcome, and embrace. Its opposite, the spirit of bigotry, is divisive, exclusive, and self-righteous.[105]

The demonic element is prominently featured in Scripture. It must not be forgotten in the evangelical revival.

Wesley was keenly aware of the ingrained egocentricity that pervades all human cultures. He himself had been through culture shock, having spent two years[106] in frontier America on the interface between ministries to Creek Indians and colonial settlers. He knew something about cross-cultural dialogue.

Wesley beheld bigotry in every society he knew. He had an especially vivid memory of the slave trade in Savannah, Georgia, and of the custom of Native Americans in roasting their prisoners to death.[107]

He was deeply concerned about the genocides of his time. He specifically spoke of the extermination of whole nations not only by pagans and Muslims but by supposedly Christian Spanish, Dutch, and English. He had a cross-cultural conception of bigotry. He was deeply aware that it pervaded the English and American cultures in which he himself had ministered. Surveying the recalcitrance of his own society, Wesley cited a long list of the ways in which bigotry had contaminated his own national environment.[108]

---

[104]"A Letter to a Roman Catholic," JWO 496 – 99, secs. 13 – 17. For other references to Roman Catholic teaching, see B 1:77 – 79, 87, 128 – 29, 508; 2:292, 374 – 75, 581; 3:450 – 51.

[105]"A Caution against Bigotry," B 1:64, sec. 1.2; cf. LJW 1:200; 2:300; 4:367.

[106]February 5, 1736 – December 22, 1737.

[107]"A Caution against Bigotry," B 1:67, sec. 1.9.

[108]"A Caution against Bigotry," B 1:67, sec. 1.10.

b. The Reproof of Prejudice

Wesley made an ardent plea for reconciling narrowly embittered partisanships.[109] *Bigots* are defined as those who have too strong an attachment to or fondness of their own party, opinion, church, race, or religion.[110] Bigotry is excessive partisanship due to an inordinate sense of the rightness of our own causes and interests. It is based on too sharp a distinction between us and them, which tempts constantly toward prejudice.[111] It is an inveterate, at times diabolical, proneness to narrow partiality. The bigot views the other party in the worse light conceivable,[112] often as an extension of supposed "humor."

The problem of bigotry among the faithful is that it undermines love and unity in the body of Christ. The bigot hesitates to admit that others who have widely different opinions could also have the same faith and be recipients of the same Spirit.

Thus bigotry is seen as an offense against the catholic spirit.[113] The text for this homily is the episode in which the disciples discovered a man "driving out demons in your name and we told him to stop, because he was not one of us" (Mark 9:38 NIV). The difference between "us" and "them" becomes easily exaggerated. In this case, the "us" referred to one who was a believer but not yet among the core of Jesus' disciples. This believer was acting in Jesus' name and accomplishing what the disciples had been unable to do. "Casting out demons" becomes in this homily a broad metaphor for any concrete, helpful, redemptive activity.[114]

Ironically, in this narrative it was Jesus' own disciples who were the bigots, saying, "They are not following us; they are so different from us."[115]

Wesley deplored any attitude that would distort human perceptions by exaggerating differences between believers, especially if these exaggerations undermined the unity of the worshiping community. He recognized that social location remains a constant temptation to bias. He was keenly aware of the obstacles to transcending one's own special economic interests.[116]

2. How the Spirit of Bigotry Is Tested

The text of "A Caution against Bigotry" leads next to Jesus' response to the bias

---

[109]Having been charged by Anglicans with excessive zealotry and disregard for parish boundaries, Wesley replied to Bishop Joseph Butler, "I am a priest of the church universal. And being ordained a Fellow of a College, I was not limited to any particular cure, but have an indeterminate commission to preach the word of God in any part of the Church of England." Henry More, *Wesley*, 1:465; 1:61n. Arguing that valid ministry should be measured by its fruits rather than merely by its form, on March 28, 1739, Wesley wrote, "I look upon *all the world as my parish*." B 25:616.

[110]"A Caution against Bigotry," B 1:76, sec. 4.1.

[111]Especially, in Wesley's setting, prejudices with respect to plausible experiential evidences of the work of God in the revival, B 2:84; 3:515; FA, B 11:280–81, 515–16.

[112]"A Caution against Bigotry," B 1:64–68, sec. 1.1–14.

[113]"A Plain Account of the People Called Methodists," J VIII:257, sec. 5.

[114]"A Caution against Bigotry," B 1:63–64, proem 1–3; cf. "Sermon on the Mount 13," B 1:687–92, a caution against false prophets; and *LJW* 2:351; 3:348.

[115]"A Caution against Bigotry," B 1:69, sec. 2.1, paraphrased.

[116]"A Caution against Bigotry," B 1:65–68, sec. 1.

of his followers. How are we rightly to respond when we see demons cast out by one whose opinions are politically incorrect or biased or ill informed?

Wesley insisted that we must first become aware of our own bigotry, of the ways in which we ourselves are often unwilling to allow the benefit of the doubt to others who view the world from a different history of valuing.[117]

Jesus gave this injunction: Do not hinder others from using whatever power God has given them. Do not be quick in judgment. When you and I differ, you pray for me that my gift may be used of God, and I will pray that yours will. "'Do not stop him,' Jesus said. 'For no one who does a miracle in my name can in the next moment say anything bad about me, for whoever is not against us is for us. Truly I tell you, anyone who gives you a cup of water in my name because you belong to the Messiah will certainly not lose their reward'" (Mark 9:39–41 NIV).

Those who, belonging to Christ, offer acts of mercy in his name, and who are being led by the Spirit who elicits faith active in love, will not go badly wrong if their hearts are right.[118] So we should not think it our major business to undermine a miracle done in Christ's name by one who appears to be outside our own fold. We should not dump out the water of mercy offered in Christ's name because a different language is used. We need to look carefully toward the correspondence between others' behavioral outcomes and their doctrinal teachings. Insofar as they correspond, the rule of Gamaliel applies: God is at work in the correspondence. Let God be the judge of it.[119]

3. How to Examine Our Own Bigotry

The homily concludes with a thoughtful self-examination seeking to track the steps of one's own bigotry. Wesley asked a tough personal question: Are you sorry when God blesses someone who holds erroneous views? Insofar as the fruits of the Spirit are manifested through constructive personal change, you do well not to forbid that person lest you sentence yourself as guilty of bigotry.[120]

The best exercise in transcending bigotry is to pray those who are different from you. Rejoice in their gifts. Enlarge their good work. Speak well of those who are different. Show them kindness.[121]

Even if you must bear the brunt of another's bigotry, do not be bigoted in return. Do not imagine that the intolerance of others justifies your own. Let them have all the bigotry to themselves. If they speak evil of you, speak all manner of good of them. Do not be phony or pretend to like what you do not like, but look for whatever is truly good in those who are dissimilar.[122]

This spirit of tolerance is deeply written into the Wesleyan evangelical revivals,

---

[117]"A Caution against Bigotry," B 1:73–75, sec. 3.
[118]Letter to John Newton, April 9, 1765, LJW 4:293.
[119]"A Caution against Bigotry," B 1:73–75, sec. 3.1–10.
[120]"A Caution against Bigotry," B 1:77, sec. 4.2–4.
[121]"A Caution against Bigotry," B 1:77, sec. 4.5.
[122]"A Caution against Bigotry," B 1:78, sec. 4.6; cf. 1:253; 3:315, 588.

which, like the Anglican ethos, was more a culture of consent than dissent. Its successors have not manifested a tradition dominated by church trials or petty divisiveness or constant ideological combat. It is a rich jewel forever subject to becoming misplaced.[123]

Further Reading on Theological Method

Theological Method

Coppedge, Allan. "John Wesley and the Issue of Authority in Theological Pluralism." In *A Spectrum of Thought.* Wilmore, KY: Francis Asbury, 1982.

Dunning, Ray. "Systematic Theology in a Wesleyan Mode." *WTJ* 17, no. 1 (1982): 15–22.

Frost, Stanley B. *Die Autoritätslehre in den Werken John Wesleys.* Munich: Ernst Reinhardt, 1938.

Gunter, W. Stephen, Ted A. Campbell, Rebekah L. Miles, Randy L. Maddox, and Scott Jones. *Wesley and the Quadrilateral: Renewing the Conversation.* Nashville: Abingdon, 1997.

Lawson, John. *Notes on Wesley's Forty-Four Sermons.* London: Epworth, 1964.

Maddox, Randy L. "Responsible Grace: The Systematic Perspective of Wesleyan Theology." *WTJ* 19, no. 2 (1984): 7–22.

Matthews, Rex D. "'Religion and Reason Joined': A Study in the Theology of John Wesley." ThD diss., Harvard University, 1986.

Moore, Robert L. *John Wesley and Authority: A Psychological Perspective.* Missoula, MT: Scholars, 1979.

Outler, Albert C. "The Wesleyan Quadrilateral in John Wesley." In *The Wesleyan Theological Heritage: Essays of Albert C. Outler*, edited by Thomas C. Oden and Leicester R. Longden, 21–38. Grand Rapids: Zondervan, 1991.

Reddish, Robert O. *John Wesley: His Way of Knowing God.* Evergreen, CO: Rorge, 1972.

Shimizu, Mitsuo. "Epistemology in the Thought of John Wesley." PhD diss., Drew University, 1980.

Thorsen, Donald A. D. *The Wesleyan Quadrilateral: Scripture, Tradition, Reason, and Experience as a Model of Evangelical Theology.* Grand Rapids: Zondervan, 1990.

Doctrinal Standards

Beet, Joseph Agar. "The First Four Volumes of Wesley's Sermons." *PWHS* 9 (1913): 86–89.

Collins, Kenneth. "On Reading Wesley's Sermons: The Structure of the Fifty-Three Standard Sermons, Ordo Salutis Displayed in the Sermons." In *Wesley on Salvation*, 129–39. Grand Rapids: Zondervan, 1989.

Cushman, Robert E. *John Wesley's Experimental Divinity: Studies in Methodist Doctrinal Standards.* Nashville: Kingswood, Abingdon, 1989.

Davies, Rupert E. "Our Doctrines." Chap. 5 in vol. 1, *A History of the Methodist Church in Great Britain*, 147–79. London: Epworth, 1965.

---

[123]"Advice to the People Called Methodists," 1745, B 9:123–31; J VIII:351–59.

————. "The People of God." *LQHR* 184 (1959): 223 – 30.

Heitzenrater, Richard. *Mirror and Memory: Reflections on Early Methodism*. Nashville: Kingswood, Abingdon, 1989.

Hughes, Henry Maldwyn. *Wesley's Standards in the Light of Today*. London: Epworth, 1921. Cf. *LQHR* 128 (1917): 214 – 34.

Lockyer, Thomas F. "What Are 'Our Doctrines'?" *LQHR* 134 (1920): 46 – 63.

Neely, Thomas. *Doctrinal Standards of Methodism*. New York: Revell, 1918.

Oden, Thomas C. *Doctrinal Standards in the Wesleyan Tradition*. Grand Rapids: Zondervan, 1988; rev. ed., Nashville: Abingdon, 2008.

Ogden, Schubert M. "Doctrinal Standards in the United Methodist Church." *Perkins Journal* 28 (Fall 1974).

Redd, Alexander. *The Problem of Methodism Reviewed: or, John Wesley and the Methodist Standards Defended*. Mount Sterling, KY: Advocate, 1893.

Rowe, G. Stringer. "A Note on Wesley's Deed Poll." *PWHS* 1 (1897): 37, 38.

Simon, John S. "John Wesley's Deed of Declaration." *PWHS* 12 (1919): 81 – 93.

Warren, Samuel. "Statement of the Principal Doctrines of Wesleyan Methodism." In vol. 1 of *Chronicles of Wesleyan Methodism*, 3 – 30. London: John Stephens, 1827.

West, Anson. "The Doctrinal Unity of Methodism." In *The Methodist Episcopal Church in the U.S.*, 245 – 55. New York: Phillips and Hunt, 1885.

Catechetics

MacDonald, James A., ed. *Wesley's Revision of the Shorter Catechism*. Edinburgh: George A. Morton, 1906.

McGonigle, Herbert. "Wesley's Revision of the Shorter Catechism." *PM* 56, no. 1 (1980): 59 – 63.

The Articles of Religion

Blankenship, Paul F. "Wesley's Abridgment of the Thirty-Nine Articles as Seen from His Deletions." *MH* 2, no. 3 (1964): 35 – 47.

Harmon, Nolan B., and John W. Bardsley. "John Wesley and the Articles of Religion." *RL* 22 (1953): 280 – 91.

Pope, William Burt. *A Compendium of Christian Theology*. 3 vols. London: Wesleyan Methodist Book-Room, 1880.

Ralston, Thomas N. *Elements of Divinity*. New York: Abingdon, 1924.

Watson, Richard. *Theological Institutes*. 2 vols. New York: Mason and Lane, 1836, 1840; edited by John M'Clintock, New York: Carlton & Porter, 1850.

Wheeler, Henry. *History and Exposition of the Twenty-Five Articles of Religion of the Methodist Episcopal Church*. New York: Eaton and Mains, 1908.

CHAPTER 6

Creation, Providence, and Evil

A. The Goodness of Creation

Wesley's teachings on God's creation and providence are concentrated in his homilies "God's Approbation of His Works," "On Divine Providence," and "The Wisdom of God's Counsels," a discourse "On God's Sovereignty," and a series on spiritual creatures. They serve as his extended comment on that article of religion that confesses that God is "maker and preserver of all things, both visible and invisible."[1] Regrettably, Wesley is seldom remembered as one who had memorable reflections on either creation or providence.

1. God's Approbation of His Works

The text of the homily "God's Approbation of His Works" is Genesis 1:31: "It was very good" [Homily #56 (1782), B 2:387 – 99; J #56, VI:206 – 15].

Everything is created "good in its kind." Viewed potentially and developmentally, each creature is created by God to be "suited to the end for which it is designed; adapted to promote the good of the whole, and the glory of the great Creator."[2] This truth was recognized as early as the first chapter of Genesis.

a. God's Enjoyment of the Goodness of Primordial Creation

What is created, insofar as given by God, is truly good in every way. "God saw all that he had made, and it was very good" (Gen. 1:31 NIV).

The creation is not by design constitutionally prone to perversion. It becomes distorted only through the exercise of idolatrous freedom. Wesley evidenced no temptations toward either Manichaean or Neoplatonic antimaterialism. There is nothing that resembled gnostic fantasies of creation itself as incorrigibly dragging the soul downward. Creation is good. God heartily approves of his own work in giving time, space, and life proportionally to diverse creatures.[3]

---

[1]XXV, art. 1.

[2]"God's Approbation of His Works," B 2:387, proem 1; cf. B 1:513 – 16; 2:387 – 99, 437 – 50, 537 – 38, 552 – 53; 4:25 – 26, 42 – 43, 63 – 64, 69 – 70, 153 – 54, 307 – 8.

[3]"God's Approbation of His Works," B 2:387 – 99; LJW 6:91.

b. Creation Fallen

Scripture distinguishes sharply between the good of creation before sin and the fallenness of creation after willed sin.

As created, each creature is fit to promote the good of the whole.[4] *As fallen*, the good of the whole has become grossly distorted. We live out of a lengthy history of sin that has taken this good creation and brought it to the lost condition in which human history is now enmeshed.[5]

No human now lives in that original unsullied state of creation. The gift of freedom has been poorly spent. In the journey from birth to emerging consciousness, we all will to assert our interests inordinately. That is a willed action even among children, as any parent can attest.

Sadly, whenever we meet other persons, we meet them always in a flawed condition. They meet us as flawed. Since Eden the course of history has been shaped by flawed persons who assert their interests inordinately. Except perhaps at birth and in the neonatal situation, we seldom get a glimpse of that primal goodness. We live in a creation originally given as good yet now fallen through a history of idolatry, pride, sensuality, and twisted imagination.[6]

Fallenness comes logically and chronologically only after creation, not as if embedded within creation or necessitated by creation. Creation as such remains good insofar *as created*, even after the fall. Never does the fall of freedom absolutely take away the image of God.

Since no finite creature was there at the creation, all creatures with physical eyes have a limited understanding of creation. All we can do is make conjectures about the goodness of original creation based on its fragmented forms of goodness in the present order of experience. But we can believe in that hypothesized original goodness because it is clearly attested in Scripture.[7]

We who now behold fallen creation are always already entangled in a protracted history of sin. Each discrete creature is always more prone to see his or her own private good more clearly than the good of the whole or the infinite Source of the whole good. Our perception of the created order is thus forever limited not merely because we are creatures but because we are creatures configured by a grim history of sin.

c. Unpolluted Air, Earth, Water, and Energy: An Ecological Axiom

We find in Wesley an uncommonly high doctrine of the original goodness of unfallen physical creation. Creation as originally given by God is "very good," having no admixture of evil, insofar as received from the hand of the Creator.

Using arguments from both reason and revelation, Wesley surveyed the know-

---

[4]*LJW* 3:333–35.
[5]"Doctrine of Original Sin," J IX:191–92.
[6]*CH*, "The Goodness of God," 7:107–29.
[7]B 2:387–99, 437–50, 537–38; 4:25–26, 42–43, 63–64.

able created order in a way that encompassed its basic constituent physical elements — the subtle combinations and variations of earth, air, fire, and water — comprising all forms of the created order in their specific permutations.[8] Each and all together were regarded as good as originally given, "all essentially distinct from each other and yet so intimately mixed together in all compound bodies that we cannot find any, be it ever so minute, which does not contain them all."[9] Wesley credited the ancient Greek physicists with perceptive insight into the basic elements of these permutations.

By *earth* the ancients symbolically pointed to all palpable matter, all physical, nonliquid, nongaseous creation. We are given the physical environment as a gift for our stewardship. As created, the earth is filled with unadulterated, untainted creaturely goods. As such, it is beautiful; though when distorted by sin, it can be terrifying.[10] There was originally no pollution in the air, and the water supported abundant forms of sea life.[11]

By *fire* we point to all of the diverse particles of energy present in creation. A splendid balance of light and fire exists in the created order. The specific distance between the sun and the earth is a spectacular example of how God has offered the earth light and fire in exquisite proportion. The sun is a precisely balanced source of good for creatures who need light and heat in specific congruity and equilibrium. The relation of earth and light elicits a veritable celebration of God's goodness in the created order.[12]

By *air* we point to the unseen movements of gaseous creation. By *water* we point to all that is liquid. By *earth* we point to all things solid. By *fire* we point to all forms of energy.

Wesley ruminated almost ecstatically on the created excellence of all biological forms, vegetable and animal, sometimes embracing curious ideas about their original goodness. Reasoning out of scriptural testimony, he posited an untrammeled innocence in the unfallen natural order in its original perfection (lacking weeds and unpleasant insects, for example, and no animals preying on one another). A world without sin is a place of incomparable happiness, since it is not spoiled by the slightest hint of twisted self-assertiveness.[13] By sleep,[14] which faintly refracts the primal condition belonging "to innocent human nature," "the springs of the animal machine were wound up from time to time."[15]

---

[8]B 2:383 – 90, 504 – 8, 573 – 74; 4:136 – 37.

[9]"God's Approbation of His Works," B 2:388, sec. 1.1.

[10]B 2:389 – 90, 506 – 8, 573 – 74; *LJW* 4:282 – 87; cf. *WHS*, 39 – 40.

[11]"God's Approbation of His Works," B 2:389 – 91, sec. 1.2 – 5; 505 – 6.

[12]"God's Approbation of His Works," B 2:392, sec. 1.7.

[13]"God's Approbation of His Works," B 2:393 – 96, sec. 1.8 – 14.

[14]On sleep, see B 2:134, 392; 3:267, 322 – 24; 4:110.

[15]"God's Approbation of His Works," B 2:392, sec. 1.7. In a letter to Hester Ann Roe dated June 2, 1776, Wesley asked, "Do you commune with God in the night season? Does He bid you even in sleep, Go on? And does He 'make your very dreams devout'?" *LJW* 6:223.

d. Pride in the Disorder of Creation

The king of Castile imagined, "If I had made the world, I would have made it better." God replied, I "did not make it as it is now."[16]

The difference between then and now is the intrusion of sin on God's good creation. This paradise became lost and fallen through pride, idolatry, vanity, sensuality, and twisted imagination.[17] Human pride imagines that it could have done a far better job than God in ordering creation and so fantasizes a reordering of all things according to our sinful imaginings. Out of this pretended improvement comes all manner of evil.[18]

The created world thus becomes distorted by intergenerational sin, as symbolized by the lengthening history of the progeny of Adam and Eve. The world we now see is not the originally good creation but a world grossly distorted by the evil that freedom has collectively chosen and rechosen. God did not unilaterally insert this evil into the world, but freedom absurdly elected it. God gives freedom, and freedom absurdly debauches the goodness of creation.

2. The Free-Will Defense

a. God Is Not the Author of Evil

The "free-will defense" stands staunchly against the pretense that God is the author of evil. This argument is featured in this homily on God's approbation of his works: World history is an accumulation of decisions in which each period affects subsequent periods, layer upon layer. "God made man upright," but man "found out to himself 'many inventions' of happiness independent of God."[19] We as a human species have outrageously worsened creation through the licenses we have taken by our idolatrous freedom. Consequently, the whole creation, the cosmos, the natural order now groans in travail. Humans have done damage to the entire original creation by our sin, and caused all creatures to suffer.[20]

The Manichaeans of Augustine's time posited a conflict built into God's creation between two equal divine forces: a good God and an evil God. History was viewed as the arena of conflict of these two.

There is not a hint of Manichaean flavor in Wesley, for whom the creation as such was unambiguously *good*. Only after the fall of freedom, when creatures, bent toward pride and idolatry, by their own self-determining freedom fall, does a train of disastrous effects follow.

Some of Wesley's contemporaries wrongly assumed that "evil must exist in the very nature of things."[21] Wesley answered, "It must, *in the present nature* of things,

---

[16]"God's Approbation of His Works," B 2:397, sec. 2.

[17]B 1:208; 2:561; 3:183 – 84; 4:341.

[18]"On Faith," B 4:190 – 97.

[19]"God's Approbation of His Works," B 2:399, sec. 2.3; Eccl. 7:29.

[20]"God's Approbation of His Works," B 2:397, sec. 2.1.

[21]Soame Jenyns, *Free Inquiry into the Nature and Origin of Evil* (n.p.: R. and J. Dodsley, 1757), 15 – 17, 108 – 9.

supposing man to have rebelled against God. But evil did not exist at all in the original nature of things."[22] The present condition of humans in history is radically fallen but not beyond divine grace.

The fundamental goodness of creation remains despite all historical absurdities. God does not take away human liberty altogether but allows it to play itself out in judgment, addressing it patiently with the call to repentance within the limits of time. Just because human freedom has muddled creation does not mean that God accedes to the disarray. God persists amid the fallenness of human history to permit this corrupted chronicle to continue, patiently offering the promise of redemption to all who are fallen. The biblical testimony of heavenly bliss at the end of history echoes the primal vision of the genesis of untainted good in divine creation.[23]

b. Countering William Law's Quasi-Manichaean Speculations

Wesley wrote an open letter to William Law on January 6, 1756 (*LJW* 3:332 – 70; J IV:466 – 509), to challenge Law's unscriptural views. Law's early works on Christian spirituality, *A Practical Treatise upon Christian Perfection* (1726) and *A Serious Call to a Devout and Holy Life* (1728), had decisively influenced the young Wesley and his colleagues in the Oxford Holy Club. By 1735, however, Law had begun to read Jacob Boehme and delve into various versions of Protestant mysticism of dubious orthodoxy, influenced by the theosophic gnosticism of Paracelsus and the far-left spiritualist wing of the Reformation. After a decade of quiescence during the 1740s, William Law began to publish his thoughts on mysticism in *The Way to Divine Knowledge* (1752), *The Spirit of Prayer* (1749 – 50), and *The Spirit of Love* (1753 – 54), in which he criticized the classic Christian understanding of the means of grace and substituted a gnostic cosmology and universalist mysticism, attesting a "Spirit of Christ" deeply hidden within every natural human being, presumably quite apart from saving grace and without need for justifying grace.

Baffled by the follies of his former mentor, by 1756 Wesley determined to write an open letter to Law, respecting his former views but admonishing him against his foolish turn toward "superfluous, uncertain, dangerous, irrational, and unscriptural philosophy," that is so "often flatly contrary to Scripture, to reason, and to itself."[24] Remembering that Law had once admonished Wesley about spoiling religion with philosophy, Wesley now turned the tables by showing this is what Law was doing:

> Reverend Sir, — In matters of religion I regard no writings but the inspired. Tauler, Behmen [Boehme], and a whole army of Mystic authors, are with me nothing to St. Paul.... At a time when I was in great danger of not valuing this authority enough, you made that important observation: "... So far as you add philosophy to religion, just so far you spoil it." This remark I have never forgotten.... But have not you?[25]

---

[22]"God's Approbation of His Works," B 2:398 – 99, sec. 2.2.
[23]"God's Approbation of His Works," B 2:397 – 99, sec. 2.1 – 3.
[24]*LJW* 3:332 – 33.
[25]Letter to William Law, *LJW*, 3:332, proem.

c. Critique of Law's Excesses

Wesley criticized Law's speculations under four headings: (1) nature antecedent to creation, (2) creation, (3) paradise, and (4) the fall. In each case, he precisely quoted and refuted Law point by point on the basis of scriptural testimony. As to Law's view that "nature as well as God is antecedent to all creatures," Wesley puzzled, "Is then nature God? Or are there two eternal, universal, infinite beings?"[26]

As to the fantastic notion that "God brought gross matter" out of the "sinful properties" the fallen angels had imparted to nature, Wesley asked Law to explain how physical elements as such can have either sin or virtue.[27]

As to how the earthly body of Adam might have contained latent evil, Wesley asked, "Was there evil in the world, and even in Adam … at his first creation?"

Wesley thought that William Law, in his cosmological speculations, had taken unconscionable liberties with both revelation and reason, had gone far beyond the plain sense of Scripture, and offered weak, inconsistent proofs.[28]

d. How Bad Philosophy Attracts Bad Divinity: Assessing a Hermaphrodite View of Adam

In Law's conjectures, Adam "had at first the nature of an angel," hence was "both male and female." Wesley questioned whether "angels are hermaphrodites," challenging Law's curious speculations that "Eve would not have been had Adam stood," that Adam would have brought forth the second Adam, Christ, without Eve, and that "Christ was both male and female."[29] It is evident that Jesus was male, not male and female, a fact that shows his true humanity. Jesus would have been hardly recognizable as human if a hermaphrodite. As to the notion that Adam "lost much of his perfection before Eve was taken out of him," Wesley asked for some shred of textual evidence on which to ground such speculation.[30]

"Bad philosophy has, by insensible degrees, paved the way for bad divinity."[31] Disastrous repercussions follow from Law's loose suppositions: "You deny the omnipotence of God" by asserting an inexorable degeneration of spiritual nature into material nature. God is limited both before and after creation.[32] There is Manichaeanism lurking in the notions that "matter could not possibly be but from sin" and the human body is "curdled spirit."[33]

---

[26]Letter to William Law, *LJW*, 3:333 – 34, sec. 1.1.

[27]Letter to William Law, *LJW*, 3:335 – 36, sec. 1.2.

[28]Letter to William Law, *LJW*, 3:338 – 43, sec. 1.3 – 4.

[29]Letter to William Law, *LJW*, 3:338 – 42, sec. 1.3 – 4.

[30]Letter to William Law, *LJW*, 3:338 – 43, sec. 1.3 – 4.

[31]Letter to William Law, *LJW*, 3:343, sec. 2.1.

[32]Letter to William Law, *LJW*, 3:343 – 44, sec. 2.1.

[33]Letter to William Law, *LJW*, 3:343, sec. 2.1; William Law, *The Spirit of Love* (1752; repr., New York: Paulist Press, 1978), 1:23.

B. Spiritual Creation

God is giver not only of physical creation but also of spiritual creation, the unseen sphere of creation not accessible to the eye. These incorporeal spiritual beings and powers are also creatures, not coeternal with God, but contingent entirely on the gift of their creation. There is a radical difference between any creature and its Creator.

1. Of Good Angels

The text of the homily "Of Good Angels" is Hebrews 1:14: "Are they not all ministering spirits?" [Homily #71 (1783), B 3:3 – 15; J #71, VI:361 – 70].

a. Why Discuss Angelic Beings?

Why speak of angels? Because Scripture takes their reality as a constant assumption.

Wesley offered two teaching homilies on angelic powers. He was not fixated on this issue, but he did have to answer questions from his community of spiritual formation. He found clearly attested in Scripture a range of spiritual creation located in the chain of being between corporeal humanity and uncreated divinity.

It would be a stupendous gap in the order of creation if the universe had inorganic matter, plant and animal life, and human life growing in complexity and spirituality, and then vaulted through the heavens all the way from human existence to God in the highest. It is more plausible to assume that there must be something in between.[34] "There is one chain of being, from the lowest to the highest point, from an unorganized particle of earth or water, to Michael the archangel. And the scale of creatures does not advance *per salturn*, by leaps, but by smooth and gentle degrees; although it is true that these are frequently imperceptible to our imperfect faculties."[35]

Wesley found solace in the text from Hebrews 1:14, which asks, "Are not all angels ministering spirits sent to serve those who will inherit salvation?" (NIV). We have now come to the juncture of discussing these incorporeal agencies in the created order — not as to whether they *empirically* can be shown to exist (a fruitless way of putting the question with respect to invisible creatures), but as to their *ministry*, what they do.

It would seem tempting to skip over this discussion of good and bad angels, but whenever I have ventured to discuss these matters with modern audiences, they have found them exceptionally intriguing. The ordinary people Wesley served were interested in these biblical questions, even though the guild biblical scholars largely ignore them. This may seem at first to be a quaint corner of Wesley's thinking, but when we empathize with his vocabulary and enter seriously into it, his language

---

[34]"Of Good Angels," B 3:4 – 15.
[35]"Of Evil Angels," B 3:16, pref. 1; cf. "God's Approbation of His Works," sec. 1.14.

becomes surprisingly plausible and capable of resonating in our contemporary culture.[36]

b. Angels Attested in Both the History of Philosophy and in Scripture

These ministering spirits were widely known and recognized in the ancient literature of Socrates, Hesiod, Plato, and Aristotle, and virtually all the classical writers of Greek antiquity. These early writings were, on this point, "crude, imperfect, and confused ... fragments of truth, partly delivered down by their forefathers, and partly borrowed from the inspired writings."[37]

They offer only a preliminary attempt to understand the unseen ministering spirits who were to be more fully attested gradually in the unfolding history of God's self-disclosure. Though many have had various opinions of angelic creation, it is only in the history of revelation that we obtain a reliable picture of their ministries.

Scripture provides "a clear, rational, consistent account of those whom our eyes have not seen or our ears heard."[38] Wesley's argument for superpersonal spiritual creatures comes from reason illumined by revelation, using the wisdom of historic tradition, and from his own experience in the evangelical revival as supporting evidence.[39] He was content to let others argue about angels from strictly rationalist or empiricist premises.

c. Scriptural Testimony to Ministering Spirits

God has the power to work either immediately (through direct means) or mediately (through other than direct means). Through ministering spirits, God has chosen to work for the good of creation through incorporeal spiritual beings, using them to draw us to God and to one another. God has endued them with "understanding, will, and liberty, essential to, if not the essence of, a spirit."[40]

The good ministering spirits can read the thoughts of human beings because they see their "kindred spirit more clearly than we see the body."[41] Their ministrations are grounded in this ability, which, having long existed through time, has accumulated wisdom from "surveying the hearts and ways of men in their successive generations."[42]

God is capable of making the "winds his messengers, flames of fire his servants" (Ps. 104:4 NIV). Angels do not need physical bodies or finite magnitude to serve the Lord.[43] They have extraordinary vision, but without physical eyes, and possess what seems to us an almost unlimited sight and perception. They communicate, yet

---

[36]"Of Good Angels," B 3:4 – 7.
[37]"Of Good Angels," B 3:4, pref. 1.
[38]"Of Good Angels," B 3:6, pref. 4.
[39]CH 7:511 – 12; cf. 4:346 – 49; JJW 6:229.
[40]"Of Good Angels," B 3:6, sec. 1.1.
[41]"Of Good Angels," B 3:7, sec. 1.2; cf. 3:72; 4:229.
[42]"Of Good Angels," B 3:8, sec. 1.3.
[43]"Of Good Angels," B 3:6, sec. 1.1.

without the sound of speech.[44] They have an extraordinary capacity to see many things at a glance that we corporeal observers miss or do not see well or wholly. With intuitive brilliance, they see at one glance the truth presented to them, as distinguished from our crude and laborious reasoning and data-gathering processes. They have immediate intellectual apprehension and the ability to penetrate human hearts. They know the hearts of those to whom they minister. They have a high degree of wisdom compared to our finite faculties.[45]

The angels are not just individually active but belong to an ordered community. Those unfallen angels who celebrate God's life are found to be continually ministering to our souls. Care of souls *is* the work of these ministering spirits. Our pastoral care is a participation in their ministry. Good angels work to enable our goodness as ministers of God the Spirit. They have a guardianship role, especially to the faithful.[46]

Ministering spirits attend our souls, addressing us in our fallen condition, never flatly overwhelming human freedom or dictating terms. They work as persuasive, not coercive, agents. The premise is synergistic (with coagency), not monergistic (with a single agent of action). They counter and thwart the destructive work of evil spiritual powers. They work to overturn the intentions and effects of evil in myriad unperceived ways.

The good angels minister in ways analogous, from our limited point of view, to the best ministries of human agents of reconciliation, yet with greater agility and subtlety. Think of the best caregivers you know, and that is something like the work of the ministering spirits of God. They minister quietly through interpersonal relationships, even when persons remain unaware of their ministries. The good angels minister not merely to the righteous but also to the unrighteous, calling them to repentance and accountability, assisting in the search for truth.[47]

The good angels work through illness toward wholeness. They minister through dreams. The faithful need not fear these ministering spirits, for they are given for our good. Through them God works in our hearts to elicit happiness and holiness. We cannot fully understand their ministrations on our behalf as long as we dwell in the body.[48]

Though not omnipresent, these ministering spirits have been given "an immense sphere of action,"[49] including governments and empires, political and economic orders, and cultural processes. But they work chiefly within the silent reaches of the human heart and through human relationships.[50] They have power to cause or remove pain, knowing all the intricacies of the human body.

44"Of Good Angels," B 3:7, sec. 1.2.
45"Of Good Angels," B 3:7 – 8, sec. 1.2 – 3.
46"Of Good Angels," B 3:11 – 12, sec. 2.
47"Of Good Angels," B 3:12 – 14, sec. 2.3 – 8.
48"Of Good Angels," B 3:11 – 12, sec. 2.2.
49"Of Good Angels," B 3:9, sec. 1.6.
50"Of Good Angels," B 3:13 – 14, sec. 2.7 – 9.

Though good, they are not to be worshiped, for only God is worthy of worship, yet God does indeed work through them. The ministering spirits are not identical to the Holy Spirit, who remains the one uncreated God through whom these creaturely spirits are sustained.[51]

d. On Guardian Angels

The text of the homily "On Guardian Angels" is Psalm 91:11: "He shall give his angels charge over thee, to keep thee in all thy ways" [Homily #135 (1726), B 4:224 – 35 (not in Jackson edition)].

Even amid wealth, power, or glory, it is scarcely possible to forget that human beings "are weak, miserable, helpless creatures," unequal to the dangers that surround us, riddled with guilt and disease. Our physical lives end "at length with a total dissolution. The meanest object of our scorn — a beast, an insect, nay, even things that themselves have no life — are sufficient either to take away ours, or to make it a curse rather than a blessing."[52]

If life is so miserable, how can God be regarded as good? Evil is permitted "to humble our natural pride and self-sufficiency." We may be tempted to be defeated by worldly powers. But "unless by our own positive voluntary act, they 'shall have no advantage over us.'" The free-will defense thwarts any hint of injustice in God.

e. Whether Incorporeal Ministering Spirits Attend Us at Certain Times

Ministering spirits "are always ready to assist us when we need their assistance, always present when their presence may be of service, in every circumstance of life wherein is danger of any sort."[53] They are to keep us in all our ways (Ps. 91:11). Whether in bodily pain or the temptation of our souls, whether we are aware of approaching evil or not, they make "their timely interposition."[54] Thus, even amid afflictions, "we cannot doubt" God's goodness insofar as we "consider what peculiar care he hath taken" for our protection by giving "his angels charge over [us], to keep [us] in all [our] ways."[55]

It would exceed the commission they have received, however, if ministering spirits absolutely prevented evil, so as to try to outwit the positive challenges of suffering and limitation. To avoid any possibility of vice is to forgo any possibility of virtue. Behavioral excellence (virtue) exists only when it faces finite obstacles. The mission of the ministering spirits is not to deliver the soul from all temptation or bodily pain, as if to coerce choice, but to accompany choice. For "where there is no choice, there can be no virtue. But had we been without virtue, we must have been content with some lower happiness than that we now hope to partake of."[56]

---

[51]"Of Good Angels," B 3:15, sec. 2.10.
[52]"On Guardian Angels," B 4:225, pref. 1.
[53]"On Guardian Angels," B 4:226 – 27, sec. 1.1.
[54]"On Guardian Angels," B 4:227, sec. 1.2.
[55]"On Guardian Angels," B 4:226, pref. 3.
[56]"On Guardian Angels," B 4:227 – 28, sec. 1.4 – 5.

f. Whether Incorporeal Ministering Spirits Know Us Better Than We Know Ourselves

Excelling in strength and wisdom, ministering spirits may alter "some material cause that else would have a pernicious effect: the cleansing [of] (for instance) tainted air."[57] They have power to raise or allay human passions. "That one immaterial being, by touching another, should either increase or lessen its motion, that an angel should either retard or quicken the stream wherewith the passions of an angelic substance flow, is not more to be wondered at than that one piece of matter should have the same effect on its kindred substance."[58] Angels may touch our affections. They may inspire good thoughts in our hearts. They may protect the righteous from spiritual dangers.[59] The faithful pray for their active presence.

Ministering spirits know us better than we know them:

> It is not improbable their fellowship with us is far more sensible than ours with them. Suppose any of them are present, they are hid from our eyes, but we are not hid from their sight. They, no doubt, clearly discern all our words and actions, if not all our thoughts too. For it is hard to think these walls of flesh and blood can intercept the view of an angelic being. But we have, in general, only a faint and indistinct perception of their presence, unless ... by an internal sense, for which human language has not any name.[60]

g. Whether Errands of Mercy Are Assigned to Incorporeal Ministering Spirits

The Omnipotent One does not arbitrarily use his own immediate power to accomplish his purpose but may employ these ministering spirits. Even if God's purpose in doing so is hidden in a "knowledge ... too wonderful for [us]" (Ps. 139:6), it "cannot be unlawful to extend our search as far as our limited faculties will permit."

God assigns mediated power to ministering spirits because they delight in finding such employment, in conducing others toward the paths of happiness.[61] "In doing good to us they do good to themselves also," for "by exercising the goodness they have already," they continually increase in their joy in serving the Lord.[62] "The greater goodwill they bear to men, the greater must be their joy when these men, in the fullness of time, are received into that glory appointed for them."[63]

Blessed is the one who enjoys the protection of ministering spirits! "No temporal evil shall befall him, unless to clear the way for a greater good!" "Let him but be true to himself, let him but fix his love on their common Creator, and nothing in the creation, animate or inanimate, by design or chance, shall have power to hurt him."

---

[57] "On Guardian Angels," B 4:229, sec. 2.3.
[58] "On Guardian Angels," B 4:230, sec. 2.6.
[59] "On Guardian Angels," B 4:231, sec. 2.8.
[60] Letter to Miss Bishop, June 12, 1773, J XIII:24.
[61] "On Guardian Angels," B 4:231–32, sec. 3.1.
[62] "On Guardian Angels," B 4:232, sec. 1.2.
[63] "On Guardian Angels," B 4:232, sec. 1.3.

God's own ministering spirits offer us "consolation among the numberless evils wherewith we are surrounded."[64]

2. Of Evil Angels

The text of the homily "Of Evil Angels" is Ephesians 6:12: "We wrestle … against principalities" [Homily #72 (1783), B 3:16 – 29; J #72, VI:370 – 80].

Originally all angels were of the same nature: spirits with justly ordered affections. They had self-determining liberty by which they could choose to be loyal to God, yet some of them absurdly chose to be disloyal.[65]

a. Whether Some Incorporeal Spiritual Creatures, Though Created Good, Have Fallen from Grace

Leaving the original ordering of God, the evil angels abandoned all goodness and took on the opposite nature: pride, arrogance, self-exaltation, envy, rage against the divine order, and despair over their condition. They are diligent in the prosecution of their design, yet God has set limits on their power to destroy. They do not merely act individually but are united to a common head, "the prince, the god of this world," Satan, the Adversary, in whose kingdom a hierarchy exists and specific tasks appear to be assigned.[66]

Like human beings, angels may fall. Some have proved corruptible. That is part of the risk of spiritual freedom. Evil angels have the same powers of intelligence, movement, and communication but are fallen from grace, and ultimately their works will be thwarted.[67] Good angels are enabled by grace to persevere.

There is a transpersonal struggle going on in the heavenly spheres between those incorporeal superpersonal agents who have fallen and those who are servants of God, doing what angels are created to do: praise God and increase the love of God in creation.[68]

The reason for the apostasy of the evil angels and the causes and precise effects of the fall of perhaps one-third of the angels remain a mystery. It may be due to jealousy or pride. They may have been envious of the Son of God, whose favor is decreed in Psalm 8:6 – 7 concerning the one who is appointed Lord "over all creatures." We might speculate that this elicited envy and pride in the firstborn creatures. They may have said in their hearts, "I will exalt my throne above the stars of God.… I will be like the most High" (Isa. 14:13 – 14).[69]

By revelation we learn the truth about these incorporeal powers, that while all were created holy, some fell. Paul summarized the apostolic teaching of fallen angels in a single sentence: "For our struggle is not against flesh and blood, but against the rulers, against the authorities, against the powers of this dark world and against

---

[64]"On Guardian Angels," B 4:234 – 35, sec. 5.
[65]"Of Evil Angels," B 3:17 – 19, sec. 1.1 – 4.
[66]"Of Evil Angels," B 3:20 – 21, sec. 2.1 – 3.
[67]On Satan's devices, see B 2:138 – 51; 4:144 – 47.
[68]"Of Evil Angels," B 3:17 – 19, sec. 1.1 – 3.
[69]"Of Evil Angels," B 3:18, sec. 1.3.

the spiritual forces of evil in the heavenly realms" (Eph. 6:12 NIV). Paul called on believers to "put on the full armor of God, so that when the day of evil comes, you may be able to stand" (v. 13 NIV). Our present wrestling is not finally against human ingenuity, evil appetites, or passions, but against powers with such superhuman force and competence that they are called in Scripture the "rulers ... of this dark world" (v. 12 NIV). Though some fallen angels remain in their citadel, others go about ruinously sowing evil.[70]

b. The Employment of Evil Angels

Evil angels constantly seek to govern the world, encouraging ignorance, unrighteousness, and error. Any weakness leaves us open to temptation, which they are clever to exploit. They attempt to extinguish the love of God when it inflames, to blind hearts to God's power and promise. They are ready to take advantage of circumstantial shortcomings and inattentiveness.[71]

Their most furious attacks are directed against the emergence of faith, hope, and love. They oppose the love of the neighbor as vigorously as the love of God, fomenting dissension, war, and conflict. They not only draw us toward doing evil but also seek to prevent us from doing good by infusing evil thoughts, eliciting doubt, and subverting good motivations. When an evil thought occurs without any obvious or reasonable connection with a previous thought, there is reason to suspect the work of evil angels. They aggravate evil passions by "touching the springs of the animal machine," easily disturbing the vulnerable equilibrium of the body-soul interface.[72]

This is why Satan is constantly viewed in Scripture as tempter and arch-deceiver.[73] Both believers and unbelievers are tempted to sin. The hosts of demonic powers are actively tempting and deceiving amid the symptoms of illness, anxiety, addictions, and psychological disturbances.[74] No good is done without the assistance of God, no evil without the tempting of the Adversary.[75]

Wesley conjectured that many illnesses of our body-soul condition (the psychosomatic interface), "both of the acute and chronical kind, are either occasioned or increased by diabolical agency; particularly those that begin in an instant." Merely describing these as nervous illnesses is a rationalization *ignotum per ignotius* (explaining something unknown by something even more unknown). "For what do we know of nerves themselves? Not even whether they are solid or hollow!"[76]

c. Spiritual Combat

Scripture calls us to put on the whole armor of God in this conflict, having the mind of Christ, calling upon his name, walking the narrow way, avoiding offense,

---

[70]"Of Evil Angels," B 3:20, sec. 1.6.
[71]"Of Evil Angels," B 3:21 – 23, sec. 2.2 – 4; cf. Letter to the Bishop of Gloucester 11:495 – 96.
[72]"Of Evil Angels," B 3:20 – 27, sec. 2.
[73]B 1:187 – 88; 3:566; 9:385; FA, B 11:123 – 24.
[74]"Of Evil Angels," B 3:20 – 27, sec. 2.
[75]"Of Evil Angels," B 3:24, sec. 2.9; cf. 1:29 – 30; FA, B 11:120 – 21.
[76]"Of Evil Angels," B 3:25 – 26, sec. 2.12.

grasping the shield of faith to cast aside the devil's fiery darts, wearing the helmet of salvation against doubt, remaining steadfast in faith even amid the roar of lions.[77] The faithful are urged to be wary of the time when Satan "transforms himself into an angel of light." Then "watch and pray that you enter not into temptation."[78]

When temptations come, they are viewed by faith as "occasions of fighting that you may conquer. If there is no fight, there is no victory."[79] The trial continues daily: "Each day will bring just temptation enough and power enough to conquer it.... The unction of the Holy One is given to believers for this very end—to enable them to distinguish (which otherwise would be impossible) between sin and temptation. And this you will do not by any general rule, but by listening to Him on all particular occasions and by your consulting with those that have experience in the ways of God."[80]

God permitted Satan to tempt and deceive Job because God knew Job would be given grace to resist temptation. God gives our freedom a wide range of operation but hedges freedom at the point at which it becomes self-destructive.[81]

The moral law functions to protect us from temptation. As a parent is gracious in instructing a child not to play near a precipice, so God is gracious in giving us the Ten Commandments, which begin, "Thou shalt not." The good parent is a living partner who knows when to say no out of love, and when to leave freedom room to play. The hedging of the Law is motivated by protecting love.

To those who asked why God bothers with these secondary incorporeal agencies and why he does not simply act unilaterally and directly, Wesley appealed to Scripture, where there is specific testimony to these superpersonal agents. They assist in accomplishing God's purposes. They remain an enduring fact of the history of revelation. God is working through good ministering spirits and spiritual powers against all residual evil spiritual powers toward a final consummation of his purpose in creation.[82]

d. In Earth as in Heaven

The text of the homily "In Earth as in Heaven" is Matthew 6:10: "Thy will be done in earth, as it is in heaven" [Homily #145 (1734), B 4:346–50 (not in the Jackson edition)].

We are called to do the will of God on earth as the angels do it in heaven. The whole scope of an ethic of obedience is implied in the text. Wesley's purpose was to show the extensive nature of angelic obedience as a pattern for the obedience of faith among humans.[83] The prototype of all prayer is "Thy will be done in earth, as it is in heaven" (Matt. 6:10).

---

[77]"Of Evil Angels," B 3:27–29, sec. 3.1–3; CH 7:250–52, 785–86.
[78]"Of Evil Angels," B 3:28–29, sec. 3.4–6.
[79]Letter to Damaris Perronet, March 30, 1771, LJW 5:234.
[80]Letter to Elizabeth Briggs, April 14, 1771, LJW 5:237.
[81]"Of Evil Angels," B 3:26, sec. 2.14.
[82]"Of Evil Angels," B 3:27–29, sec. 3.
[83]"In Earth as in Heaven," B 4:348, pref.

There are three defining aspects in angelic obedience: doing *what* God wills, *in the manner* God wills, and *with the motive* God intends. The obedience of faith follows the same pattern. Negatively, faith seeks "to do *nothing but* what is the will of God." Positively, faith seeks "to do *all* that is the will of God: i.e., contained in the Scriptures," as interpreted by the ancient Christian writers, whether left to human reason for contextualization, or whether indirectly bidden by God in obedience to the "laws of the church and state." In any case, we are called to do all that is God's will *as* he wills it, "in that measure and with that affection only," and with "right motive ... because he wills it."[84]

"Angels do all that is the will of God, and that only," precisely *as God wills it*, "in that measure and with that affection only," and with the "right motive, i.e., that we do all, and do all thus, only because he wills it."[85]

Given these parameters, Wesley asked, is such obedience possible for the faithful in this life? "Without idly disputing whether we can do thus or no, let us do what we can. And we can, if we will, make his will at least the sine qua non in all our actions. And if we do this, we shall in time do more."[86]

All who follow Christ are invited to say with him first, "Not my will," and on this basis, "but thine, be done" (Luke 22:42). "So far only as self goes out," and self-will is conquered, can God come in. We are being called to "do the will of God on earth as it is done in heaven."[87]

C. Providence

1. On Divine Providence

The text of the homily "On Divine Providence" is Luke 12:7: "Even the very hairs of your head are all numbered" [Homily #67 (1786), B 2:534–50; J #67, VI:313–25].

a. Only God Could Give a Full Account of Providence

Much in God's purposeful activity remains for finite creatures a mystery. This is for a good reason: only the eternally Omniscient One could offer a reliable account of God's "manner of governing the world." Only the eternally Omnipresent One could adequately grasp the originating vision and goal and intermediary links and overall design of providence. Sufficient intimations of this governance, however, have been given in general outline in Scripture, which is viewed as the veritable "history of God."[88]

Although the Hebraic-Christian teaching of providence has been intuitively grasped by the wise of all ages from Cato to the Chickasaws, and indistinctly attested by ancient poets and philosophers, it awaited the history of Israel to become more

---

[84]"In Earth as in Heaven," B 4:349, sec. 2, italics added.
[85]"In Earth as in Heaven," B 4:348–49.
[86]"In Earth as in Heaven," B 4:349, sec. 3.3.
[87]"In Earth as in Heaven," B 4:349–50, sec. 3.
[88]"On Divine Providence," B 2:536, sec. 4.

explicitly understood.[89] Among the foremost classic Christian doctrines, "there is scarce any that is so little regarded, and perhaps so little understood" as providence.[90]

As sole Creator who has "called out of nothing, by his all-powerful word, the whole universe, all that is," God daily sustains creation "in the being which he has given it."[91] The same one who created all, maintains all, as omnipresent participator in and omniscient discerner of all that is.[92] At every moment, God sustains what God has created, even if miserably fallen.[93]

The guiding text of the homily on providence is "Indeed, the very hairs of your head are all numbered. Don't be afraid; you are worth more than many sparrows" (Luke 12:7 NIV).

God's care extends not only to the macrocosmic design of the whole but to every microcosmic expression, each discrete happening, as symbolized by a particular hair on a specific head. Every distinct aspect of creaturely being is quietly upheld in being by providence, for "nothing is so small or insignificant in the sight of men as not to be an object of the care and providence of God."[94] Though it is beyond "our narrow understandings" how all this works together, we may learn personally to trust the Orderer and Sustainer.[95] This is learned behavior: to trust God without being able to see as God sees.

The eternal, all-knowing God sees at each moment the mutual interconnections of each diverse creature and of the whole as it works together.[96] This knowledge includes the "inanimate parts of creation," as well as plants, animals, incorporeal spirits, and humans with all their thoughts, feelings, and conditions. God "sees all their sufferings, with every circumstance of them."[97] "His tender mercies are over all his works" (Ps. 145:9).[98]

"It is hard, indeed, to comprehend this; nay, it is hard to believe it, considering the complicated wickedness, and the complicated misery, which we see on every side. But believe it we must, unless we make God a liar; although it is sure, no man can comprehend it.... Can a worm comprehend a man? How much less can it be supposed that a man can comprehend God!"[99]

b. Whether Freedom and Moral Agency Are Consistent with Providence

Providence does not eliminate but rather guards freedom, even when freedom falls. Sin emerges as a toxic waste product of freedom. Free will does not contradict

---

[89]"On Divine Providence," B 2:535 – 36, secs. 1 – 4; cf. FA, pt. 2, B 11:227.
[90]"On Divine Providence," B 2:537, sec. 7.
[91]"On Divine Providence," B 2:537 – 38, secs. 8 – 9; cf. "Spiritual Worship," B 3:91.
[92]"On Divine Providence," B 2:537 – 39, secs. 8 – 12.
[93]B 1:523 – 26; 2:534 – 50, 577 – 82; 3:595 – 608; 4:365 – 66; JWO 187 – 88.
[94]"On Divine Providence," B 2:537, sec. 6.
[95]"On Divine Providence," B 2:538 – 39, secs. 9 – 11.
[96]"On Guardian Angels," B 4:233 – 34; "The One Thing Needful," B 4:356; LCM, J X:70 – 71.
[97]"On Divine Providence," B 2:539, sec. 12; cf. "On Visiting the Sick," 3:391.
[98]"On Divine Providence," B 2:542, sec. 16.
[99]"On Divine Providence," B 2:540, sec. 13.

providence. Those given the gift of freedom must live with the consequences of abusing it.[100]

Suppose one imagines that it would be better to have a world that has no freedom in it — only stones, no choices. That is not the kind of world God has chosen to create, as is evident from the actual history of stones and of human freedom. God creates free human beings both with the capacity to enjoy life with him and an aptitude for distorting the created world.[101]

It is theoretically conceivable that God could decree the immediate destruction of all forms of evil. But if the possibility of vice were absolutely destroyed, so also would be the possibility of virtue, since virtue and vice are connected expressions of freedom. We cannot have it both ways: both freedom and the protection of freedom from all its potential follies. If we have a world in which freedom can exercise itself in the direction of virtue, we must allow those conditions in which freedom might fall into vice. God does not *desire* to see freedom fall, but in the interest of freedom, he *permits* the conditions in which freedom is able to fall. Otherwise we would be hard-pressed to explain the obvious fact that freedom has indeed fallen in this world.[102] God does not permit any temporal evil that does not "clear the way for greater good."[103]

Had God abolished sin by fiat, he would be repudiating his own wisdom in creating free companionate beings. Providence is not viewed simply as the unilateral decree of God but rather as working synergistically amid complex layers of causality.[104] It is God's way of working within the free dynamics of self-determination embedded in natural causality so as to elicit our free responses through grace.[105]

Human choosing is governed by its Orderer as having rational freedom, "not as stock or stone."[106] Providence acts not only through the reliable rules of natural causality but amid a freewheeling, proximately indeterminate history, hedging and persuading and constraining human folly.

In responding to the constant permutations of freedom in history, God does not ever abdicate his own character or abandon his purpose in creation, for God cannot "deny himself ... counteract himself, or oppose his own work."[107] God "has never precluded himself from making exceptions" to the laws of nature "when so ever he pleases."[108]

---

[100]"On Divine Providence," B 2:541, sec. 15.

[101]"On Divine Providence," B 2:540–41, secs. 14–15.

[102]"The Image of God," B 4:294–95. For an illustration of how God's providence permitted the independence of the American colonies to work itself out toward a greater end, see "The Late Work of God in North America," B 3:594–608.

[103]"On Guardian Angels," B 4:234.

[104]For comments on Arminianism and synergism, see *LJW* 5:89; 6:331; 7:247; B 9:65; *JJW* 2:473.

[105]"On Divine Providence," B 2:541, secs. 12–13; for a further distinction between creation and providence, see "Thoughts upon God's Sovereignty," J X:361.

[106]"On Divine Providence," B 2:540–41, sec. 15.

[107]"On Divine Providence," B 2:539–41, secs. 13–15.

[108]"On Divine Providence," B 2:546, sec. 22.

c. Complementary Spheres of Providence

There are three concentric circles in which the providence of God is working with varied tempo and intention:

all of nature and human history (general providence)
all the baptized who have been claimed into the redemptive community (professing providence)
and especially in all those who, having confirmed and earnestly received their baptism and having been justified, are actively responding to sanctifying grace (perfecting providence)[109]

In the last of these circles are those who indeed worship the revealed God in spirit and in truth.[110]

First, the whole of nature and history is the peripheral circle, the widest arena of God's sustaining and providing. There we see his caring action. God foresees the needs of all things, according to their grace-given placement in the order of creation. God, whose "love is not confined," does not simply create and abandon but sustains, nurtures, and cares for the created order in that way that best suits the whole.[111]

This is what has been usually called "general providence,"[112] though Wesley had his mind trained on seeing the general always in particulars: "God acts in heaven, in earth, and under the earth, throughout the whole compass of his creation; by sustaining all things, without which everything would in an instant sink into its primitive nothing; by governing all, every moment superintending everything that he has made; strongly and sweetly influencing all, and yet without destroying the liberty of his rational creatures."[113]

Second, this providential activity, which is generally present in all nature and human history, is more specifically and intensively effective in the *worshiping* community, where the Word is proclaimed and the sacraments administered. This smaller circle of providence encompasses all the baptized who profess to believe in Christ, who by honoring God receive from him "a nearer concern for them."[114]

Third, the providence that is beheld generally in all of humanity, and more intensively within the worshiping community, is most powerfully discerned in those who actively and *intentionally share life in Christ*. Within this professing community, there are some who vitally live their faith, live out their daily walk in Christ, and most truly embody testimony to God's saving work everywhere. There may be others who are attached superficially to the covenant community but have not responded in faith to its Word and sacraments. Within the baptized community there are wheat and tares.[115]

---

[109]"Spiritual Worship," B 3:94, sec. 9; J VI:428.
[110]"On Divine Providence," B 2:541–42, secs. 16–18.
[111]"On Divine Providence," B 2:542, sec. 16.
[112]Cf. B 2:56–57, 544–48; FA, B 11:226–27, 530–31.
[113]"On the Omnipresence of God," B 4:42–43, sec. 2.1.
[114]"On Divine Providence," B 2:542–43, sec. 17.
[115]"On Divine Providence," B 2:543, sec. 18.

This active third circle of providence circumscribes those who, having committed themselves radically to reorder their lives in relation to God's self-giving, have set themselves to a disciplined life in Christ. They are the living believers whom Wesley denoted as "real Christians," who "worship God not in form only but in spirit and in truth."[116] This community that embodies faith active in love is where the providential action of God is most emphatically witnessed and experienced. This is the arena of God's providential activity where he is most actively sanctifying and completing his purpose in humanity.

It is on this interior circle, where faith becomes active in love, that much of the ensuing discussion of providence is focused.[117]

2. Special Providence

a. Distinguishing General and Special Providence

Wesley was suspicious of any notion of *general providence* that might implicitly deny special providence.[118] *Special providence* refers to the caring of God in specific ways toward particular persons in specific situations. If God is to act in history to redeem what is lost, this must come to focus in actual concrete events, in unrepeatable times and places where that divine caring is made known and experienced.[119]

God does not neglect the whole in caring for the part or the part in caring for the whole. A general providence that excludes particular providence is "self-contradictory nonsense."[120] We cannot reasonably posit God's provision of the general laws of nature and then absolutely disallow that God may act toward the special fulfillment of his will in particular situations.[121] That would disavow God's omnipotence.

"Either, therefore, allow a particular providence, or do not pretend to believe any providence at all. If you do not believe that the Governor of the world governs all things in it, small and great; that fire and hail, snow and vapour, wind and storm, fulfil his word; that he rules kingdoms and cities, fleets and armies, and all the individuals whereof they are composed (and yet *without forcing the wills of men, or necessitating any of their actions*), do not affect to believe that he governs anything."[122]

b. Discerning Special Acts of Providence

The recognition of special providence is a highly personal form of knowing. Wesley was convinced that his own ministries were abundantly accompanied by special evidences of quiet providential ordering. Almighty God is free to break

---

[116]"On Divine Providence," B 2:543, sec. 18.

[117]"On Divine Providence," B 2:543–44, secs. 18–19.

[118]"On Divine Providence," B 2:546; cf. FA, pt. 2, B 11:226–27; LCM, J X:71; "Wandering Thoughts," 2:132; *JJW* 4:211, July 6, 1781. Wesley thought the idea of general providence could devolve into "a sounding word which means just nothing," "The Nature of Enthusiasm," B 2:56.

[119]"On Divine Providence," B 2:546–48, secs. 23–26; cf. 2:56–57, 544–48; FA, B 11:226–27, 530–31.

[120]"On Divine Providence," B 2:548, sec. 26.

[121]"Principles of a Methodist Farther Explained," B 9:207–22, 396–97; 11:147–53, 468–69, 512–17.

[122]"An Estimate of the Manners of the Present Times," J XI:160, sec. 13, italics added.

through the usually reliable arena of natural causality.[123] To construct a view of reality that omits any possibility of divine intervention requires an arbitrary narrowing of reality.[124]

Wesley was intensely interested in investigating paranormal activities, special acts of providence, from healings to earthquakes, seeking to discern the contours of God's judgment and grace in history.[125] When he visited his bands, he asked each one how God was enabling and hedging their way, and how they were interpreting the providence of God in their personal experience.[126] This encouraged believers to further trust God's providing and to become aware of each unfolding gift of providence. Believers are called to receive everything excepting sin as given by the hand of God.[127]

God's care for the world in general and the faithful in particular calls us to wholly trust the Sustainer of all things, to thank God for constant providential care, to walk humbly as we celebrate God's personal interest in creatures, and to use the means of grace provided.[128] Those who obstinately turn their backs on providence make themselves vulnerable to despair. Those who order their lives around it are in that measure opened to unexpected blessings. A special form of happiness comes from knowing that God is caring for us even under conditions of adversity.[129]

If special providences are ruled out by some logic alien to Scripture, then "the hairs of our head are no longer numbered, and not only a sparrow, but a city, an empire, may fall to the ground, without the will or care of our heavenly Father."[130] The general providing activity at times has special expressions of the divine intentionality in discrete providential events.

Scripture maintains that

providence extends to every individual in the whole system of beings which [God] hath made; that all *natural causes* of every kind depend wholly upon his will; and he increases, lessens, suspends, or destroys their efficacy, according to his own good pleasure; that he uses *preternatural causes* at his will, — the ministry of good or of evil angels; and that he hath never yet precluded himself from exerting his own immediate power, from *speaking* life or death into any of his creatures, from *looking* a world into being or into nothing.[131]

---

[123]"Serious Thoughts Occasioned by the Late Earthquake at Lisbon," J XI:1 – 13.

[124]"On Divine Providence," B 2:546 – 47, secs. 22 – 25.

[125]"Serious Thoughts Occasioned by the Late Earthquake at Lisbon," J XI:3 – 4.

[126]Cf. "The Providentially Protected Person," in *The Elusive Mr. Wesley: John Wesley, His Own Biographer*, ed. Richard Heitzenrater (Nashville: Abingdon, 1984), 125 – 30.

[127]"The Nature of Enthusiasm," B 2:56 – 57.

[128]"On Divine Providence," B 2:548 – 50, secs. 27 – 29.

[129]These same ideas of providence are embedded in Homily #39, "The Catholic Spirit," B 2:79 – 80, in a series of personal questions assumed to be affirmatively answered by anyone whose life is hidden in Christ: "Dost thou believe that he now 'upholdeth all things by the word of his power'? And that he governs even the most minute, even the most noxious, to his own glory, and the good of them that love him?"

[130]To those who allow "only a general Providence," Wesley confessed, "I do not understand the term." FA, B11:227, J VIII:159.

[131]FA, B 11:227, J VIII:159.

Wesley was vexed that so "few persons understand … the doctrine of a Particular Providence … at least, not practically, so as to apply it to every circumstance of life." He was particularly irritated to hear God's "government of the world continually found fault with."[132] Yet at times an excessive or highly subjective stress on special providence caused Wesley to caution against "enthusiasm."[133]

3. On God's Sovereignty

a. Thoughts on God's Sovereignty

We next focus on "Thoughts upon God's Sovereignty" [J X:361 – 63].

God creates according to his sovereign will and governs justly all that has been created.[134] God does not overleap and displace human freedom by coercing human decision making. Rather, he supplies humanity with sufficient grace to which freedom can respond and for which freedom is accountable.

It is no diminution of the sovereign freedom of God to hold that human beings are morally free and responsible. Only an incomparably wise and powerful God could abide having vulnerable human freedom in a good universe. Wesley posited a divine freedom that transcends all human freedom while still preserving moral accountability.[135]

No finite creature is in a moral position to ask the Creator whether the creation was created justly or not, for creation is always sheer gift. There is no reasonable basis for the contingent creature to lodge a complaint of injustice toward the sovereign Creator.[136]

Prior to creation, God was free to create as he pleased. Having created, as Governor, God does not act by fiat as "a mere Sovereign … but as an impartial Judge, guided in all things by invariable justice," which presupposes "free-agency."[137] "In some cases, mercy rejoices over justice.... God may reward more, but he will never punish more than strict justice requires." It belongs to the omniscient justice of God to reproach no one "for doing anything which he could not possibly avoid" or for "omitting anything which he could not possibly do."[138]

b. Whether Miracles Have Ceased

Here we will look at Wesley's "Letter to the Rev. Dr. Conyers Middleton Occasioned by His Late 'Free Inquiry'" (LCM), dated January 4, 1749 [J X:1 – 79; LJW 2:312ff.; last section in JWO, 181ff.; first part reprinted as "A Plain Account of Genuine Christianity"].

Dr. Conyers Middleton of Trinity College, Cambridge, published in 1748 A Free

---

[132]Letter to Ebenezer Blackwell, August 31, 1755, LJW 3:139.
[133]"The Nature of Enthusiasm," B 2:56 – 57.
[134]JWO 435 – 36, 452 – 53, 486.
[135]J X:361 – 62.
[136]J X:361.
[137]J X:362.
[138]J X:363.

Inquiry into the Miraculous Powers Which Are Supposed to Have Subsisted in the Christian Church, Etc., in which he argued that no authenticated miracles took place after the time of the apostles.[139] His deeper motive was to discredit ante-Nicene sources altogether by tendentiously showing them to be already fomenting religious corruption. Wesley thought the essay important enough to cause him to cancel a planned trip to Holland and set immediately to answer it, spending "almost twenty days in that unpleasing employment."[140]

Wesley narrowed the debate to the central point in dispute: "whether the testimony of the Fathers be a sufficient ground to believe that miraculous gifts subsisted at all after the days of the Apostles."[141] Wesley challenged each shred of proposed evidence presented by Middleton, who sought to prove that whatever miraculous powers might have been imparted to the apostles were withdrawn from the postapostolic writers, who turned out to be "credulous and superstitious." Middleton offered only weak arguments that miraculous powers were withdrawn in the midst of intensely increasing persecution. He had charged the patristic writers with encouraging the worst medieval corruptions, such as monasticism, relic worship, and praying for the dead, yet his evidences were flimsy and his arguments disconnected.[142]

A devastating critique is offered of the scholarship underlying the five proposals of Middleton's *Free Inquiry*. Wesley showed that Middleton himself quoted numerous sources (Theophilus of Antioch, Tertullian, Minucius Felix, Origen, Cyprian, Arnobius, Lactantius) contradicting his own original assertion that miracles ceased after the time of the apostles. A very loose reading of Ignatius "convinces me you have not read ... one page of it."[143] Meanwhile, "the farther you go, the more things you imagine ... yourself to have proved."[144] Wesley defended the character and integrity of Clement of Rome, Polycarp, Justin Martyr, and Irenaeus as trustable writers willing to die for the truth.[145]

Middleton was naively fixated on "gleaning up every scrap of heathen scandal and palming it upon us as unquestionable evidence."[146] So what if Celsus represented Christian wonder-workers as common cheats, and Lucian viewed them as money-hungry con artists? This did not constitute reliable evidence. Using bad translations, paraphrases, misquotations, wrong attributions, thrown-together selections, inconsistencies, and non sequiturs, Middleton had constructed his case tendentiously. Wesley, the itinerant preacher of the revival, was directly taking on a leading Cambridge teacher whom many regarded as an expert in patristic studies. "Poor Celsus had not a second; though he multiplies, under your forming hand, into

---

[139]*LJW* 1:235; 2:88, 101, 105 – 6, 207, 210, 229, 350, 362.
[140]*JJW* 3:390.
[141]LCM, J X:5.
[142]LCM, J X:7 – 14.
[143]LCM, J X:19.
[144]LCM, J X:24.
[145]LCM, J X:16 – 24.
[146]LCM, J X:25.

a cloud of witnesses."[147] "You are resolved to draw out of the well what was never in it."[148]

The incidental inaccuracies of Justin Martyr and Irenaeus cannot be used to discredit all of their testimony to the miraculous in their times. That the Fathers studied demonic influences does not consign them to the "grossest credulity."[149] Middleton fantasized superstitious jugglers and swindlers and charlatans at every turn, yet "there is no more proof of their ever existing, than of a witch's sailing in an egg-shell."[150]

Even if some of the early Christian writers were at times mistaken, that "by no means proves that they were all knaves together." Middleton had "promised great things, and performed just nothing" with a "lame piece of work." Wesley said, "At every dead lift you are sure to play upon us these dear creatures of your own imagination ... your tenth legion."[151]

c. Countering Naturalistic Reductionism

Simplistic naturalistic reductions for various types of miracles are less plausible than the original reports. The casting out of demonic powers cannot be reduced to epileptic fits or ventriloquism.[152] The healing miracles reported in the postapostolic period cannot be reduced to the natural efficacies of oils.[153] The serious historian does not select only those data that reinforce his predisposing prejudices. Admittedly, the heathen as well as early Christians claimed miraculous cures, and oil may cure some diseases by natural efficacy. We do not know the precise bounds of natural causality, yet "all this will not prove that no miraculous cures were performed ... in the three succeeding centuries" after the apostles.[154] The visions and ecstasies of early church writers were not of the same kind as those of the Delphic Pythia or the Cumaean Sibyl.[155]

There is no evidence that visions and prophecies were "contrived" by church leaders. To make his case, Middleton had to invent numerous "additions of his own" to the text "in order to make something out of nothing."[156]

As to the gift of tongues, many cases may have gone unrecorded, but Irenaeus wrote that many in his day spoke with tongues. And it is simply "an historical mistake" to assume that "this gift has never once been heard of" since the Reformation, for "it has been heard of more than once, no farther off than the valleys of Dauphiny" less than fifty years ago.[157]

---

[147]LCM, J X:26–27.
[148]LCM, J X:29.
[149]LCM, J X:36.
[150]LCM, J X:37.
[151]LCM, J X:38.
[152]LCM, J X:44–46.
[153]LJW 1:235; 2:88, 101, 105–6, 207, 210, 229, 362, 350.
[154]LCM, J X:41.
[155]LCM, J X:47.
[156]LCM, J X:48.
[157]LCM, J X:54.

It is a futile effort to try to prove that martyr apologists were frauds. For "they were hated.... And this very hatred would naturally prompt [opponents] to examine the ground of the challenges daily repeated by them they hated; were it only that, by discovering the fraud ... they might have had a better pretense for throwing the Christians to the lions."[158] There is no room to "doubt of the truth of the facts therein asserted, seeing the apologists constantly desired their enemies 'to come and see them with their own eyes' — a hazard which those 'crafty men' would never have run, had not the facts themselves been certain."[159]

Further Reading on Creation and Providence

Collins, Kenneth. *A Faithful Witness: John Wesley's Homiletical Theology*, 25 – 29. Wilmore, KY: Wesleyan Heritage, 1993.

Lipscomb, Andrew A. "Providence of God in Methodism." In *Wesley Memorial Volume*, edited by J. O. A. Clark, 383 – 403. New York: Phillips & Hunt, 1881.

Miley, John. *Systematic Theology*. Reprint, Peabody, MA: Hendrickson, 1989.

Pope, William Burt. *A Compendium of Christian Theology*. 3 vols. London: Wesleyan Methodist Book-Room, 1880.

Rack, Henry D. "Piety and Providence." In *Reasonable Enthusiast*, 420 – 71. Philadelphia: Trinity Press International, 1985.

Ralston, Thomas N. *Elements of Divinity*. New York: Abingdon, 1924.

Slaatte, Howard A. *Fire in the Brand: Introduction to the Creative Work and Theology of John Wesley*, 115ff. New York: Exposition, 1963.

Summers, Thomas O. *Systematic Theology*. 2 vols. Edited by J. J. Tigert. Nashville: Methodist Publishing House South, 1888.

Watson, Richard. *Theological Institutes*. 2 vols. New York: Mason and Lane, 1836, 1840; edited by John M'Clintock, New York: Carlton & Porter, 1850.

Wood, R. W. "God in History: Wesley a Child of Providence." *MQR* 78 (1929): 94 – 104.

D. Theodicy

Theodicy means an attempt to justify God in full recognition of the presence and power of evil. A theodicy offers reasoning about how evil and suffering are to be understood in relation to reasoning about divine justice, power, and love. In his homilies "The Promise of Understanding" and "The General Deliverance," and in numerous letters, Wesley explicitly set forth a penetrating theodicy. At age twenty-six, Wesley wrote to his father a searching theological reflection on evil [Letter to His Father, January 15, 1731, on Archbishop William King's *Origin of Evil*, B 25:264 – 67], which we will now examine.

---

[158]LCM, J X:60.
[159]LCM, J X:60 – 61.

1. Whence Comes Evil?

a. Unde Malum?[160]

How came evil into the world?[161] The Manichaean supposition of "two supreme, independent principles is next door to a contradiction in terms.... Nay, if there can be two essentially distinct absolute infinities, there may be an infinity of such absolute infinities."[162] "It is just as repugnant to Infinite Goodness to create what it foresaw would be spoiled by another as to create what would be spoiled by the constitution of its own nature.... But if it could be proved that to permit evils in the world is consistent with, nay, necessarily results from, infinite goodness, then the difficulty would vanish."[163]

Why does God permit pain?

Pain is necessary to make us watchful against it, and to warn us of what it tends toward, as is the fear of death likewise, which is of use in many cases that pain does not reach. From these all the passions necessarily spring.... But if pain and the fear of death were extinguished, no animal could long subsist. Since therefore these evils are necessarily joined with more than equivalent goods, then permitting these is not repugnant to, but flows from, infinite goodness. The same observation holds as to hunger, thirst, childhood, age, diseases, wild beasts, and poisons. They are all therefore permitted because each of them is necessarily connected with such a good as outweighs the evil.[164]

Why does God permit the free exercise of human liberty?

By liberty I mean an active, self-determining power, which does not choose things because they are pleasing, but is pleased with them because it chooses them.... That man partakes of this principle I conclude, (1) because experience shows it; (2) because we observe in ourselves the signs and properties of such a power. We observe we can counteract our appetites, senses, and even our reason if we so choose; which we cannot otherwise account for than by admitting such a power in ourselves.... If, therefore, this be the noblest of all our faculties, then our chief happiness lies in the due use of [this liberty].[165]

This liberty sometimes yields "pain, namely when it falls short of what it chooses, which may come to pass if we choose other things impossible to be had, or inconsistent with each other, or such as are out of our power.... And into these foolish choices we may be betrayed either by ignorance, negligence, by indulging

---

[160]"Unde Malum, or Whence Comes Evil? A Response to Archbishop William King's De Origine Mali," LJW 1:64, 68; 8:254; B 2:234.

[161]"Evil is a deviation from those measures of eternal, unerring order and reason not to choose what is worthy to be chosen ... [thus] we may fairly account for the origin of evil from the possibility of a various use of our liberty." Letter to His Father, December 19, 1729, on Humphrey Ditton's view of the origin of evil (B 25:242).

[162]Paraphrasing Humphrey Ditton, in Letter to His Father, December 19, 1729, B 25:241.

[163]Letter to His Father, January 15, 1731, B 25:264–67; cf. B 4:279–80, 285–86.

[164]Letter to His Father, January 15, 1731, B 25:265.

[165]Letter to His Father, January 15, 1731, B 25:265–66, paraphrasing William King.

the exercise of liberty too far, by obstinacy, or habit; or lastly by the importunity of our natural appetites. Hence it appears how cautious we ought to be in choosing."[166]

b. Three Possible Ways God Could Have Hindered Creatures from Abusing Their Liberty

Pretend insofar as possible to put yourself in God's place by asking what God's options were in allowing liberty to become abused. There are three ways by which God might have hindered his creatures from thus abusing their liberty:

1. *By not creating any being free.* But had this method been taken, then
   - the whole universe would have been a mere machine;
   - that would have been wanting which is most pleasing to God of anything in the universe — namely, the virtuous freedom of his reasonable creatures;
   - his reasonable creatures would have been in a worse state than they are now; for only free agents can be perfectly happy, as without a possibility of choosing wrong, there can be no freedom.
2. *By overruling this power* and constraining them to choose right. But this would have been to do and undo, to contradict himself, to take away what he had given.
3. *By placing them where they should have no temptation to abuse it.* But this, too, would have been the same in effect as to have given them no liberty at all.[167]

Without allowing freedom to fall, God would have deprived humanity of its most distinctive gift. Rather, God honored humanity by granting liberty the possibility of choosing wrongly, with its train of painful consequences.

2. The Promise of Understanding in the Future

The text of the early homily "The Promise of Understanding" is John 13:7 (paraphrased): "What God does we know not, but shall hereafter" [Homily #140 (1730), B 4:279 – 89 (not in the Jackson edition)].

How adequately can we know the purposes of God in permitting freedom to fall? Wesley found comfort in the eschatologically oriented New Testament text: "You do not realize now what I am doing," Jesus said as he washed the feet of Peter who resisted him, "but later you will understand" (John 13:7 NIV). From this interchange, Wesley meditated on the prevailing ignorance of human finitude.

a. The Desire to Know: Ordinate and Inordinate

Rightly bounded, the desire to know is pleasurable and fruitful. This desire prompts us to improve our reasoning, awakens curiosity, and readies us to receive knowledge. "So long as this is contained within proper bounds and directed to proper objects, there is scarce in the mind of man a more delightful or more useful inclination" than the desire to know. It is "one of the earliest principles in the soul."[168]

---

[166]Letter to His Father, January 15, 1731, B 25:266; for subsequent reference to the origin of evil, see B 2:401 – 3, 434, 476; *LJW* 1:44, 64n, 68, 305, 309; 5:117; *JJW* 8:285.

[167]Letter to His Father, January 15, 1731, B 25:267, paraphrasing William King, italics added.

[168]"The Promise of Understanding," B 4:281, pref. 1.

This pleasurable desire to know, which when bounded makes joyful the heart and enlightens the eyes, may become idolatrously fixed on improper objects so as to elicit pain. When this desire extends itself beyond its proper boundaries, the searching is never content, ever unsatisfied.[169]

Wesley was intrigued by the scriptural paradox that we are able to know so little in this life, yet we are promised full knowing at the final resurrection. No one can in this flesh "find out the Almighty to perfection," yet this is no intrinsic tragedy or evil, for we are scripturally promised that we shall adequately "know hereafter."[170]

b. Present Deficits in our Knowledge of Nature

Wesley set forth a series of scriptural arguments on why finite minds cannot know how the infinite God has ordered the world, the heavens, the heart, grace, or life in the Spirit; why it is impossible to say why evil is permitted a temporary place in creation; why God has not made humanity from the outset perfect; why inequalities are permitted among free creatures shaped by varied temperaments; and why God permits the noblest of creatures to remain so long in such wretched ignorance.

No finite mind can fully grasp how God has ordered the world, even if fragmentary evidences of this ordering abound "daily before our eyes."[171] From the far reaches of our cosmological ignorance to the inward depths of our self-ignorance, the liability is the same: we can know *that* the cosmos and the self are ordered but not exhaustively *why*.

Wesley employed Newton's theory of gravity as an example: It is clear *that* there is an attraction, a "tendency in every natural body to approach to every other," that there is a secret chain by which all parts of the universe are meaningfully connected. But when we ask *how* this tendency has become universally balanced and *what* the universal cohesion and spring of the whole of nature precisely is, we can appeal only to such rational concepts as a "law of nature" or to such metaphors as "the finger of God." At some point our knowledge of the "infinite variety" and "perfect regularity" of natural processes comes to its limit.[172]

c. Whether the Springs of Human Action Are Unsearchable

The psychosomatic interface is just as much a mystery to human knowing as is the heavenly panoply. "Who knows how the thought of [a man's] inmost soul immediately strikes the outmost part of his body? How an impression made on the outmost part of his body immediately strikes his inmost soul,"[173] as in the case of a blush, for example, or a prick of the skin? How is life knit with the body? In what way is spirit enclosed in matter? These are open to empirical inquiry. We are not without rational competencies to describe some aspects of this interface, but finally

---

[169]B 1:208; 2:561; 3:183—84; 4:341.
[170]"The Promise of Understanding," B 4:282, pref. 5.
[171]"The Promise of Understanding," B 4:282, sec. 1.1.
[172]"The Promise of Understanding," B 4:283, sec. 1.1; on gravitation see B 3:93; 4:283.
[173]"The Promise of Understanding," B 4:283, sec. 1.2.

"man is all a mystery to himself. *That* God does work wonderfully in him he knows, but the *manner* of his working he cannot know; it is too wonderful for his present capacity. Whether he surveys his own hand or heart or head, he sees numberless footsteps of the Almighty, but vainly does he attempt to trace them up to their spring: 'clouds and darkness are round about him.' "[174]

Moreover, the springs of grace are unsearchable. Effectual prayer avails much, "but how it avails we cannot explain. How God acts upon us in consequence of our friends' prayers ... we cannot know."[175] All whys beg for eschatological reference.

d. Viewing Natural, Moral, and Penal Evil Eschatologically

Why and how God acts and hedges and opens and closes doors remains in this time and space unknowable but is *promised to be known hereafter.* At present

> we cannot say why God suffered evil to have a place in his creation; why he, who is so infinitely good himself, who made all things "very good" ... permitted what is so entirely contrary to his own nature, and so destructive of his noblest works. "Why are sin and its attendant pain in the world?" has been a question ever since the world began, and the world will probably end before human understandings have answered it with any certainty.[176]

Wesley's theodicy argued that

> all evil is either natural, moral, or penal; that natural evil or pain is no evil at all if it be overbalanced with the following pleasure; that moral evil, or sin, cannot possibly befall anyone unless those who willingly embrace, who choose it; and that penal evil, or punishment, cannot possibly befall any unless they likewise choose it by choosing sin. This entirely cuts off all imputation on the justice or goodness of God, since it can never be proved that it is contrary to either of these to give his creatures [the] liberty of embracing either good or evil, to put happiness and misery in their own hands, to leave them the choice of life and death.[177]

But "why did God give them that choice? It is sure, in so doing he did not act contrary to any of his attributes." But might God have compounded us in some other way? Suppose God had determined that man could be happy completely apart from his own choice, "to have let him know only life," "to have tied him down to happiness, to have given him no choice of misery." Such choicelessness could hardly be termed human. "The All-wise could not do anything without sufficient motives.... But what they are is hid from human eyes ... reasons they are which the ear of man hath not heard, nor can it yet enter into the heart to conceive."[178]

---

[174]"The Promise of Understanding," B 4:284, sec. 1.2; Ps. 97:2, italics added.
[175]"The Promise of Understanding," B 4:284, sec. 1.4.
[176]"The Promise of Understanding," B 4:285, sec. 2.1.
[177]Ibid.
[178]"The Promise of Understanding," B 4:285 – 86, sec. 2.1.

e. Why Inequalities and Boundaries Prevail in Temporal Creation

Even among those who choose the blessed, holy walk, there are inequalities that none can explain. Even if we are given life within specific bounds, God has not "so bounded any of his rational creatures" but that they may obtain some degree of happiness. Such bounds elicit the virtues of empathy and perseverance.

In much suffering we may "commonly trace the immediate reason of the suffering. We may commonly observe that [the] particular affliction under which a man labors either is pointed at the particular vice to which he naturally inclines, or is conducive to that virtue he particularly wants. But if we move one step further, we are lost again. We cannot tell why it was that he was suffered to be naturally inclined."[179] Even if I can identify that my suffering is due to pride, which has the good purpose of bringing me to humility, "yet the difficulty recurs — 'But why did the good God suffer me to be so prone to pride?'" I am left to exclaim, "How unsearchable are his judgments, and his ways past finding out!" (Rom. 11:33).[180]

f. Why Ignorance of the Causes of Evil Remains Our Portion in This Life

Wesley offered four arguments[181] in defense of God permitting human ignorance:

1. Such "ignorance may teach us the usefullest knowledge, may lead us to humility, that, conscious how little we can know of him, we may be the more intent upon knowing ourselves." By coming to terms with "our utter inability to understand ... we may seriously apply to what we are able to understand — the manner and reasons of our own [acting]." What else could teach us a more realistic assessment of ourselves "than to have so many instances daily before us of the imperfection of our noblest endowment? If reason, boasted reason, be so imperfect, what must be the meaner parts of our frame?"[182]

2. By pride of knowing the angels fell, so lest human creatures also would fall by too much knowledge, "God peculiarly guarded" humanity against such profusion of knowledge that would tempt toward pride. Hence a blessing flows precisely from our ignorance, which we in our inexperience have difficulty grasping.[183] *By limiting our knowledge, God is thereby limiting our temptation to pride.* We are thus taught humility precisely by "the present weakness of our understanding," which calls us to acknowledge our limits more readily and hence points toward repentance.[184]

3. Between birth and death, we are called to "live by faith, not by sight" (2 Cor. 5:7 NIV). God's central design is not that we now see and know but that we freely believe, with "such an assent as we were free to give or withhold as depended wholly

---

[179]"The Promise of Understanding," B 4:286, sec. 2.2.
[180]"The Promise of Understanding," B 4:286–87, sec. 2.2.
[181]Wesley divided these arguments into three, with points 1 and 2 being held together in this passage as a single argument.
[182]"The Promise of Understanding," 4:287, sec. 3.1.
[183]B 2:131–35; 3:172, 191–92; cf. 2:429–30; 4:344.
[184]"The Promise of Understanding," B 4:288, sec. 3.2.

on our choice. And this intention of our Creator is excellently served by the measure of understanding we now enjoy. It suffices for faith but not for knowledge. We can believe in God — we cannot see him."[185]

4. The most compelling apology for the justice of relative human ignorance is grasped only by being viewed eschatologically: *We shall know hereafter.* We are ignorant now in order to provide

> an entertainment for heaven. And what an entertainment! To have the curtain drawn at once, and enjoy the full blaze of God's wisdom and goodness! To see clearly how the Author of this visible world fastened all its parts together ... that amazing union between the body and the soul of man, that astonishing correspondence between spirit and matter, between perishing dust and immortal flame! ... why he suffered sin and pain to mingle with those works of which he had declared that they were very good! What unspeakable blessings those are which owe their being to this curse; what infinite beauty arises from, and overbalances this deformity ... fitly reserved for that state wherein, being clothed with glory and immortality, we shall be ... pure and strong enough to see God![186]

E. Evil

1. On Natural Evil

Wesley found in the tragic occurrence of a devastating earthquake in Portugal an occasion for calling England to come to its senses ["Serious Thoughts Occasioned by the Late Earthquake at Lisbon" (1755), J XI:3 – 10]. The time for repentance is always limited.[187]

Among disasters that Wesley regarded as evidences of divine judgment — and thus a merciful call to repentance — were war, pestilence, severe storms, and most stunningly, earthquakes.[188] He went to great lengths to inquire empirically into the causes of the fallen rock at Whitson Cliffs ("I walked, crept, and climbed round and over a great part of the ruins"), seeking natural causation yet never being fully satisfied that the event could be reduced to "merely natural cause."[189]

Wesley would not leave romanticists in a false peace. "What think you of a comet? ... The late ingenious and accurate Dr. Halley (never yet suspected of enthusiasm) fixes the return of the great comet in the year 1758 [three years hence]; and he observes that the last time it revolved, it moved in the very same line which the earth describes in her annual course round the sun," which would 'set the earth on fire.'[190]

Allowing that there are natural causes in disasters, "they are still under the direc-

---

[185]"The Promise of Understanding," B 4:288, sec. 3.2.

[186]"The Promise of Understanding," B 4:288 – 89, sec. 3.3.

[187]The supposed cause of divine judgment in Lisbon's case was in Wesley's view probably the Portuguese Inquisition; cf. *JJW* 4:141; 5:40.

[188]Concerning earthquakes, see B 2:390, 507; *LJW* 3:156; 6:150, 284; *JJW* 3:453 – 57; 4:117 – 20; *CH* 7:727.

[189]"Serious Thoughts Occasioned by the Late Earthquake at Lisbon," J XI:3, 4; cf. XI:496 – 504.

[190]"Serious Thoughts Occasioned by the Late Earthquake at Lisbon," J XI:9.

tion of the Lord of nature; nay, what is nature itself, but the art of God, or God's method of acting in the material world."[191] Those who live in friendship with God need "not fear, though the earth be moved, and the hills be carried into the midst of the sea."[192]

2. The Groaning of Creation and the General Deliverance

The text of the homily "The General Deliverance" is Romans 8:22: "The whole creation groaneth, and travaileth in pain together until now" [Homily #60 (1781), B 2:437–50; J #60, VI:241–53].

a. Toward a Future Ecology

Closer to a philosophical ecology than anything else found in Wesley, the homily on "The General Deliverance" views plant and animal life in relation first to the original human condition prior to the fall, then after the fall, and finally in the light of the resurrection. The predicament of plants and animals and even of the inorganic world is viewed in the context of salvation history—creation, fall, the history of sin, redemption, and consummation.

The mercy of God is over all of his works: rocks, plants, animals, humans, angelic creatures.[193] Therefore we are being called to express the same goodness and mercy toward creation that God has shown toward us, to be merciful in whatever sphere of responsibility we are given—not only with respect to our own human suffering, but with respect to nonhuman creation's suffering as well.

b. The Great Chain of Being

Wesley posited a great chain of being in which the one who is incomparably good brings forth a created order (not an emanation) that exhibits vast variety and complexity, wherein less conscious elements are ordered to benefit, enable, and serve more freely conscious elements.[194] As plants sustain and provide energy for animal life, so animals provide sustenance for human life.[195]

Inorganic matter[196] sustains and feeds organic matter, which in turn is the basis of a food chain that sustains animals, who in turn supply sustenance for human beings who live precariously in this curious juxtaposition of finitude and freedom, this special arena of creation with our roots in nature yet with astonishing capacities for imagination, reason, and self-determination. Humanity experiences the psychosomatic interface that straddles finitude and freedom, standing in the middle of creation, "a creature capable of God, capable of knowing, loving, and obeying his Creator."[197]

---

[191]"Serious Thoughts Occasioned by the Late Earthquake at Lisbon," J XI:6, 7.

[192]"Serious Thoughts Occasioned by the Late Earthquake at Lisbon," J XI:10; see also Charles Wesley: "The Cause and Cure of Earthquakes," J VII:386–99.

[193]"The General Deliverance," B 2:437, proem 1.

[194]"The General Deliverance," B 2:348–41, proem 1.1–2; see also B 2:396–97, 436; 3:464.

[195]"The General Deliverance," B 2:441, sec. 1.5.

[196]B 11:269.

[197]"The General Deliverance," B 2:439, sec. 1.2.

c. The Human Composite: Antecedent to the History of Sin

Human creation is viewed as a distinct composition (Lat. *compositum*), a unique interfacing of body and spirit, finitude and freedom. Like animals, we have bodies, but unlike animals we have linguistic, rational, imaginative, and spiritual capacities transcending brute creation. Animals do not have those competencies to the degree that we do. Human freedom has capacities for refracting the goodness and mercy of God that nonhuman creatures in various degrees lack.[198] "Man is capable of God" in far greater measure than nonhuman creation.[199] Like angelic creation, we have spiritual capacities, yet unlike angelic powers, we have physical bodies situated in time.

Before the history of sin began to unfold, humanity in its original condition had unfallen freedom, deathless life, and no guilt or anxiety.[200] Each creature reflects the divine glory in its own way, humans by imaging the moral nature of God,[201] and animals by their vital life.[202] In paradise, humans were perfectly happy, reflecting the image of God, with freedom of choice, without which they would have been "as incapable of vice or virtue as any part of the inanimate creation. In these, in the power of self-motion, understanding, will, and liberty, the natural image of God consisted."[203]

d. The Original Plant and Animal Creation

Humanity stood right at the cosmic center as steward and name giver, being given responsible dominion over this created order.[204] No animal has ever received a name except by humans, who were thereby being given the task of stewardship of the whole plant and animal world.[205] Through humanity the blessings of God were intended to flow to other creatures. In this way, nonhuman creatures have from the outset been dependent on the destiny of humanity for their happiness.[206]

Humanity's goodness lies in reflecting God's goodness. The creatures' goodness is in serving the whole of the created order in their appropriate and proportional way. Every creature is gifted with some particular way of serving the whole. No creature serves the whole in the same way any other creature does. Brute creation prior to the fall is viewed biblically as a garden in which there is plenty of food, pleasure, gratitude, and immortality.

What happened when humanity willed to disobey and broke this intended relationship? The consequences for the whole chain of being were disastrous. Through sin human life has made itself incapable of transmitting these blessings that were

---

[198]"The General Deliverance," B 2:439, sec. 1.2.
[199]"The General Deliverance," B 2:441, sec. 1.5.
[200]"The General Deliverance," B 2:438, sec. 1.1.
[201]"The New Birth," B 2:188, sec. 1.1.
[202]*LJW* 3:108; *SS* 2:230n.
[203]"The General Deliverance," B 2:438–39, sec. 1.1; cf. "The End of Christ's Coming," B 2:474, sec. 1.3.
[204]"The General Deliverance," B 2:440, sec. 1.3.
[205]On stewardship, see B 1:548–49; 2:266–67, 276–98; 3:231–32, 239–40; 4:183–84.
[206]"The General Deliverance," B 2:440–41, sec. 1.3–5.

intended for the benefit of other creatures.[207] In what follows we see the outlines of a primitive Wesleyan anticipation of an environmental theology and ethic.

e. The Creation Groaning in Travail: Romans 8:19 – 22

In Romans 8, Paul compared the present sufferings of the cosmos to the glory to be revealed. The whole creation is groaning in travail, in pain awaiting this glory.[208] "I consider that our present sufferings are not worth comparing with the glory that will be revealed in us" (Rom. 8:18 NIV). The glory to be revealed in us is the work of the Holy Spirit that is already in process but not yet complete. Paul had in mind the whole physical cosmos, including inorganic, organic, and animal life: "The creation waits in eager expectation for the children of God to be revealed. For the creation was subjected to frustration, not by its own choice, but by the will of the one who subjected it, in hope that the creation itself will be liberated from its bondage to decay and brought into the freedom and glory of the children of God. We know that the whole creation has been groaning as in the pains of childbirth right up to the present time" (Rom. 8:19 – 22 NIV).[209]

This means that the physical cosmos, with all its living creatures, awaits the resurrection. It is worth paying particular attention as to how this correlates with the present ecological crisis. Wesley developed a distinctive notion of the inchoate hunger of animal creation for the resurrection. The whole cosmos is awaiting this final manifestation of divine mercy, which is already in the process of coming.[210]

f. The Failure of Humanity to Communicate Divine Blessings to Brute Creation

Much unnecessary suffering and pain in the biosphere is due to human sin. For this reason, "the creation was subjected to frustration, not by its own choice" (Rom. 8:19 NIV). These animals did not get a chance to choose but were subjected by the wills of those who subjected them — namely, humanity, once splendid but then absurdly fallen. The history of sin subjected other nonhuman life forms to the human fate.[211] So when human beings fall by their own choice, the animal and plant world suffer for our collective intergenerational human choices.

The history of sin thus forms the definitive juncture, a hinge for the subsequent conveyance of design and meaning between Creator and brute creation.[212] "As all the blessings of God in paradise flowed through man to the inferior creatures; as man was the great channel of communication, between the Creator and the whole brute creation; so when man made himself incapable of transmitting those blessings, that communication was necessarily cut off."[213]

[207]"The General Deliverance," B 2:442, sec. 2.1.
[208]"The General Deliverance," B 2:438, proem 2.
[209]LJW 3:107.
[210]"The General Deliverance," B 2:438 – 39, sec. 1.1 – 2.
[211]"The General Deliverance," B 2:442, sec. 5.
[212]"The General Deliverance," B 2:441, sec. 1.5.
[213]"The General Deliverance," B 2:442, sec. 2.1.

Human sin comes to have devastating effects on plant and animal life. Because we have lost the source of our blessedness, we are no longer able to be a source of blessing for the plant and animal world. In this way, plant and animal life to some degree share the lost blessedness and operative misery of humanity.[214] The biosphere has come to depend on the capacity of the human mind and spirit to reflect the holiness and goodness of God, and to suffer when this fails to occur.[215]

g. The Wesleyan Ecological-Eschatological Theodicy for Brute Creation

In our inattentiveness to our true good, we, as warned, fell and lost our holiness and blessedness, and destined the body toward death. When we lose our original trust-filled liberty, the beasts lose their more limited spheres of enfranchisement. They are deprived of their proximate blessedness by the human fall. So animal and plant life on this vulnerable earth has become profoundly implicated in the history of sin. There is suffering not only in human history but also in the whole of the natural order as a result of our sin.[216]

If the creator of all things does not despise anything that has been made, and wills that all creatures be happy, how has it happened that there is so much travail in natural creation? Why do so many evils oppress and overwhelm creatures (plants, animals, and humans)?

The answer cannot be given within the bounds of history, but only in relation to the end of history. There is no adequate answer to the question of theodicy except in eschatological reference. We gain no adequate grip on the problem of suffering without seeing it in relation to the last judgment.

Suffering must now be understood in relation to a gradually unfolding process that is only now being revealed. Those who demand immediate rational answers to why we suffer rule themselves out of this eschatological perspective. In Wesley's view, the sufferer's suffering cannot be understood apart from its social history. Each sufferer has identity only within a particular social matrix. You cannot pluck sufferers from their time nor detach them from their history, which is a very long and complicated history involving free agents who sin and whose sins affect other choices and subsequent chains of sin in succeeding generations. Sin is not a simple problem to be solved individualistically. The history of sin has a devastating impact on human nature.[217]

h. The Groaning of Fallen Creation: On Animal Pain

We are talking about the crisis of the plant and animal world. We and they live in a fallen world, the only world we have ever seen. "We" in the corporate, representative, Adamic sense were once in the garden, but "I" as an individual was not born in that time. You and I were born into a world in which animals are deprived

---

[214]In this way misery is the "daughter of sin." B 2:410; 4:299.

[215]"The General Deliverance," B 2:438, proem 2.

[216]"The General Deliverance," B 2:44 2 – 5, sec. 2; cf. B 2:400, 428 – 29, 509; 4:285.

[217]"The General Deliverance," B 2:442 – 45, sec. 2.

of their original condition by the human fall. Intuitively, most animals know this and instinctively flee from humans. Fallen humanity is the common enemy of birds, beasts, fish, and plants. The hunting of animals is viewed as prima facie evidence of the fallenness of humanity. The human shark has become the prototype predator in this strangely deformed order.[218]

Wesley thought that a few domesticated animals have regained some capacity to refract their original disposition.[219] Even those "friendly creatures," the "generous horse," toward which Wesley had deep lifelong affection, "that serves his master's necessity or pleasure with unwearied diligence," and "the faithful dog, that waits the motion of his hand, or his eye" — they too suffer variously from the distortions of human freedom. Much of the rest of the animal world is filled with savagery and cruelty. They live by destroying each other. The human fall diminishes their original beauty and splendor. Though lacking the guilt and anxiety that characterize human freedom, they experience many other forms of bodily pain through human sin.[220]

The whole creation groans under the power of sin. It is groaning as if "in the pains of childbirth right up to the present time" (Rom. 8:22 NIV). Meanwhile we ourselves "groan inwardly" (v. 23 NIV), waiting eagerly for our adoption as children of God. We look toward the consummation of a process of redemption of our bodies that is begun but yet not complete. "In this hope we are saved" (v. 24 NIV).[221]

i. The General Deliverance and Brute Creation

Will brute creation always remain in its present condition? We can only imagine that, judged empirically, apart from God's promises, it always will remain as it now is. But on the basis of scriptural revelation, a general deliverance is promised for all creation. The animal creation is destined to be restored when and to the extent that human existence is restored to its original creation of imaging the moral goodness of God.[222]

Wesley was a different kind of ecologist who was trying to place ecological reflection in the context of the history of sin, the divine-human reconciliation, and the eschatological vision of general deliverance. There follows an extended, almost surreal, vision of what the restored creation will be like in its recovered beauty, liberty, true affections, and original vigor. His was not an argument for animal rights but rather an argument for eschatological theodicy that affects brute creation. The future of animal and plant life is seen in relation to the beginning and the end, especially the resurrection. The eschatological destiny of plant and animal life is contingent on the restoration of the fallen human will, which itself has caused the fallenness of plant and animal life.[223]

---

[218]"The General Deliverance," B 2:442–44, sec. 2.2–4.
[219]"The General Deliverance," B 2:442, sec. 2.2.
[220]"The General Deliverance," B 2:444, sec. 2.3.
[221]"The General Deliverance," B 2:445, sec. 3.1.
[222]"The General Deliverance," B 2:445, sec. 3.1.
[223]"The General Deliverance," B 2:444–48, sec. 3.

"Creation itself will be liberated from its bondage to decay" (Rom. 8:21 NIV). Paul was speaking here not only about the liberation of human history, but by it the liberation of the cosmos and all its creatures, which will be included and brought into the "glorious freedom of the children of God" (v. 21 NIV). The restoration of the freedom of the children of God will have spectacular influence on the cosmos itself.[224]

j. The Justice of God amid the Alienation of Creaturely Life

We are now called to understand our present ecological accountability within creation as a final accountability to which we will be called on the last day. God's mercy will finally extend over all God's works. God's justice continues in the midst of the alienation of creaturely life and will eventually work itself out.[225] Meanwhile, we are encouraged to be merciful as God is merciful.

The promise of general deliverance softens our hearts toward the little ones for whom the Lord cares. It enlarges our hearts toward those whom God does not forget. It reminds us that we are different from nonhuman creatures yet even in our differences akin to them, and we are given a mediating role in relation to them. It encourages us to hope, to look forward to the time of deliverance God has prepared.[226] Brute creation has something at stake in the future hope that is proclaimed in the gospel — to be delivered from its present bondage, and to share in the recovery of the glorious liberty of the children of God.[227] In the final redemption of humanity, God may raise brute creatures higher in their scale of being than was their primitive condition before the fall. If human consciousness in the glorious resurrection will rise to a new level of agility and spirituality like the angels, so may an analogous transmutation occur in animal life:[228] "May I be permitted to mention here a conjecture concerning the brute creation? What if it should please the all-wise, all-gracious Creator to raise them higher in the scale of beings" so that "something better remains after death for these poor creatures" — would not that nullify the objections to the lack of divine justice in the matter of animal pain?[229]

As God is in time turning the fall toward the final advantage of the whole creation, and not merely of human history, so in the general deliverance, he promises to enhance the glory of nonhuman creatures in a way that will transcend their original condition.[230] Here we have a wonderful vision of animals being blessed by the recovered holiness, happiness, and goodness of humanity, now by grace made more able to reflect the holiness and goodness of God. The original garden existence will be restored, in which there is no sorrow or pain or death, and where there is order, freedom, harmony, celebration, and incomparable beauty.[231]

---

[224]"The General Deliverance," B 2:445–47, sec. 3.1–5.
[225]"The General Deliverance," B 2:445–48, sec. 3.
[226]"The General Deliverance," B 2:447–49, sec. 3.5–8.
[227]"The General Deliverance," B 2:445, sec. 3.1, 2.
[228]"The General Deliverance," B 2:448, sec. 3.6.
[229]Ibid.
[230]Cf. "The Great Assize"; "God's Love to Fallen Man."
[231]"The General Deliverance," B 2:445–46, sec. 3.2, 3.

In this way, the doctrines of creation and eschaton become intimately tied together. Eschatology requires a universal vision of history. That essentially is what eschatology is, a panoramic view of universal history as seen from its end. It is an attempt to see present history in relation to the end of history, and the end in relation to its beginning. A Christian understanding of history from beginning to end is an eschatology.[232]

Further Reading on Theodicy

Bowmer, John. "John Wesley's Philosophy of Suffering." *LQHR* 184 (1959): 60–66.

Collins, Kenneth. *A Faithful Witness: John Wesley's Homiletical Theology*, 29–34. Wilmore, KY: Wesleyan Heritage, 1993.

Hubbartt, G. F. "The Theodicy of John Wesley." *AS* 12, no. 2 (1958): 15–18.

Miley, John. *Systematic Theology*. Reprint, Peabody, MA: Hendrickson, 1989.

Oord, Thomas Jay. "A Process Wesleyan Theodicy: Freedom, Embodiment, and the Almighty God." In *Thy Name and Nature Is Love: Wesleyan and Process Theologies in Dialogue*, edited by Bryan P. Stone and Thomas Jay Oord, 193–216. Nashville: Kingswood, 2001.

Pope, William Burt. *A Compendium of Christian Theology*. 3 vols. London: Wesleyan Methodist Book-Room, 1880.

Ralston, Thomas N. *Elements of Divinity*. New York: Abingdon, 1924.

Summers, Thomas O. *Systematic Theology*. 2 vols. Edited by J. J. Tigert. Nashville: Methodist Publishing House South, 1888.

Walls, Jerry. "The Free Will Defense: Calvinism, Wesley and the Goodness of God." *Christian Scholar's Review* 13 (1983): 19–33.

Watson, Richard. *Theological Institutes*. 2 vols. New York: Mason and Lane, 1836, 1840; edited by John M'Clintock, New York: Carlton & Porter, 1850.

---

[232]"Scriptural Christianity," B 1:169–72, sec. 3.

CHAPTER 7

Man

A. Human Existence: Created, Fallen, and Redeemed

The self cannot be understood as if abstracted out of that history in which selfhood is *given by God, fallen into sin, and redeemed by grace.* To understand my human existence, I must see my individual existence in relation to my social history, a history of sin.

Wesley's anthropology constantly returned to this threefold sociohistorical interpretation of human existence: created in the image of God, fallen by its own volition, restored and reclaimed by God's mercy. This is most tightly summarized in the language of the Articles of Religion and Doctrinal Minutes, and set forth more fully in selected teaching homilies, especially "The Image of God," "What Is Man?" (two discourses), "Heavenly Treasure in Earthen Vessels," "Human Life a Dream," "On the Deceitfulness of the Human Heart," "On the Fall of Man," "Spiritual Idolatry," and "The One Thing Needful." It is fully elaborated in Wesley's major extended theological treatise, *The Doctrine of Original Sin.*

1. The Anthropology of the Articles of Religion

a. Far Gone from Original Righteousness and Inclined to Evil Continually

What God gives in human nature is good as created but becomes distorted by intergenerational human decision into a condition of corporate wretchedness and misery. The seventh of the Twenty-Five Articles of Religion rejects the romantic optimism that holds to the Pelagian view of humanity (that it was by the moral example of Adam that distortions in consciousness came to be learned). The article sets forth the Pauline-Augustinian-Reformation teaching of sin, rejecting Pelagianism as not sufficiently attentive to the corporate and historical nature of sin, for "original sin standeth not in the following of Adam (as the Pelagians do vainly talk)."[1]

Biblical teaching holds that sin east of Eden "is the corruption of the nature of every man, that naturally is engendered of the offspring of Adam, whereby man is very far gone from original righteousness, and of his own [fallen] nature inclined to

---

[1]XXV, art. 7; cf. *LJW* 2:23; 4:158; 6:175.

evil, and that continually." Present human existence is far gone from that unblemished integrity. We do not merely stumble or fall inconsequentially, so we might voluntarily backtrack and correct it at any moment. That is not the way history works. Rather, it is as though humanity has already voluntarily fallen down a huge cliff and cannot get back up to the starting place, the Eden of original righteousness.[2]

This *fallen* creature is "of his own nature inclined to evil, and that continually." Insofar as human nature resists prevenient and sustaining grace, it is incessantly drawn by a persistent *yetzer hara* (inclination to evil), which is evidenced in the actual history of idolatry, pride, and sensuality so characteristic of human history. Later we will see how persistently Wesley emphasized prevenient grace as always working to redeem what has become fallen, but that is a doctrine of redeeming grace, not fallen human nature.

b. Human Nature as Created and Human Nature as Fallen

Note that Wesley, like Augustine and Calvin, used the term *human nature* dialectically in two different ways: human nature *as created* and human nature *as fallen*. The created nature of humanity is capable of reflecting the goodness of God but has become disastrously fallen into syndromes of sin that have become repeatedly reinforced by personal choice and passed on persistently from one generation to the next, through families, social structures, economic orders, and interpersonal relationships, and through each sinner's own individual free will. Evil has become invasive of the very nature of fallen humanity — unremitting, continuous, ubiquitous.

This is why sin is universal in human history. Sin has been transmitted to all descendants of Adam and Eve so as to become a kind of "second nature" to human progeny. The result is a disastrous practical impairment but not complete destruction of the original righteousness given in creation. The ravages of sin are manifested in the continuous proneness of the will to fall ever again into sin. This is an exceedingly serious conception of human fallenness. Human existence is alienated not only on the scale of the individual person but as a whole federal history, a sociohistorical type under the head, Adam.

2. Free Will after the Fall (Article 8)[3]

"The condition of man after the fall of Adam is such that he cannot turn and prepare himself by his own natural strength and good works to faith and calling upon God; wherefore we have no power to do good works, pleasant and acceptable to God, without the grace of God preventing us that we may have a good will, and working with us when we have that good will" (art. 8). Apart from grace, it is not possible not to sin (*non posse non peccare*) after the fall. Once caught in this intergenerational syndrome of sin, sinners as social creatures do not escape their determinants and consequences. By their own natural strength, there is no way to

---

[2]B 1:118, 495 – 96; cf. *CH* 7:213, 652, 691.
[3]Anglican article 10 became the eighth article of Wesley's twenty-four.

happiness in the absence of grace-enabled faith, hope, and love. The human spirit is entangled in a maze of self-deceptions.

The resultant impairment: we are unable to change ourselves, to reverse our fallen trajectory; hence when considered apart from grace, "There is no one who does good, not even one" (Rom. 3:12 NIV, from Ps. 53:1).[4]

Fallen men and women cannot turn to repent without grace preceding them. There is no way to get back to the original condition of righteousness by dint of our own earnest moral calisthenics or social enterprise or political fortitude. Whatever natural strength we might seem to have had to do good works has become radically blemished, unable to call on God, execute or even properly envision a good work. There is no way for sinners to achieve a good will or sustain it without grace preceding.

Only on these terms (grace-enabled faith active in love) may sinners will that which is good and pleasing to God. Insofar as sinners have a good will, it emerges only through cooperation with divine grace moving ahead of them, with and through their fallen freedom.

> Supposing a man to be now void of faith and hope and love, he cannot effect any degree of them in himself by any possible exertion of his understanding and of any or all his other natural faculties, though he should enjoy them in their utmost perfection. A distinct power from God, not implied in any of these, is indispensably necessary before it is possible he should arrive at the very lowest degree of Christian faith or hope or love.... He must be created anew.[5]

B. The Image of God

1. In His Own Image

The text of the homily "The Image of God" is Genesis 1:27: "God created man in his own image" [Homily #141 (1730), B 4:290–303 (not in the Jackson edition)].

If made in the image of God, "whence flow those numberless imperfections that stain and dishonor" human nature? Human beings are so prone to sickness, pain, ignorance, and unruly passions that it may seem far more plausible to many to think they are at times rather made in the image of animal or demonic creation.[6]

"'God created man upright; in the image of God created he him; but man found out to himself many inventions.' Abusing the liberty wherewith he was endowed, he rebelled against his Creator, and willfully changed the image of the incorruptible God into sin, misery, and corruption."[7]

---

[4]Wesleyan anthropological assumptions are rehearsed pithily in the article of the E. U. B. Confession that says humanity is "fallen from righteousness and, apart from the grace of our Lord Jesus Christ, is destitute of holiness and inclined to evil. Except a man be born again he cannot see the kingdom of God. In his own strength without divine grace man cannot do good works pleasing and acceptable to God. We believe however that man influenced and empowered by the Holy Spirit is responsible in freedom to exercise his will for good."

[5]Letter to John Smith, June 25, 1746, *LJW* 2:71.

[6]"The Image of God," B 4:292, proem 1–3.

[7]"The Image of God," B 4:293, proem 4, conflating Gen. 1:27 and Eccl. 7:29; B 4:294–303; 11:269.

a. Whether Humanity Was Originally Made Righteous in the Image of God

Human beings were originally made in the image of God, able to distinguish truth from falsehood, able to perceive things as they were, able to judge justly and swiftly, able to name things congruently with sufficient *understanding*, "not arbitrarily, but expressive of their inward natures." In these ways they resembled and refracted God's own wisdom and justice.[8]

Along with clear understanding, human beings were originally given "a *will* equally perfect" so long as it "followed the dictates of such an understanding." Hence all the *affections* of man and woman, under the conditions of original righteousness, were rationally ordered around a single affection: love. "Love filled the whole expansion of [man's] soul; it possessed him without a rival. Every movement of his heart was love."[9]

"What made his image yet plainer in his human offspring" was "the liberty he originally enjoyed; the perfect *freedom* implanted in his nature, and interwoven with all its parts." He could either "keep or change his first estate: it was left to himself what he would do; his own choice was to determine him in all things. The balance did not incline to one side or the other unless by his own deed."[10]

As a result of an "unerring understanding, an uncorrupt will, and perfect freedom," human beings were *happy*, for their "understanding was satisfied with truth," their will with good, and they were "at full liberty to enjoy either the Creator or the creation; to indulge in rivers of pleasure, ever new, ever pure from any mixture of pain."[11]

b. A Conjecture on How the Death of Original Righteousness Occurred Gradually as through Heart Disease

"The liberty of man necessarily required that he should have some trial, else he would have had no choice." The tree of knowledge of good and evil was prohibited. The consequence of eating from it was clearly stated: "You will certainly die" (Gen. 2:17 NIV). "Yet man did eat of it, and the consequence accordingly was death to him and his descendants, and preparatory to death, sickness and pain, folly, vice, and slavery."[12]

Wesley offered a specific conjecture on the transition of the psychosomatic interface from its original to its fallen condition. As "compound of matter and spirit," it was ordained that "neither part of the compound should act at all but together with its companion." The body had been prepared for immortality, with the vessels containing the bodily juices "ever clear and open." By merely eating of the

---

[8]"The Image of God," B 4:293–94, sec. 1.1; cf. "Justification by Faith," B 1:184, sec. 1.1. On humanity as originally "capable of God," see B 2:439–41, 448–49.

[9]"The Image of God," B 4:294–95, sec. 1.2.

[10]"The Image of God," B 4:295, sec. 1.3, italics added.

[11]"The Image of God," B 4:295, sec. 1.4, italics added.

[12]"The Image of God," B 4:296, sec. 2; "Justification by Faith," B 1:185, sec. 1.5.

forbidden fruit of "whose deadly nature [man] was forewarned seems to have contained a juice, the particles of which were apt to cleave to whatever they touched." Entering the body, they were prone to "adhere to the inner coats of the finer vessels, to which again other particles that before floated loose in the blood, continually joining, would naturally lay a foundation for numberless disorders." Every day they "lose something of their spring.... The smaller channels would gradually fill up," leading to death.[13] Deadly lipid buildup in arterial vessels causing heart disease were here being intuitively described with considerable accuracy. The arterial disease that Adam and Eve got from the forbidden fruit, slow in coming, could have been avoided.

c. The Consequences of the Fall for Human Understanding, Will, Liberty, and Happiness

With the psychosomatic "instrument being now quite untuned," four consequences of the fall ensued:

1. The *understanding* "mistook falsehood for truth," perceiving as if "through a glass darkly," followed by doubt, error, confusion and slowness, now "unable to trace out fully" the nature of things once understood so well.[14]
2. The *will*, its guide blinded, became "*now* seized by legions of vile affections. Grief and anger and hatred and fear and shame, at once rushed in upon it.... Nay, love itself, that ray of the Godhead, that balm of life, now became a torment. Its light being gone, it wandered about seeking rest and finding none; till at length" it resorted to "the guilded poison of earthly enjoyments."[15]
3. *Liberty* "went away with virtue." "The subject of virtue became the slave of vice."[16]
4. "The consequence of ... being enslaved to a depraved understanding and a corrupted will could be not other than the reverse of that *happiness* which flowed from them when in their perfection." Thus it was "not the good God, but man himself made man what he is now."[17]

2. Whether the Image of God May Be Recovered

Human *understanding* must be brought by humility to repentance, true self-knowledge, and faith. The will then must be redirected by the renewed understanding toward charity, "to collect the scattered beams of that affection which is truly human, truly divine," forgiving as we have been forgiven. By being restored "first to knowledge, and then to virtue," we are delivered to "*freedom* and *happiness* ... that liberty which not only implies the absence of all pain, unless what is necessary to future pleasure, but such a measure of present happiness as is a fit introduction to

---

[13]"The Image of God," B 4:296–97, sec. 1.1.
[14]"The Image of God," B 4:298, sec. 2.2.
[15]"The Image of God," B 4:298, sec. 2.3.
[16]"The Image of God," B 4:298–99, sec. 2.4.
[17]"The Image of God," B 4:299, sec. 2.5; for further reference to the consequences of the fall, see B 1:185–87; 2:189–90, 400–412, 467–68, 476–77, 508–9; 4:162–63, 295–99; *LJW* 3:340, 373.

that which flows at God's right hand for evermore!"[18] This restoration is available to all who will gladly receive the means of grace.[19]

a. The One Thing Needful: The Restoration of the Fallen Image

The text of the homily "The One Thing Needful" is Luke 10:42: "One thing is needful" [Homily #146 (1734), B 4:351 – 59 (not in the Jackson edition)].

Though humanity was created in the image of God, sin has profoundly effaced that image, as evidenced by the loss of freedom, now so bound by "heavy chains" of "vile affections" that it is not possible even to "lift up an eye, a thought to heaven." "The whole head is sick, and the whole heart faint" (Isa. 1:5).[20]

The one thing needful: "to recover our first estate ... to be born again, to be formed anew after the likeness of our Creator ... to re-exchange the image of Satan for the image of God, bondage for freedom, sickness for health ... to regain our native freedom."[21] This is "our one great business ... the one work we have to do."

b. The One End of Our Creation and Redemption

"The one end of our creation" is that we might love God supremely and all things in God, for *love* is perfect freedom, the very image of God. "Love is the health of the soul, the full exertion of all its powers, the perfection of all its faculties."[22]

The one end of our redemption is that we be restored to health and freedom, that every spiritual sickness of our nature might be healed. This is the purpose of the incarnation, life, death, and resurrection of Christ: to proclaim liberty to captives, to enjoin what is necessary for our recovery and reform what is obstructive of it.[23]

The one end of all God's providential dispensations is "solely our sanctification; our recovery from that vile bondage, the love of his creatures, to the free love of our Creator."[24]

The one end of the operations of the Spirit in us is to do this one thing needful, "to restore us to health, to liberty, to holiness."[25]

C. What Is Man? Two Discourses

1. Man in Space, Man in Time (First Discourse)

a. Of the Finite Magnitude of Human Existence in the Universe as Viewed Physically

The text of the first discourse on "What Is Man?" is Psalm 8:3, 4: "What is man?" [Homily #103 (1787), B 3:454 – 63; J #103, VII:167 – 74]. Wesley placed human life within the universe of space and the fleeting nature of time.

---

[18]"The Image of God," B 4:299 – 300, sec. 3.1 – 3.
[19]B 2:482 – 83; 4:299 – 301, 354 – 55.
[20]"The One Thing Needful," B 4:354, sec. 1.3; Isa. 1:5.
[21]"The One Thing Needful," B 4:355, sec. 1.5; cf. 2:483.
[22]"The One Thing Needful," B 4:355, sec. 2.1, 2, italics added.
[23]"The One Thing Needful," B 4:356, sec. 2.3.
[24]"The One Thing Needful," B 4:356 – 57, sec. 3.4.
[25]"The One Thing Needful," B 4:357, sec. 2.5.

Wesley sought to view the stature of moral, corporeal, rational creatures in comparison to the whole cosmos and eternity. However important human life is to us, when temporally and physically viewed, it takes up only a small speck of space and a fleeting streak of time in an immense cosmos.

The location of human existence within time and space in this vast universe was being more adequately understood in Wesley's experimentally oriented century than before. "What is the space of the whole creation, what is all finite space that is, or can be conceived, in comparison of infinity?"[26] Reason, when taken alone, suggests "that so diminutive a creature would be overlooked" by the "One that inhabiteth eternity," especially when we consider duration.[27]

b. The Duration of Human Existence in the Universe as Viewed Temporally

As to duration, humans at best may live about fourscore years, but what does that add up to against the actual cosmic scale? The brevity of human life is viewed by Wesley not merely in relation to prehistoric time but more so in relation to the infinite duration of eternity. So he took as his text "When I look at your heavens, the work of your fingers, the moon and the stars that you have established; what are human beings that you are mindful of them, mortals that you care for them? Yet you have made them a little lower than God, and crowned them with glory and honor. You have given them dominion over the works of your hands" (Ps. 8:3–6 NRSV).

From Cyprian, Wesley refashioned this comparison: "Suppose there was a ball of sand as large as the globe of earth, and suppose one grain of this were to be annihilated in a thousand years; yet that whole space of time where this ball would be annihilating ... would bear ... infinitely less proportion to eternity, than a single grain of sand would bear to that whole mass."[28] Augustine marveled that sinful humanity is allotted any portion at all of space and time. Even when viewed against the immensity of creation, "so small a portion" it is.[29]

2. On the Greatness of the Human Soul within Space and Time

So small and brief is human life that it may seem inconsequential. Viewed materialistically, this can only lead the most glorious of all creatures to despair over the human condition.[30]

Only when humanity is beheld in relation to God, who cares infinitely for sinners, does the true greatness of the human appear.[31] The value of even a single soul is so great that it exceeds the whole of the material order. "The body is not the man," who is "not only a house of clay, but ... an incorruptible picture of the God of glory, a spirit that is of infinitely more value than the whole earth, or more value than the

---

[26]"What Is Man?" Ps. 8:3, 4, B 3:457, sec. 1.6.

[27]"What Is Man?" Ps. 8:3, 4, B 3:458, sec. 1.7; Isa. 57:15.

[28]"What Is Man?" Ps. 8:3, 4, B 3:458, sec. 2.3.

[29]*Confessions*, 1.1, 3:459n.

[30]"What Is Man?" Ps. 8:3, 4, B 3:459–60, sec. 2.4–5.

[31]B 2:284, 289–90, 382; 4:22–25, 30–31, 292, 298.

sun, moon, and stars, put together, yea, than the whole material creation," since "not liable either to dissolution or decay."[32] That is intended not to be a diminution of matter but an exaltation of the true value of the soul,[33] of every individual soul to whom God's mercy is graciously offered in Jesus Christ, to whom the good news of God's coming is continuously addressed. That which makes the body alive is valuable beyond compare, because God acts graciously first to offer life, then to justify the life of the sinner when fallen, and finally to sanctify the life of the justified. The living soul of the human person is of a higher order than physical creation, and more durable.[34]

So humanity is a subject of intense interest to God.[35] To eliminate any remaining shadow of fear, God gave his Son to suffer death on the cross "for us ... and for our salvation."[36]

3. Suppose There Were Other Worlds

Wesley approached again the puzzling question of the possible plurality of inhabited worlds, "a favorite notion with all those who deny the Christian Revelation," because it seems to afford them a plausible critique of divine justice.[37] In his time, whether other worlds might exist in the cosmic expanse and how that might affect Christian testimony was being debated. One leading speculator, Christian Huygens, hypothesized that the moon might be populated, and maybe other unknown worlds in the cosmos existed. But even Huygens, "before he died, doubted of this whole hypothesis."[38]

Resisting the temptation to speculate on matters about which little evidence was available, Wesley argued from the key theological premise that the creation is one creation of the one God, leaving it as a matter of empirical inquiry as to whether other unknown spaces within creation exist or are populated. It would be as easy for God to "create thousands or millions of worlds as one."[39] Whether one or many, the same comparison prevails; the whole of human history is infinitely shorter in time than eternity and of less magnitude in space than infinity.[40]

4. I Find Something in Me That Thinks (Second Discourse)

a. The Human Composite of Body and Soul

The second discourse on "What Is Man?" continues with the same text: Psalm 8:4: "What is man?" [Homily #116 (1788), B 4:19 – 27; J #109, VII:225 – 30].

I am doubtless "a curious machine, 'fearfully and wonderfully made,'" but there

---

[32]"What Is Man?" Ps. 8:3, 4, B 3:460, sec. 2.5.
[33]B 2:284, 289 – 90, 382; 4:22 – 25, 30 – 31, 292, 298.
[34]Cf. Augustine, "On the Greatness of the Soul"; Thomas Aquinas, "On the Soul."
[35]"What Is Man?" Ps. 8:3, 4, B 3:460 – 61, sec. 2.5 – 8.
[36]BCP, Communion, Nicene Creed.
[37]"What Is Man?" Ps. 8:3, 4, B 3:461, sec. 2.9.
[38]"What Is Man?" Ps. 8:3, 4, B 3:462, sec. 2.11.
[39]"What Is Man?" Ps. 8:3, 4, B 3:462, sec. 2.12.
[40]"What Is Man?" Ps. 8:3, 4, B 3:461 – 63, sec. 2.8 – 14.

is far more to me.[41] There is no denying that "the human body is composed of all the four elements [air, earth, fire, water] duly proportioned and mixed together … whence flows the animal heat."[42] But "Who am I?" goes beyond the reductionist explanations. All such reductionisms fail to understand the relation of soul and body, by reducing soul to body. Such attempts were constantly emergent in the tradition of British empiricism (as represented by the traditions following Hobbes and Hume).[43]

Thus, when we seriously ask anew the ancient psalmist's question — "Who am I?" or "What is man?" (Ps. 8:4), or what is the constitutional nature of human existence? — the inquiry remains perennially pertinent amid the continuing challenges of reductive naturalism and materialism.

So what am I besides mud and bones? Wesley said, "*I find something in me that thinks*; which neither earth, water, air, fire, nor any mixture of them, can possibly do," and something that perceives objects by the senses,[44] "forms inward ideas of them. It *judges* concerning them,… *reasons*,… reflects upon its own operations,… endued with imagination and memory."[45] My passions and affections are "diversified a thousand ways. And they seem to be the only spring of action in that inward principle I call the soul."[46]

b. On Human Liberty

The human self, having *liberty*, is capable of determining itself freely within the constraints of natural causality, according to its perceived good. We are capable of using our freedom to determine ourselves responsively or nonresponsively in relation to the grace offered. We are not flatly determined by external circumstances.[47] The soul is free, hence capable of shaping itself in response to different contingencies.[48] Human liberty has both the power of choosing either to do or not to do (liberty of contradiction) or to do this or the contrary (liberty of contrariety).[49] Contrariety is the ability to choose, whereas contradiction is the ability to act on that choice or to refrain from the exercise of choice.[50]

The purpose of human life is to love and enjoy God and serve the Creator through the full use of our redeemed powers. The human problem is that we have rebelled against this intended way of ordering our lives. The felicity for which

---

[41]"What Is Man?" Ps. 8:4, B 4:20, sec. 1; cf. 3:9, 24; LJW 3:336.

[42]"What Is Man?" Ps. 8:4, B 4:20, sec. 2.

[43]B 4:29 – 30, 49 – 51, 200; 11:56 – 57.

[44]B 1:409; 2:285, 288 – 89, 294; 4:21; on animal senses, see B 2:394 – 95.

[45]"What Is Man?" Ps. 8:4, B 4:21, sec. 5, italics added.

[46]"What Is Man?" Ps. 8:4, B 4:22, sec. 7.

[47]On chance, see LJW 1:103; 6:339; 7:45.

[48]"The General Spread of the Gospel," B 2:488 – 90, secs. 9 – 12.

[49]TUN, J X:468 – 69, sec. 3.9; cf. B 1:130n, 576n. "I am full as certain of this, that I am free … to speak or not … to do this or the contrary, as I am of my own existence. I have not only what is termed a 'liberty of contradiction' — a power to do or not to do; but what is termed, a 'liberty of contrariety,' — a power to act one way, or the contrary." "What Is Man?" Ps. 8:4, B 4:24, sec. 11; see also "The End of Christ's Coming," sec. 1.4 – 5; and TUN, sec. 3.9.

[50]"What Is Man?" B 4:24, sec. 11; cf. "The End of Christ's Coming," sec. 1.4, 5; TUN, sec. 3.9.

our lives are fashioned is thwarted by our own freedom, intergenerationally and socially conceived. We humans are an unhappy lot as long as the purpose of our lives remains obstructed and unfulfilled. The way to happiness is holiness, whereby we are enabled again to reflect God's image as holy.[51]

c. The Psychosomatic Interface

Human existence is characterized by a continuing dialectical struggle between this earthly natural body and the living self's capacity for reason, conscience, and imagination. This is what we mean by the body-soul composite.[52] Soul enlivens body, awakens body to life, transcends sheer corporeality. Soul is not dependent on body for its life; rather, body is dependent on soul for its life. Body and soul are intimately united in human freedom, each affecting the other so profoundly and constantly that sickness can at times be brought on through demoralization. Acts of spiritual insight, courage, and will can overcome some forms of illness. The body, lacking soul, has no capacity for self-motion.[53]

From the enlivening Spirit, "the source of all the motion in the universe," the soul has "an inward principle of motion, whereby it governs at pleasure every part of the body," excepting those involuntary motions "absolutely needful for the continuance of life," such as blood circulation, inhaling, and exhaling. "Were it otherwise, grievous inconveniences might follow," such as losing one's life through inattention.[54]

That "*I* am something distinct from my body," is evident from the fact that "when my body dies, I shall not die."[55] Though human existence is rooted in the body and nature, it is yet capable of transcending that rootedness by reason, imagination, and consciousness. Death is the separation of soul and body, in which the body dies and the soul lives on. Only God knows precisely when death occurs, but in general terms death occurs when life (*psuche*, "soul") leaves the body.[56] In the resurrection, the unity of soul and body is recovered in its intrinsic psychosomatic interface in a glorified body.

For one end only is life given to the body: to prepare for eternity. "You were born for nothing else ... you were not created to please your senses," but "by seeking and finding happiness in God on earth, to secure the glory of God in heaven."[57]

5. Human Life a Dream

The text of the homily "Human Life a Dream" is Psalm 73:20: "As a dream when one awaketh, so, O Lord, when thou awakest, thou shalt despise their image" [Homily #124 (1789), B 4:108 – 19; J #124, VII:318 – 25].

---

[51]"What Is Man?" Ps. 8:4, B 4:24, sec. 11.

[52]B 4:279 – 83; cf. 2:129 – 34, 382 – 83, 405 – 6, 438 – 39.

[53]*TJW*, 177 – 79.

[54]"What Is Man?" Ps. 8:4, B 4:22 – 23, secs. 8, 9.

[55]"What Is Man?" Ps. 8:4, B 4:23, sec. 10.

[56]Whether this occurs precisely at the point of the ending of respiration, or circulation of blood, or rigor mortis, we cannot say. "What Is Man?" Ps. 8:4, B 4:23 – 25, secs. 10 – 12.

[57]"What Is Man?" Ps. 8:4, B 4:26, sec. 15.

a. Dream Life and Real Life

This homily springs out of a single penetrating metaphor — the relation of dream life and real life. Temporal life is like a dream. When I wake up, what I was dreaming about is not there anymore. It has vanished. The analogy is between the transiency of life and the durability of eternity. Real life is eternal. Human life is like a dream in relation to the eternal. It is ephemeral, passing. The life that awaits is everlasting.[58]

As long as the psalmist meditated on the "prosperity of the wicked" (Ps. 73:3 NRSV), the arrogant scoffers whose "hearts overflow with follies" (v. 7 NRSV), he was wearied by this thought of the temporality of creatures — that is, he said, "until I went into the sanctuary of God; then I perceived their end. Truly you set them in slippery places; you make them fall to ruin" (vv. 17 – 18 NRSV). For they can be swept away in a moment. "They are like a dream when one awakes; on awaking you despise their phantoms" (v. 20 NRSV).[59] The psalmist's thoughts show "how near a resemblance there is between human life and a dream."[60]

b. The Ephemeral Quality of Dreaming

Wesley offered some intriguing observations on the origin of dreams.[61] Few human phenomena are more mysterious. Whence come dreams? From diverse strata of causal determinants: through the body and physical condition; through the recollected passions of the previous day; perhaps even through incorporeal spiritual powers that should not be ruled out as having a potential effect on the shaping of dreams.[62] Though God may at times speak through dreams, we are always susceptible to misjudge God's address in dreams, instances of which are abundantly attested in Scripture.[63]

The more interesting question is whether we can know we are dreaming while still in the dream state. Rather, the dream is best recognized only in relation to the contextual real life in which it is occurring. "It is a kind of parenthesis, inserted in life, as that is in a discourse, which goes on equally well either with it or without it." By this we may know a dream: "by its being broken off at both ends," by its radical contingency in relation with the real things that flow before and after.[64]

God, who sees everything in simultaneity, sees creation in something like the manner in which we see in a dream, with many things happening simultaneously, not merely linearly but all at once. The dream thus signals some remnant of the eternal in human life. Wesley was here comparing dreaming to time not eternity,

---

[58]"Human Life a Dream," B 4:109 – 10, secs. 1 – 2; cf. *CH* 7:398.

[59]"Human Life a Dream," B 4:109 – 10, sec. 1.

[60]"Human Life a Dream," B 4:110, sec. 2.

[61]See also B 2:54, 130, 289, 577; 4:108 – 19; 11:496 – 97.

[62]Cf. *JJW* 4:229 – 30; 6:495 – 96.

[63]"Human Life a Dream," B 4:110 – 11, secs. 3 – 5. Dreams are "not simply to be relied upon without corroborating evidences." *JJW* 2:226.

[64]"Human Life a Dream," B 4:111, sec. 5.

but even dreaming holds some affinity to eternity in the sense that it is a fleeting reflection of eternity still existing within the conditions of the history of sin.[65]

c. The Resemblance of Human Life to a Protracted Illusion

Wesley's real interest was in neither the origin nor the interpretation of dreams, but on the dream as an archetype of illusion, and human life in this fallen world as a protracted illusion.[66] Though this may sound at first as if it resonates with the Eastern religions' view of *maya* (illusion), Wesley's stronger motive was present awakening, while time remains, to the decisive conditions of this worldly reality, so as to be prepared for eternity.[67]

A dream is a condition in which imagined events are presented to our minds in sleep but have no palpable being except in the imagination. The dream state is a fantasy, a play with the energies of human experiences. Precisely that ephemeral —as passing as a dream—is temporal life compared to eternity.

We awaken from temporal life into eternity.[68] The resemblance is between the fleeting nature of the dream and the infinite continuation of eternal life.[69] In such an awakening, we would perceive our old lives and world with entirely new eyes. We have no more to do with those poor transient shadows. Now we see, hear, and feel but without that body of clay. Now we are all eyes, all ears, all perception.[70] In this new world of spiritual realities in eternity, the matters of this visible world would not be taken with absolute seriousness or finality.[71] Wesley was not demeaning the value of current life in this analogy but elevating it by placing it in its eternal context.

d. Dream and Reality: An Analogy between Temporality and Eternity

The vital question: Where would you stand if your "dream of life" were to end now unexpectedly? How would you value your earthly treasures and accomplishments? To know real eternal life is far more consequential than to be great in the eyes of the world while spiritually dead.[72] Will our affections be so turned to those things above that when we awake from the dream of earthly life, we will relish life in the light of God? Or will our affections be so fixated on those transitory shadows of this dream life that when we awake we will want to flee the light of heaven? How different will be the awakening of those who yearned for eternity as opposed to those who yearn now for earthly things.[73]

At some point, each of us must awaken from dream life to real life, from temporality to eternity. Religion provides the foundation and means for correlating these two worlds and lives: temporal and eternal. The good news that God is with

---

[65]"The General Deliverance," B 2:436 – 50.
[66]"Human Life a Dream," intro., B 4:109.
[67]B 4:112 – 18.
[68]*JJW* 1:245; 5:68, 229.
[69]"Human Life a Dream," B 4:112, secs. 6 – 7.
[70]"Human Life a Dream," B 4:112 – 13, sec. 7.
[71]"Human Life a Dream," B 4:113, sec. 8.
[72]"Human Life a Dream," B 4:113 – 15, secs. 9 – 10.
[73]"Human Life a Dream," B 4:115 – 17, secs. 12 – 13.

us brings eternal life already into the sphere of temporality in the incarnate Lord.[74] We retain a constant sense of the connection between heaven and earth when we remember that our present lives are comparatively but a dream and that soon we will awake to real life.[75] The homily ends with a fervent plea to take time seriously, hence this life seriously, in relation to eternal life. For the dream of corporeal life will be over soon. Perhaps tonight your soul may be required of you.

6. Heavenly Treasure in Earthen Vessels

The text of the homily "Heavenly Treasure in Earthen Vessels" is 2 Corinthians 4:7: "We have this treasure in earthen vessels" [Homily #129 (1790), B 4:161 – 67; J #124, VII:344 – 48].

a. Man as a Riddle to Himself

Man has long been a "riddle to himself," a vexing mixture of "nobleness and baseness." The deeper our self-exploration proceeds, the more mysterious we may become to ourselves.[76]

The biblical account is clarifying: the reason for human greatness is that humanity is made in the image of God; the reason for human baseness is that freedom has fallen. By juxtaposing the creation with the fall of humanity, "the greatness and littleness, the dignity and baseness, the happiness and misery, of [man's] present state, are no longer a mystery, but clear consequences of his original state and his rebellion against God. This is the key that opens the whole mystery, that removes all the difficulty," by showing the difference between what God originally made and "what man has made himself."[77]

Though fallen into a dismal history of sin and rebellion against God, the human self is being made capable by grace of reflecting to a greater or lesser extent the image of God. This is the mystery of human existence, its grandeur and misery, its glory and shame. This is the wonderful *compositum* of *humanum* — the human capacity for reflecting the goodness of God precisely while rooted in the natural causality and time, and prone to sin. This is what we are made up of, a tautly nuanced conflation of opposites, a blend of God's grace working within distorted human freedom — made in the image of God yet fallen into a history of sin. I not only have a body but more so am a body, subject to the vicissitudes of history.[78]

b. The Treasure We Now Have

Paul provided the prevailing metaphor for grasping this compositum of opposites: "We have this treasure in jars of clay to show that this all-surpassing power is from God and not from us" (2 Cor. 4:7 NIV). The "we" is first considered as "all humanity" and then as those born anew through saving faith.

---

[74]"Human Life a Dream," B 4:117 – 18, secs. 14 – 16.
[75]"Human Life a Dream," B 4:118 – 19, secs. 16 – 18.
[76]"Heavenly Treasure in Earthen Vessels," B 4:162, proem 1.
[77]"Heavenly Treasure in Earthen Vessels," B 4:162 – 63, proem 2, 3; 2:188 – 89, 540 – 41; 4:293 – 95.
[78]"Heavenly Treasure in Earthen Vessels," B 4:163, sec. 1.1.

The treasure in which all humanity now already shares is the "remains of the image of God": first, the treasure of *liberty*, a spiritual nature with free will, characterized by understanding, liberty, self-moving, and self-governing power;[79] and second, the treasure of a *natural conscience* able roughly to discern between good and evil. Conscience, that form of consciousness that accuses and excuses us, bears testimony to the splintered image of God in us, even though forever being diluted and distorted by willed sin and quasi-conscious self-deception. These treasures of liberty and conscience are found among all, including theists, nontheists, Muslims, pagans, and "the vilest of savages."[80] They indicate the remnant of the divine image still remaining even amid fallen human history. "Such treasure have all the children of men, more or less, even when they do not yet know God."[81]

The treasure that Christian believers have received is the fullness of *justification by faith*, whereby believers are born anew from above. The love of God is shed abroad in their hearts. In them is being renewed the whole image of God, not merely a remnant.[82] They have faith in God's working in them, "a peace which sets them above the fear of death," a "hope full of immortality."[83] The treasure of the reborn is God the Son forming in them — a spiritual nature capable of refracting divine goodness, always placed within natural causal determinants, yet graciously made capable of attesting God in time.

c. In Earthen Vessels

We have this treasure in earthen vessels. We are mortal, corruptible, and in fact corrupted as an entire human history.[84] We are capable of taking this treasure and grossly distorting it. The treasure is lodged within brittle, vulnerable bodies subject to sickness, error, and death. Not only is the body debased and depraved, but the mind, by which the direction of the soul is guided, is also disordered toward error "in ten thousand shapes."[85]

God permits such a treasure still to be lodged in such poor earthen vessels "to show that this all-surpassing power is from God and not from us" (2 Cor. 4:7 NIV).[86] The main design of God is to keep these temporal, bodily vessels humble, so that whatever comes — limitation, weakness, affliction — we shall by our weakness learn where our strength lies.[87]

---

[79]*LJW* 7:16.

[80]"Heavenly Treasure in Earthen Vessels," B 4:163, sec. 1.1, 2. When Wesley spoke of the honesty of the heathen (B 1:131–32, 135, 669), their proximate justice (B 1:500–501, 655–56), their sincerity (B 1:263, 307), and their structures of morality (B 1:488–89; 2:66–67, 472–73; 3:199–200), and of preparatory virtues of refined heathen (*LJW* 8:219), he was assuming the crucial premises of liberty and conscience as preparation for the gospel.

[81]"Heavenly Treasure in Earthen Vessels," B 4:163, sec. 1.1, 2.

[82]"Heavenly Treasure in Earthen Vessels," B 4:163–64, sec. 1.2, 3.

[83]"Heavenly Treasure in Earthen Vessels," B 4:164, sec. 1.3.

[84]B 1:177–78; 2:406–8; 3:195–96, 456–60.

[85]"Heavenly Treasure in Earthen Vessels," B 4:164–66, sec. 2.1, 2; on total depravity see "The Righteousness of Faith," sec. 1.4–6, cf. *SS* 1:141n; *LJW* 5:231.

[86]"Heavenly Treasure in Earthen Vessels," B 4:166–67, sec. 2.4.

[87]"Heavenly Treasure in Earthen Vessels," B 4:166–67, sec. 2.4–7.

Human reason, will, and memory, however distorted, remain a transcript of the triune God:

> You, whom he ordained to be Transcripts of the Trinity…
> You, of reason's powers possessed,
> You, with will and memory blest:
> You, with finer sense endued,
> Creatures capable of God;
> Noblest of his creatures, why,
> Why will you for ever die?[88]
> And when we rise in love renewed, our souls resemble thee,
> An image of the triune God to all eternity.[89]

7. Countering the Overreach of Natural Science

a. On Necessity

Wesley discusses the idea of necessity in two essays: "Thoughts upon Necessity" [J X:457–74] and "A Thought on Necessity" [J X:474–80]. Wesley was especially interested in the analogies between pseudoreligious monergistic reductionisms, such as absolute double predestination, and pseudoscientific materialistic monergisms, such as those of David Hartley and Lord Karnes — people who in Wesley's day were saying what the B. F. Skinners and Bertrand Russells have asserted in our time.

Wesley could not believe "the noblest creature in the visible world to be only a fine piece of clock work." Rather, the human person is a free agent, "self-determined in action," not determined by another. Adam's prototypical sin was to plead coercion by another: "It is true, I did eat; but the cause of my eating, the spring of my action, was in another."[90]

b. Types of Naturalistic Reductionism: Ancient, Scientific, and Religious

Among leading ancient theories of necessity were the Manichaeans, who made a whole dualistic system of such a denial, and the Stoics, who saw human action fatefully bound up in an indissoluble chain of causes and effects.[91] David Hartley argued that all our thoughts depend on vibrations in the brain, from which proceed reflections, passions, dispositions, and actions.[92] If so, all behavior would then be determined by causes external to the self. Even virtues and vices are hypothesized as being caused by vibrations of the brain.[93]

Similarly, Lord Karnes described the universe as an immense machine, an amazing piece of clockwork consisting of innumerable wheels fitly framed, into which are

---

[88]*CH* 7:88, cf. 390, 395, 527.
[89]*CH* 7:390.
[90]TUN, J X:457, sec. 1.1.
[91]TUN, J X:457, sec. 1.2; cf. B 1:76n, 386n; 2:130n, 285n; 3:493n.
[92]David Hartley, *Observations on Man* (London: S. Richardson, 1749).
[93]"A Thought on Necessity," J X:474–75.

squeezed human beings. People think they are free but are not.[94] Amid all supposed "rational" schemes, reason itself remains impotent as it considers free will.[95]

Predestinarians are partly responsible for setting a disastrous pattern for scientific inquiry in their assertion that "whatever happens in time was unchangeably determined from all eternity.... The greatest and the smallest events were equally predetermined.... It follows that no man can do either more or less good, or more or less evil, than he does."[96] Wesley sought to refute both scientific and religious determinisms.

c. Countering Naturalistic Reductionism

If people were governed by materialistic causes wholly external to themselves (whether physical, psychological, sociological, or economic), then there could be no moral good or evil, no virtue or vice, hence no judgment to come, contrary to the biblical view of human accountability.[97] Absurdities necessarily follow from the scheme of necessity.

"It is not easy for a man of common understanding ... to unravel these finely woven schemes.... But he knows, he feels, he is certain, they cannot be true; that the holy God cannot be the author of sin."[98] Even Hartley admitted that "upon this scheme, all the moral constitution of our nature is overturned ... man is no longer a moral agent."[99] With human freedom misplaced, human dignity is lost.[100]

Wesley said, "If I cannot believe what I feel in myself, namely, that it depends on me, and no other being, whether I shall now open or shut my eyes, move my head hither and thither, or stretch my hand or my foot, if I am necessitated to do all this, contrary to the whole both of my inward and outward sense, I can believe nothing else, but must necessarily sink into universal skepticism."[101]

Jonathan Edwards seems to have found a way to maintain both necessity and moral culpability. Yet "Edwards' whole mistake," in Wesley's view, was that the will on this "supposition, is irresistibly impelled; so that [people] cannot help willing thus or thus. If so, they are no more blamable for that will than for the actions which follow it. There is no blame if they are under a necessity of willing. There can be no moral good or evil, unless they have liberty as well as will."[102]

Against naturalistic determinisms, Wesley argued that people can resist their motives at times, even when they want to proceed with an action. It is not the case that "choice must be determined by that motive which appears best upon the

---

[94]Henry Home Lord Kames, *Essay on Liberty and Necessity* (Edinburgh, 1731); see Wesley, "A Thought on Necessity," J X:474–80.

[95]TUN, J X:477–78.

[96]TUN, J X:459, sec. 1.7.

[97]TUN, J X:463–64, sec. 3.1–2; cf. B 3:493, 498–99; 4:50.

[98]TUN, J X:463, sec. 3.1.

[99]TUN, J X:465, sec. 3.3.

[100]B 2:486; 4:151.

[101]TUN, J X:472, sec. 4.3.

[102]TUN, J X:467, sec. 3.7.

whole," for people evidently choose at times against their better motives. The very thing we desire most to do, we do not. People are not passive in receiving all sensory impressions. Human judgments may be changed. The mind has the intrinsic power of cutting off the connection between the judgment and the will. People's outward actions do not necessarily follow their will.[103]

Rather, God created human beings with understanding, will, and liberty. The understanding needs the will to execute its decisions, and the will needs liberty to determine itself. To deny liberty is to deny the essence of the human spirit. God does not necessitate humans to be happy any more than to be miserable. That depends on what they do with their freedom, by grace.

Further Reading on the Human Condition

Barker, Joseph. *A Review of Wesley's Notions Concerning the Primeval State of Man and the Universe.* London, ca. 1855.

Collins, Kenneth. *A Faithful Witness: John Wesley's Homiletical Theology*, 105 – 24. Wilmore, KY: Wesleyan Heritage, 1993.

Matsumoto, Hiroaki. "John Wesley's Understanding of Man." In *Japanese Contributions to the Study of John Wesley*, 79 – 96. Macon, GA: Wesleyan College, 1967. Also in *WQR* 4 (1967): 83 – 102.

Miley, John. *Systematic Theology.* Reprint, Peabody, MA: Hendrickson, 1989.

Outler, Albert C. "Diagnosing the Human Flaw: Reflections upon the Human Condition." In *Theology in the Wesleyan Spirit*, 23 – 45. Nashville: Tidings, 1975.

Pope, William Burt. *A Compendium of Christian Theology.* 3 vols. London: Wesleyan Methodist Book-Room, 1880.

Prince, John W. "Theory of Human Nature." In *Wesley on Religious Education*, 13ff. New York: Methodist Book Concern, 1926.

Ralston, Thomas N. *Elements of Divinity.* New York: Abingdon, 1924.

Reist, Irwin W. "John Wesley's View of Man: Free Grace versus Free Will." *WTJ* 7 (1972): 25 – 35.

Shelton, R. Larry. "Wesley's Doctrine of Man." *PM* 55, no. 4 (1980): 36, 37.

Summers, Thomas O. *Systematic Theology.* 2 vols. Edited by J. J. Tigert. Nashville: Methodist Publishing House South, 1888.

Vogel, John Richard. "Faith and the Image of God." Master's thesis, DePauw University, 1967.

Walls, Jerry. "The Free Will Defense: Calvinism, Wesley and the Goodness of God." *Christian Scholar's Review* 13 (1983): 19 – 33.

Watson, Richard. *Theological Institutes.* 2 vols. New York: Mason and Lane, 1836, 1840; edited by John M'Clintock, New York: Carlton & Porter, 1850.

---

[103]TUN, J X:472, sec. 4.3; on the distinction between inward and outward sin, see B 1:239 – 40, 245 – 46, 336 – 44; 2:215 – 16.

CHAPTER 8

Sin

Wesley dealt first with voluntary sin and then with original sin.

A. On the Deceitfulness of the Human Heart

The text of the homily "On the Deceitfulness of the Human Heart" is Jeremiah 17:9: "The heart is deceitful above all things, and desperately wicked: who can know it?" [Homily #128 (1790), B 4:149–60; J #123, VII:335–44].

1. Why Optimists Forever Misjudge the Human Heart

Inordinate optimism about progress in history was a characteristic of Wesley's age. Many believed that human beings are naturally good, virtuous, wise, and happy — far from being prone to sin. The cultured despisers of his day engaged in "labored panegyrics" on the dignity of human nature and absence of sin.[1] After such deep drafts of optimism, it seems that the wise men of Wesley's era might have learned little more than the pagans of old.[2]

Today we remain captive to extravagant illusions about our autonomous human potential. The pious Lord Karnes and the skeptical David Hume were more inclined to blame God for sin than to call human will to account. The fault seems to be with the Creator for creating the problem in the first place.[3] Wesley pointed out the typical evasions. Some plead psychological determinations: "I often act wrong, for want of more understanding." Others plead somatic or physical determinations: "I frequently feel wrong tempers," but they do not regard this as a sin, "for it depends on the motions of my blood and spirits, which I cannot help."[4] Others argue sociological determinations, that individual human beings cannot be blamed for the evil so widely evident and disbursed in the world. Others go so far as to exaggerate demonic determinations, saying that it is Satan who "*forces* men to act as they do; therefore they are unaccountable."[5] Even Satan, remarked Wesley, never uttered such a blasphemy.

---

[1]"On the Deceitfulness of the Human Heart," B 4:150–51, proem 1–3.
[2]"On the Deceitfulness of the Human Heart," B 4:149–51, proem 3.
[3]"On the Deceitfulness of the Human Heart," B 4:151, proem 3.
[4]Ibid.
[5]"On the Deceitfulness of the Human Heart," B 4:151, proem 4, italics added.

2. Toward Scriptural Realism about the Human Heart: Why Desperately Wicked?

The scriptural view of the origin of sin gives an entirely different account: "The heart is deceitful above all things and beyond cure. Who can understand it?" (Jer. 17:9 NIV). The subject is the human heart, described first in this homily as desperately wicked, then as deceitful above all things, and finally as so deceitful that none of us can know ourselves apart from saving grace.

Why this desperate wickedness? We do well not to focus too quickly on particular sins that are "no more than the leaves, or, at most, the fruits" that spring from the root of sin: pride and self-will, inordinately loving the creature above the Creator. They spring from centering our valuing on ourselves, from judging everything by how it affects us individually, our own interests, our own passions, our own destinies.[6] We love created goods so excessively that we exalt their limited, finite values to the ultimate level of an idol. In doing so, we fail to stand accountably before the source and ground and giver of the world, and hence the whole cosmos suffers from our spiritual disorder.[7] It is this heart of sin that gives rise to individual acts of sin.[8] All sinners have their center in "idolatry, pride, either thinking of themselves more highly than they ought to think, or glorying in something which they have received, as though they had not received it ... seeking happiness out of God."[9]

Despite differing individually in a thousand ways, everyone is like everyone else in "enmity against God."[10] Such is the universal human condition: "No crime ever prevailed among the Turks or Tartars, which we cannot parallel in every part of Christendom."[11]

To this is added another frightful dimension: the attested world of superpersonal, noncorporeal, disembodied intelligences determined to usurp both human freedom and divine power. That is what the archdeceiver and his affiliated powers seek to do, said Wesley, quoting Scripture. We do not hear a lot of loose talk of Satan by Wesley. But the demonic distortion of legitimate power he took seriously. It stands as background to any serious discussion of personal and social sin.[12] When Satan asserted his self-will and self-pride into human history, the history of sin was launched and soon covered the whole world, infecting every facet of the human condition.

3. Why Deceitful above All Things?

As a result, it is folly to think that if we earnestly seek self-understanding apart from divine grace, we will achieve it easily. For our hearts are deceitful. If "'every

---

[6]On self-will see B 1:337 – 38; 3:353 – 55; 4:152 – 54.
[7]"On the Deceitfulness of the Human Heart," B 4:152, sec. 1.1.
[8]Ibid.
[9]"On the Deceitfulness of the Human Heart," B 4:154, sec. 1.4.
[10]"On the Deceitfulness of the Human Heart," B 4:155, sec. 1.4; Gen. 6:5.
[11]"On the Deceitfulness of the Human Heart," B 4:156, sec. 2.4.
[12]"On the Deceitfulness of the Human Heart," B 4:154, sec. 1.3.

imagination of the thought of man's heart is evil,' only evil, and that continually," self-knowledge is hard to come by.

This deceit leads us to imagine that we are much wiser and better than we are. It leads us to deceive not only ourselves but others who depend on our truth telling. Often truth seekers do not even recognize their own untruthfulness. Wesley was as intensely interested in the psychology of self-deception as Kierkegaard and Freud would later be.[13] "Who can discover it in all the disguises it assumes, or trace it through all its latent mazes?"[14] How artfully we conceal from others, and from ourselves.

Why are so few conscious of this self-deception? We might have learned long ago from Scripture that the heart is deceitful "in the highest degree, above all that we can conceive. So deceitful, that the generality of men are continually deceiving both themselves and others ... not knowing either their own tempers or characters, imagining themselves to be abundantly better and wiser than they are." No one is "willing to know his own heart" except the person humbly taught of God, who comes in the incarnation as Servant Messiah.[15]

Socrates extolled knowledge of oneself, assuming that the unexamined life is not worth living. Wesley puzzled about the extent to which we in our fallen condition are even able to adequately know ourselves, because we see ourselves constantly from the vantage point of our own narrow self-interests and egocentricities. This ruse tends to trap us in a hedge of layered self-deceptions.[16]

4. Toward the Mending of the Self-Deceived Will

But thanks be to God, even this desperate state can be overcome through saving faith. In those born of God, the "heart is 'renewed in righteousness and true holiness.'"

Wesley then made a decisive qualification: "Yet the heart, even of a believer, is not wholly purified when he is justified. Sin is then overcome, but it is not rooted out; it is conquered but not destroyed. Experience shows him, first, that the roots of sin, self-will, pride, and idolatry remain still in his heart. But as long as he continues to watch and pray, none of them can prevail against him. Experience teaches him secondly, that sin ... cleaves to his best actions."[17]

None of us can know our own hearts; only the One who made them can. Nothing can cure them but convicting, justifying, and sanctifying grace. Without the help of grace, we remain self-deceived and a mystery to ourselves. Only through the disclosure of God's love can we know ourselves rightly.

How desperate we are without God. "He that trusteth in his own heart is a

---

[13]B 3:98 – 99; 4:149 – 60.
[14]"On the Deceitfulness of the Human Heart," B 4:157, sec. 3.5.
[15]"On the Deceitfulness of the Human Heart," B 4:155, sec. 2.1.
[16]*LJW* 6:139; on delusions of the senses, see B 3:538.
[17]"On the Deceitfulness of the Human Heart," B 4:157, sec. 2.5.

fool."[18] Those who are wise in their own eyes are most foolish. "At what distance from wisdom must that man be who never suspected his want of it? And will not his thinking so well of himself prevent his receiving instruction?... No fool is so incapable of amendment as one that imagines himself to be wise."[19] Those who most assuredly think they are standing alone are on the slipperiest ground.[20] The faithful can only cry to God to search their hearts and lead them into the way of understanding.

Wesley echoed cautiously the realistic hopes for modest improvements of the human condition through scientific inquiry and technological innovation. He was not resistant to the natural sciences of his day and saw them as an attempt to understand God's providential ordering of nature and history. But this attempt does not suffice to alter those who are addictively prone to distortions of pride and carnality.[21]

Christ came to enable us to know ourselves completely. However desperately wicked human pride may be, it is constantly being addressed by divine forgiveness. It is the self-assertive sinner to whom God reaches out to reconcile, pardon, redeem, and sanctify inside out.[22]

B. On the Fall of Man

The text of the homily "On the Fall of Man" is Genesis 3:19: "Dust thou art, and unto dust shalt thou return" [Homily #57 (1782), B 2:400–412; J #57, VI:215–24].

1. Why Does God Allow Misery and Heartache in the World He Loves?

"Why is there *pain* in the world, seeing God is 'loving to every man, and his mercy is over all his works?' Because there is sin. Had there been no sin, there would have been no pain. But pain (supposing God to be just) is the necessary effect of sin. But why is there sin?"[23] Because man and woman, having spirit, will, reason, and liberty, akin to God, nonetheless "chose evil." This is Scripture's "plain, simple account of the origin of evil." Without it man remains an "enigma to himself."[24]

Sin began with Eve's unbelief and Adam's idolatry, with Eve believing the Tempter rather than God, and Adam loving creatures idolatrously more than God.[25] Only this deadly combination of two wills of male and female together initiated this loss of original righteousness. As we will see later, Adam was responsible for headship, so all responsibility cannot be shifted to Eve. But for Eve, the pain and curse of childbearing ensue. And for Adam, the sweat of hard labor followed this free choice

---

[18]"On the Deceitfulness of the Human Heart," B 4:159, sec. 3.1.
[19]"On the Deceitfulness of the Human Heart," B 4:159, sec. 3.2.
[20]"On the Deceitfulness of the Human Heart," B 4:160, sec. 3.3.
[21]"On the Deceitfulness of the Human Heart," B 4:159–60, sec. 3.
[22]*CH*, "Exhorting and Beseeching to Return to God," B 7:79–94.
[23]"On the Fall of Man," B 2:400; cf. *LJW* 1:88, 97, 102.
[24]"On the Fall of Man," B 2:401, proem 1; cf. *LJW* 3:375–87.
[25]"On the Fall of Man," B 2:401–3, sec. 1.1.

of evil. The loss of innocence meant the loss of happiness. Prior to the fall there was no inequality of women and no hard labor for men.[26]

2. The Consequence of Sin for the Body-Soul Composite

a. Dust and Spirit

God did not make human beings as "mere matter, a piece of ... clay; but a spirit, like himself, although clothed with a material vehicle."[27] Humans are not merely dust, but dust shaped by living soul. The interface of body and soul is the human spirit.

Being trapped in a syndrome of rebellion holds many possibilities for stumbling and falling. Given the momentum of the history of sin, soon "every child of man is in a thousand mistakes, and is liable to fresh mistakes every moment," not merely out of ignorance, but in collusion with the whole of human history's willingness to ignore the divine will.

The psychosomatic equilibrium (body/soul; soma/psyche) easily tilts out of kilter. The living soul plays itself out "upon a set of material keys" and cannot "make any better music than the nature and state of its instrument allows." Thinking becomes distorted by the passions of the corruptible body, which "hinders the soul in its operations: and, at best, serves it very imperfectly. Yet the soul cannot dispense with its service."[28]

b. To Dust You Shall Return

As an outcome of a history full of this self-assertion, "we are all traveling toward death." Death comes to all humans.[29] The execution of the decree of death is built into the very nature of the human body after the fall. This body consists of "innumerable membranes exquisitely thin" that are filled with circulating fluids, which reach their full measure of functioning in youth and early adulthood. By middle age, the body acquires some stiffness and stenosis, and after sixty years or so, "wrinkles show the proportion of the fluids to be lessened." There is a diminution of the juices, "finer vessels are filled up," and in "extreme old age the arteries themselves ... become hard" and "death naturally ensues." From the outset of life, "we are preparing ... to return to the dust from whence we came!"[30]

Yet God does not despise the work of his hands but provides a remedy for all who are fallen by bearing our sins in his body on the tree.[31] As God is just in punishing sin, so he is merciful in providing a universal remedy, in his Son through his Spirit, for a universal evil. The righteousness of one suffices as justification for all.[32]

---

[26]"On the Fall of Man," B 2:403–5, sec. 1.2–3.

[27]"On the Fall of Man," B 2:409, sec. 2.6.

[28]"On the Fall of Man," B 2:403, sec. 2.2.

[29]"On the Fall of Man," B 2:407, sec. 2.4. Excepting special biblical examples of those who so walked with God that they may not have died—Enoch, Elijah, and John the apostle—the sentence of death for sin is passed on all of Adam's and Eve's posterity.

[30]"On the Fall of Man," B 2:407–8, sec. 1.5; cf. 3:269–70.

[31]"On the Fall of Man," B 2:410, sec. 2.8.

[32]"On the Fall of Man," B 2:411–12, sec. 2.9.

C. Spiritual Idolatry

1. Keep Yourselves from Idols

The text for the homily "Spiritual Idolatry" is 1 John 5:20 – 21: "Keep yourselves from idols" [Homily #78 (1781), B 3:103 – 14; J #78, VI:435 – 44].

To make an idol first requires something good, some gift of the creaturely order that we then take to be better than it is and elevate to a pretended deity. An idol is anything that tempts the heart away from centeredness in God, any good thing in the creaturely environment that is capable of being adored,[33] anything good enough in this world to seem worthy of worship out of twisted desire, shaped by the figments of imagination and pride.[34]

"Spiritual idolatry" is sharply distinguished from triune "spiritual worship."[35] Wesley entreated, "Keep yourselves from idols" (1 John 5:21). Our idols become implacable "rivals of God."

The possibility of making idols is endless. But Wesley thought they were usually made according to one of three motivations: as objects of *sense, pride, or imagination*.[36] This threefold pattern was summarized in 1 John 2:16: "For everything in the world — the *cravings* of sinful man, the *lust* of his eyes and the *boasting* of what he has and does — comes not from the Father but from the world" (NIV [1984], italics added).[37] Wesley called this the three layers of rebellion (*triplex concupiscentia*): sensuality (lust), pride (boasting), and imagination (cravings).

2. Idolatry in the Form of Sensuality

The proximate goodness of sensuality tempts us to be dragged down into the false imagination that what life really amounts to is our own sensory experiences and physical satisfactions, of which we seem never to get enough.[38] *The idolatry of sense* feeds off of the desire of the flesh, "the cravings of sinful man" ("all that panders to the appetites," 1 John 2:16 NEB). We may idolize good things like sex, food, security, money, or any material good. We are sensory beings, so we love these good things. The problem is that we may love them in such a way that instead of seeing them in relation to their giver, we pretend that they are good in and of themselves. That is the sensual side of the problem of idolatry.

We are tempted to worship sensory objects linked with the fulfillment of bodily appetites. Exaggerating their goodness, we make idols of those things that make

---

[33]See also "Original Sin," sec. 2.7; "On the Deceitfulness of the Human Heart," sec. 1.4; and "On the Wedding Garment," sec. 12, on the theme of idolatry.

[34]"The Unity of the Divine Being," B 4:65 – 67, secs. 12 – 18; J VII:267 – 69.

[35]Written on the same text, 1 John 5:20 – 21, at the same time, Christmas season of 1780, and published together in *Arminian Magazine*.

[36]These three forms of idolatry are also considered in "Spiritual Idolatry."

[37]Wesley concurred with Augustine that "all sins may be included within these three classes of vice," Augustine, *Enarratio in Psalmum*, 8.13, MPL 36:115; "The Way to the Kingdom," sec. 2.2, and "The Almost Christian," B 1:137n, sec. 2.1; cf. B 1:409; 3:89, 282, 351, 534 – 35; 4:65, 182 – 83.

[38]"The Unity of the Divine Being," B 4:64 – 66, secs. 11 – 13.

our lives temporally more comfortable or pleasant. Sensuality is prone to become a spiritual disease of both rich and poor, either of whom can become inordinately attached to worldly things.[39]

3. Idolatry in the Form of Pride

If the idols of sensuality exploit our capacity for bodily and corporeal life, the idols of pride exploit our capacity for self-transcendence.[40] While sensuality pulls us inordinately downward, pride raises us inordinately upward, beyond our limits and competence. Pride tempts us toward the pretension that we have no limitations.[41]

In our pride, we absurdly imagine our egocentric selves to be the center of all other values, so that we ourselves become adversaries to the true God by boasting of who we are and what we do. By *the pride of life* we seek our happiness through the praise of others. We exalt our finitude to the laughable pretense that other values revolve around us.[42]

Prototypical pride is seen in the demonic aspiration of the fallen angels who desire despairingly to be God. From this absurdity springs the lie that has saturated human history,[43] the pretense that creatures can feign being God. As a result, we assess each value only in relation to its value for ourselves.[44]

4. The Idols of Imagination

Pride and sensuality pull us in two conflicting directions, intensified by the exercise of the idolatrous imagination.[45] Idolatry escalates the objects of fancy by the devices of the imagination. We fantasize finite creatures as God. We prolifically imagine that which is not God as if it were truly God.

Imagination is a marvelous human faculty capable of engaging in a relation with possibility — with what might occur.[46] But when imagination takes over inordinately and becomes controlled by idolatrous sensuality and pride, this elicits anxiety and guilt. The escalated imagination of sensory ecstasy or egocentric pride may lead toward compulsive addictions to lust and hubris.

The wonderfully created capacity of imagination in this way falls increasingly into distortions as great as its native powers. By imagination we come to love more that which is less worthy of love than God.

Sensuality and pride, when intensified by the idolatrous imagination, are basic

---

[39]"The Unity of the Divine Being," B 4:65, sec. 12.

[40]B 1:197 – 98; 1:337 – 38; 2:179; 4:287 – 88.

[41]Idolatry as sense, imagination, and pride is also discussed in "The Unity of the Divine Being."

[42]"On the Education of Children," B 3:348 – 49, secs. 5 – 16; J VII:89 – 94; FA, J VIII:141.

[43]On the spiritual pride of the English, see B 11:238 – 39; of ancient Israel, see B 11:2008 – 9; of the Methodists, see B 11:387 – 89. In these passages, Wesley countered the common modern complaint that religious discussions of pride are characteristically neglectful of social self-criticism, and of one's own social location or tradition.

[44]"The Unity of the Divine Being," B 4:65, sec. 12.

[45]LJW 4:305; 5:336; B 1:338 – 39; 3:106 – 7, 183 – 84, 524 – 25; 4:123 – 24; 11:128.

[46]On the right use of imagination, see B 2:294.

ingredients in the oft-repeated, ever-unfolding fall of human history.[47] The idolatry of imagination feeds off of *the desire of the eye*, in finding gratification in grand and beautiful objects, apparel, and amusements.

A key feature of Wesley's psychological analysis of imagination is the crucial function of novelty in the idol-making process. The aesthetic imagination is constantly hungering for something new to enjoy, so it is immersed in diversions and amusements and the pleasure that is taken in seeking curiosities. Novelty appears to heighten the pleasure of music, poetry, and philosophy.

Wesley was well aware of the intimate connection between idolatry and education superficially conceived. Academics are "so far from suspecting" this relationship that "they seriously believe it is a matter of great praise to 'give ourselves wholly'" to the quest for novel ideas.[48]

5. Inordinate Love of Money and Sex

The inordinate love of the world is most clearly seen in the human fixation on the *love of money*, not merely money functionally understood, but the obsession with money, seeking money for its own sake, and thus placing happiness precisely in acquiring or possessing it. This is "effectually to renounce the true God, and to set up an idol in his place."[49]

Even more compulsively, the inordinate love of the world may appear in distortions of the good gift of *sexuality*, in fixing our love on beloved human creatures, not with a pure heart grounded in enduring covenant love, but by making of another little more than an immediate object of fleeting pleasure for oneself. Wesley admonished spouses not to "put a man or a woman in the place of God.... Let this be carefully considered, even by those whom God has joined together."[50] The goal of good habituation is happiness. Idolatry, always looking better than it is, never elicits happiness.[51]

6. Whether Penitent Faith Can Break the Bondage of Idolatry

We keep ourselves from idols first by becoming deeply convicted that no idol can bring the happiness it promises.[52] Idolatry is initially combated by praying for the grace to become aware of our own temptations and then for the grace to trust in God instead of the gods.[53] We do not overcome idolatry without coming to our senses, awakening from sleep, choosing the better way, and resolving to seek happiness in the true ground of happiness.[54]

---

[47]"The Unity of the Divine Being," B 4:65 – 66, secs. 12 – 14.
[48]"Spiritual Idolatry," B 3:106 – 9, sec. 1.7 – 14.
[49]"Spiritual Idolatry," B 3:110, sec. 1.17.
[50]"Spiritual Idolatry," B 3:111, sec. 1.18.
[51]"Spiritual Idolatry," B 3:110 – 11, sec. 1.17 – 18.
[52]"Spiritual Idolatry," B 3:111, sec. 2.1.
[53]*PW* 7:194.
[54]"Spiritual Idolatry," B 3:113, sec. 2.3.

No idolatry can be overcome without *repentance*, which becomes filled with consciousness of our own impotence, guilt, and the madness of idolatry. So "cry for a thorough knowledge of yourself.... Pray that you may be fully discovered to yourself, that you may know yourself as also you are known."[55] Only on the basis of such realistic awareness of our own impotence to change our idolatries can they be overcome by grace through the *faith* that exclaims, "Lord, I would believe! Help thou mine unbelief. And help me now!"[56]

Further Reading on Sin

Arnet, William. "The Wesleyan/ Arminian Teaching on Sin." In *Insights into Holiness*, edited by K. Geiger, 55–72. Kansas City: Beacon Hill, 1962.

Collins, Kenneth. *John Wesley on Salvation*, chap. 1. Grand Rapids: Zondervan, 1989.

Cox, Leo George. "John Wesley's Concept of Sin." *BETS* 5 (1962): 18–24.

Fletcher, John. *An Appeal to Matter of Fact and Common Sense: A Natural Demonstration of Man's Corrupt and Lost Estate*. Bristol, UK: William Pine, 1772.

Outler, Albert C. "Diagnosing the Human Flaw." In *Theology in the Wesleyan Spirit*, 23–24. Nashville: Tidings, 1975.

---

[55]"Spiritual Idolatry," B 3:113, sec. 2.4.
[56]"Spiritual Idolatry," B 3:114, sec. 2.5.

CHAPTER 9

Original Sin

A. The Doctrine of Original Sin according to Scripture, Reason, and Experience

1. Why Wesley Wrote His Longest Treatise on Sin

Nothing in human history is more original than sin. The underlying reason for giving so much attention to the study of original sin is not a fixation on sin itself but on theodicy and redemption.

Wesley thought that a solid doctrine of original sin was required for two reasons: first, to free God of the charge of being responsible for humankind's sinful condition, and then to exalt the gospel of justification, new birth, and especially, transforming, sanctifying grace.[1]

a. The Doctrine of Original Sin according to Scripture, Reason, and Experience

Wesley wrote only one full-length systematic treatise, and it happened to be on a perennially unpopular topic — original sin.[2] It comprises most of the ninth volume of the Jackson edition [1756 – 57, J IX:191 – 464], a large tome with almost three hundred packed pages devoted to exhaustive exegetical analysis. The few who have carefully read it discover the side of Wesley most frequently ignored by his modern romantic sycophants and by those who imagine him to be Pelagian. The secondary literature has focused so much more on his soteriology and ecclesiology that it has almost totally ignored his most detailed treatise — on original sin.

This extensive tome is among the most demanding and intricate of Wesley's writings. The reader must pay astute attention to the quotation marks to identify who is quoting or refuting whom. There are profuse quotations without the benefit of modern stylistic conventions.[3]

---

[1]*DOS*, pt. 2, J IX:273 – 85, sec. 2.

[2]For references to original sin apart from *DOS*, see *JJW* 3:374; 4:199; B 1:64 – 65, 185 – 89, 211 – 13, 225 – 29; 2:170 – 85; 4:152 – 55; 9:50 – 52; 11:163 – 64, 519 – 20; *LJW* 4:48, 67.

[3]The annotated Bicentennial edition of the treatise on original sin will make it easier for the reader to discern the difference between Wesley's own views and those numerous points where he is quoting others either favorably or unfavorably.

Though some of the material from part 1 of *The Doctrine of Original Sin* found its way into one of the *Standard Sermons*, Homily #44, "Original Sin,"[4] do not assume that it is merely a summary of the longer treatise.

Though Wesley liked to write with a tight economy of style and scale, in *The Doctrine of Original Sin*, he was determined to go into whatever length required to nail down his historical, exegetical, and ethical points. Here he functioned more than elsewhere as a deliberate systematic theologian reflecting on all the attending issues relating to the depth of the human predicament.[5]

However closely argued, this inquiry is addressed less to the academic world than to the leadership of those in Wesley's direct connection of spiritual formation —his societies and bands[6]— as a caveat against diluted views of sin. And he still is capable of making contact with minds seeking his counsel in modern times.

But why write on original sin so extensively? Wesley saw the problem of sin as a profound dilemma requiring probing, untiring analysis. Here he was less than ever willing to suffer fools gladly.

Even today it is not unusual to hear Wesley or Wesleyans polemically dismissed as romantic, naturalistic, humanistic Pelagians, despite all disclaimers. This dismissal shows a failure to take Wesley seriously on original sin.

b. A Dismal Subject

Some people imagine that Wesley espoused an optimistic view of human nature. This treatise deserves to be read by anyone thinking such foolishness. Temperamentally, Wesley was indeed inclined toward the possibilities of grace, rather than forever bemoaning the endless consequences of fallen human nature. He was engaged in the lifelong act of reconstruction of the human condition, both personal and social. He did not hesitate to seek the inclusive reformation of the human character. Amid the characteristic optimism of his period, however, he appears as a realistic and tough-minded analyst of sin and at times a grieving observer of inexorable human fallenness.[7]

We will not penetrate far into Wesley's theology until we take seriously his doctrine of original sin.[8] It is, he admitted, a dismal subject, but one that must be presupposed in any effort to understand other essential Christian doctrines, such as incarnation, justification, and redemption. Those who have no way to grasp the perplexity, depth, and recalcitrance of human sin have little motivation to speak of Christ on the cross. We cannot get to atonement or redemption until we take seriously the predicament to which Christ is an answer. It is a foundational locus of theology.

---

[4]"Original Sin" (1759), B 2:170 – 85; J VI:54 – 65.

[5]*DOS*, pt. 1, pref. 5, J IX:194.

[6]Though Wesley often spoke in first person to John Taylor, and though the argument was couched in an academic format, more so than usual for Wesley, it was nonetheless a moral admonition for those who might otherwise be led astray.

[7]*DOS*, pt. 1, pref., J IX:193 – 95.

[8]Wesley viewed original sin as a "grand doctrine," *LJW* 4:146, 153, 237; 5:327; 6:49, among the doctrinal essentials.

c. Whether the Origin of Sin Is a Fit Subject for Serious Inquiry

In public worship, Christians confess their sins. My sins, not those of others, are the focus of the act of confession of sin.

Sometimes in modern forms of common worship, we have tended to circumvent entirely the act of confession — one of the least Wesleyan aspects of Wesley's modern progeny. The subject of original sin so avidly neglected by modern Christianity was not neglected by Mr. Wesley. Few liberal Protestants have ever heard a sermon on original sin, except in the guise of a political appeal against economic injustice or war or racism or social oppression.

Wesley anticipated modern analyses of the dynamics of the psychogenetic transmission of neurotic patterns as well as the social and intergenerational consequences of injustice. Modern psychologically oriented Christians familiar with the ideas of repression, the unconscious, and neurotic behavior, those who know much about how psychological dysfunction gets passed on from parents to children, often know almost nothing about classic Christian understanding of intergenerational transmission of evil.[9]

2. Whether Sin Is a Socially Transmitted Disease[10]

The dynamics of social and class transmission of economic oppression are well known to modern Christians, especially among those who refuse to take original sin seriously. Yet these modern views of social location and class conflict were astutely anticipated by classical Christianity generally and by Wesley in particular during the early phase of the Industrial Revolution, and are reflected with special discernment in Wesley's teaching on original sin.[11] Long before Marx or Lenin or Niebuhr or Gutiérrez, Wesley and others before him (notably John Chrysostom, Augustine, Gregory the Great, and Thomas Aquinas) were speaking of social location, economic interest, and class conflict as basic distorting influences on our perception of reality, falsifying our capacity to see the common good.

The implicit intergenerational doctrine of sin that became secularized in Marx and Freud was explicitly anticipated by Wesley and other Christian teachers. These modern categories of interpretation may still be somewhat useful in explicating the Christian doctrine of original sin. Yet they are finally inadequate, refusing as they do to understand the human condition as a voluntary alienation standing in final relation to the ground and source of life. This is worth noting in a preliminary manner so that some readers may make contact with Wesley's view of original sin in a way they might not otherwise be able to recognize.

We imagine that our modern psychological analyses of the human predicament are unprecedented in their accuracy and acumen. Freud had a complex analysis of the origins of neurosis, especially as it emerged out of relations with

---

[9] Albert C. Outler, *Theology in the Wesleyan Spirit* (Nashville: Tidings, 1975), chap. 1.
[10] On sin as disease, see B 1:404, 586; 2:184, 342; 3:134–35, 533–34; 4:86–87.
[11] *DOS*, pt. 1, J IX:208–38, sec. 2.1–15.

primary persons, key voices that shape the growth of individual consciousness. Long before Freud, the classic Christian tradition had understood that sin is socially and interpersonally transmitted, that parental inputs affect neurotic responses, yet never unilaterally and never without the collusion of our own freedom. The intergenerational transmission of distorted sexuality is another way of talking about original sin.[12]

Many imagine that our modern sociological analyses of the human predicament are unprecedented. Marx offered a complex economic analysis of the origins of social conflict, especially as it emerged out of class consciousness and oppressive economic patterns. Yet centuries before Marx, the classic Christian tradition had understood how profoundly sin is socially and economically transmitted, and that class biases misshape the truth of our relations with one another. Our location in a socioeconomic order powerfully impacts our ways of thinking about moral judgments and ideas. We become natively biased in relation to our own class. The intergenerational transmission of unjust economic and class oppressions is a surrogate speech for original sin, but far less profound than that of classic Christianity.

Consciousness raising was for Marx the raising of the consciousness of the underclass to become outraged at the injustices of class oppression, calling upon people to unite and break their chains of economic bondage through revolution. Now we find that their revolution over time became a poverty machine, which itself has required the release of new freedoms to overcome. Such is the history of sin. Rightly understood, original sin is not alien to modern consciousness. Even when we hear nothing of sin from modern pulpits, it is a deeply familiar modern theme in our culture.

Wesley shied away from theorizing about a glib unilateral explanation of the transmission of sin: "The fact I know, both by Scripture and by experience. I know it is transmitted; but how" precisely it is transmitted is shrouded under "the mystery of iniquity.[13]

Modernity does not use the term *sin* to talk about sin, but sin nonetheless remains an intense modern preoccupation. We cannot open our eyes without seeing how deeply our society is in trouble — our cities, our sexuality, our compulsions. Our sense of sin is deep-seated. Wesley regarded the doctrine of original sin as the first line of defense against the deadly optimisms of the Enlightenment. To the extent that he failed, the task must again be undertaken in our time.[14]

Wesley asked, "What is the real state, with regard to knowledge and virtue, wherein mankind have been from the earliest times? And what state are they in at this day?"[15]

---

[12]B 1:533 – 41; *SS* 1:382.
[13]Letter to John Robertson, September 24, 1753, 3:107; cf. "The Mystery of Iniquity," B 1:32 – 34; 2:466 – 68; *CH* 7:115 – 17.
[14]*DOS*, pt. 1, J IX:230 – 38, sec. 2.12 – 15.
[15]*DOS*, pt. 1; J IX:196.

3. Combating the Deist Denial of Original Sin: A Searching Response to John Taylor

Wesley never imagined that he was doing any original thinking in his explication of the traditional doctrine of original sin. Rather, he thought of himself merely as defending the received faith against crypto-Arians of his time, as represented by a leading deist, John Taylor (1694–1761) of Norwich, a proto-Unitarian who had written a popular book in 1740 titled *The Scripture-Doctrine of Original Sin, Exposed to Free and Candid Examination*,[16] in which he challenged the basic premise of original sin. Wesley thought that Taylor was working out of a deistic theism, a Pelagian anthropology, a reductionist Christology, a works-righteousness ethic, and a universalist eschatology, all of which were undermining substantive Christian teaching.[17] Wesley considered Taylor's unitarianism as tending toward antinomianism, toward the trivializing of Christ's work on the cross, the weakening of Christ's deity, and finally the impugning of God's character by making God responsible for present human sinfulness.[18]

Taylor viewed sin benignly as an imbalance of appetites propagated by habit, following the classical Greek views of habituated vice.[19] It was an "old Deism in a new dress; seeing it saps the very foundation of all revealed religion, whether Jewish or Christian.... If, therefore, we take away this foundation ... the Christian system falls at once."[20]

All of these tendencies to which Wesley was trying to respond remain epidemic in popular modern Christianity. If so, it may be that this least-read treatise on original sin is among his most relevant for contemporary audiences.[21]

Wesley considered Taylor's views as a deadly toxin being diffused insidiously throughout the church, to which an antidote was urgently needed. "I verily believe no single person since Mahomet has given such a wound to Christianity as Dr. Taylor," whose books "have poisoned so many of the clergy, and indeed the fountains themselves — the universities in England, Scotland, Holland, and Germany."[22] In the absence of an adequate rejoinder by others, Wesley believed he "dare not be silent any longer." He considered it his solemn pastoral duty to admonish and amend these misunderstandings on behalf of all who looked to him for spiritual

---

[16]John Taylor, *The Scripture-Doctrine of Original Sin, Exposed to Free and Candid Examination* (London: J. Waugh, 1740). A second edition in 1741 contained a supplement replying to Jennings and Watts; a third edition appeared in 1746, eleven years before Wesley entered the fray.

[17]Taylor's other works include *The Scripture-Doctrine of Atonement* and *The Lord's Supper Explained upon Scripture.*

[18]*LJW* 3:180, 208; B 1:461; 3:474; 4:100, 151n, 522.

[19]Opposing all federalist interpretations of Adam's sin, and viewing all guilt as personal and nontransferable, Taylor concluded, "If we come into the world infected and depraved with sinful dispositions, then sin must be natural to us; and if natural, then necessary; and if necessary, then no sin." Taylor, *Scripture-Doctrine of Original Sin*, 129.

[20]*DOS*, pref. 4, J IX:194.

[21]*DOS*, pref., J IX:192–94.

[22]Letter to Augustus Toplady, December 9, 1758.

counsel.[23] Wesley's refutations were complemented by David Jennings's *Vindication*[24] and John Hervey's dialogue, *Theron and Aspasio*, as well as careful studies of original sin by Isaac Watts,[25] Samuel Hebden,[26] and Thomas Boston.[27]

All this is, by way of preface, to put Wesley's treatise in its setting. It reveals the Anglican evangelist in a complex theological debate in which he sincerely thought that the integrity of Christian teaching was decisively at stake. Insofar as the presupposition of original sin is misplaced, all else becomes more difficult to understand in theology.[28]

B. Evidences of Sin Displayed in the History of Sin

1. Human History Attests the Universality of Corruption

We see Wesley's quadrilateral theological method more consciously unfolding here than anywhere else in his writings. We see him first working with historical arguments, then experiential and sociological arguments, and then most clearly with scriptural and patristic exegesis of Scripture.

Wesley began with historical testimony to original sin, setting forth massive layers of historical evidence for the universality of human misery and sin.[29] It was this first portion of *The Doctrine of Original Sin* that Wesley reprinted separately in 1762 under the ironic title of *The Dignity of Human Nature*.

It would be foolish to expect that an eighteenth-century mind could have already grasped in detail the psychological and social analyses of the nineteenth and twentieth centuries. We do not expect persons to know methods and worldviews that emerge only after they die. Yet those who dismiss Wesley often do so on such absurd grounds. Modern chauvinism, which imagines a sense of the moral superiority over all premodern modes of consciousness, views Wesley's historical arguments as quaint and dismissible, at times even humorous.

It requires a deeper empathy than modern chauvinist contempt for antiquity to get back into Wesley's frame of reference so as to grasp what he was seeing about

---

[23]*DOS*, pref. 2, J IX:193. In his journal of August 28, 1748, Wesley noted that he had encountered at Shackerley some "disciples of Dr. Taylor; laughing at Original Sin, and consequently, at the whole frame of Scriptural Christianity." He said when he returned to Shackerley on April 10, 1751, "Being now in the very midst of Mr. Taylor's disciples, I enlarged much more than I am accustomed to do on the doctrine of Original Sin; and determined, if God should give me a few years' life, publicly to answer his new gospel."

[24]David Jennings, *A Vindication of the Scripture-Doctrine of Original Sin* (London, 1740).

[25]Isaac Watts, *The Ruin and Recovery of Mankind* (London, 1740).

[26]Samuel Hebden (1692–1747) was an independent minister of Wrentham, Suffolk. He wrote *The Doctrine of Original Sin, as Laid Down in the Assembly's Catechism, Explained*.

[27]Thomas Boston, *Human Nature in Its Fourfold State*, 10th ed. (Edinburgh, 1753), extracted in *DOS*, pt. 7. Jonathan Edwards did not publish *The Great Christian Doctrine of Original Sin Defended* until 1758.

[28]*DOS*, pref., J IX:193–95.

[29]Note the full title *The Doctrine of Original Sin according to Scripture, Reason, and Experience*. The role of tradition, particularly patristic tradition, is here viewed under the category of exegesis of Scripture. In a similar sense, tradition is rightly viewed under "experience," inasmuch as it attests the experience of the historic Christian community, particularly in its classical consensual phase.

the universal evidences of social and personal corruption. Only those who survey the human condition from its earliest times see the depth of its predicament, with its perennial tendency to misjudge the attainability of knowledge and virtue.[30]

2. Whether Human Corruptibility and Misery Are Found Universally

With the primordial fall of freedom into corruption, the consequences have pervaded everything that has happened subsequently within the intensely interconnected story of human history. Each one's personal decisions affect the succeeding flow of interpersonal and social sin. The wonderful capacity for imagination becomes distorted by pride and sensuality, turning the heart toward thinking and doing evil continually so that all flesh becomes adulterated. Total depravity does not mean that there is nothing good in human creation, but that sin taints every corner and aspect of human choosing.

a. The History of Sin Displayed in the Old Testament

Story after story reveals this corruption. The primary scriptural text Wesley was working out of was Genesis 6:5: "And God saw that the wickedness of man was great in the earth, and that every imagination of the thoughts of his heart was only evil continually." Already "the contagion had spread itself through the inner man; had tainted the seat of their principles, and the source of their actions."[31]

Wesley's survey of the history of sin is hardly a cheery argument. Its very purpose is to prove historically the universality of pride and sloth, not just among pagans, but among those also to whom saving grace has been extended, yet who have turned again to apostasy and fallenness. In Wesley's thinking about the whole course of human history, the biblical narrative formed the core of it, though not its entirety. He was far better educated in classical Hellenistic and Roman literary sources in their original Greek and Latin than standard guild academics today.[32]

The story of Noah offers a summary way of talking about the general corruption of history, the radical deterioration of God's gift of accountable freedom. When Plan A (paradise) degenerated to rebellion, Plan B (expulsion from paradise) was put in effect. When Plan B failed, Plan C was required — a flood, a new beginning, a rainbow covenant, and a new promise. Noah attested not only the negation of the old but a new beginning as well, a new covenant with all humanity, not just with a particular people.[33]

After the flood, the relentless story of corruption continued, scene upon scene: The account of the Tower of Babel typifies the universality of the corruption of language. Human speech becames confused, twisted, and contaminated. Idolatrous human beings did not communicate well with one another. That remains a

---

[30]*DOS*, pt. 1, J IX:196, sec. 1.1.
[31]*DOS*, pt. 1, J IX:197, sec. 1.1, quoting John Hervey, *Theron and Aspasio*, Dialogue 11; cf. *LJW* 6:121.
[32]*DOS*, pt. 1, J IX:196–97, sec. 1.1–2.
[33]*DOS*, pt. 1, J IX:197, sec. 1.3.

profound evidence of the general fallenness of humanity.[34] There is no hint in the earliest accounts of ancient history that primitive humanity was ever pervasively reformed. Sodom, having not even ten righteous persons, was destroyed by fire and brimstone. In Canaanite culture, sin was attested at every hand. War, torture, infanticide, and exploitation abounded.[35]

The calling of Abraham offered a new beginning for the covenant people, but again sin came to reign even among the progeny of Israel. Though one might have expected them to excel in virtue because of God's law and promises, they behaved much like those who had never known God. The covenant of law was given to bless the people and offer the promise of happiness, but they repeatedly neglected it and returned inveterately to sin.[36] The syndrome of idolatry led to Babylonian captivity, which should have corrected it but did so only temporarily. Captivity had the redemptive intent of bringing the faithful back to the covenant promise. Faith was recovered in captivity, only to be lost again in idolatry and national waywardness.[37]

b. The History of Sin Displayed in the New Testament

The story of actual human history apart from grace is a story of sin winning again and again. Jesus himself set forth a dismal picture of the persistent deteriorations of history. He viewed the religious leaders of his time as whitewashed sepulchres "full of dead men's bones" (Matt. 23:27), displaying every imaginable stench of uncleanness.[38]

The apostle Paul offered the definitive text for original sin in Romans 1 and 2: we are given human existence as good, but we worship the creature rather than the Creator. Out of our persistent idolatries, all other forms of human distortion emerge, from the collapse of natural sexuality to every other imaginable offense.[39]

c. The History of Sin Displayed in Ancient History

Wesley then turned to Greco-Roman history, asking the same questions of Hesiod, Homer, Aeschylus, and the ancient historians, poets, and tragedians. These led to the same dismal conclusion: no society recorded in ancient history comes even close either to moral accountability or happiness. Even the best of societies are attended by painful human costs. Even the best of persons lived within profoundly narrowed horizons. The supposed virtues of Rome were given the lie by the cruelty of its most noble citizens, such as Cato and Julius Caesar. Of Pompey, Wesley observed, "a less amiable character is not easy to find."[40]

Infant sacrifice through exposure was in Wesley's mind a particularly horrid example of an accepted unjust social practice in Rome. To this he added the torture

---

[34]Ibid.
[35]*DOS*, pt. 1, J IX:200, sec. 1.8.
[36]*DOS*, pt. 1, J IX:198, sec. 1.4.
[37]*DOS*, pt. 1, J IX:200–201, sec. 1.8–10.
[38]*DOS*, pt. 1, J IX:201, sec. 1.11; Matt. 23:27.
[39]*DOS*, pt. 1, J IX:202–3, sec. 1.12.
[40]*DOS*, pt. 1, J IX:202–4, sec. 1.12–13.

of victims in war, as well as abusive political and sexual practices. Wesley was a sensitive moral historian who hated injustices. He was a good Oxford classics scholar who had read Thucydides, Tacitus, and Cicero from early school days in their original Greek and Latin. He found no part of the story they told untainted by sin. The universality of sin is evident to anyone who reasonably looks at the evidence.[41]

We see this especially when we view human history lengthening out over many generations. Original sin implies that no one can enter history as if starting with an absolutely clean moral slate, as if nothing unseemly had ever happened before. Previously distorted human history happened before I got here. I am not personally responsible for the choices of others, but their choices affect me. Their history has entered into my history. The experience of my parents' generation has entered decisively into my history.

In this way, human fallenness has a social and historical character. Whole societies can affect the form sin takes in a given period. Modern individuals think of themselves under a radically individualistic premise. But Scripture thinks corporately about human life. Sin has vast incalculable intergenerational effects.[42]

C. Sociological Evidences of the Universality of Human Corruption

1. The Universality of Sin in Nontheistic Cultures

If it seems that Wesley was functioning as an amateur social anthropologist, it is only fair to remember that the methods of field anthropology had not yet been invented in the modern sense. The term *heathen* referred descriptively to those who did not share the premises of Western theism.[43] Wesley inquired first into the moral happiness of nontheistic cultures and then of theistic cultures.

Wesley followed Edward Brerewood's population geography in concluding that if the world were divided into thirty parts, nineteen would be heathen, six Islamic, and only five Christian.[44] Christians of all confessions added up to a minority in his day. More ominously, a disturbing percentage of those formally viewed as baptized Christians obviously would fall far short of the mark of effective moral accountability.[45]

Wesley's intention in part 1.2 of *The Doctrine of Original Sin* was to present a multicultural survey of human societies, asking whether any have surmounted the outrageous effects of sin. He ranged widely in remarking on cultures about which he had more firsthand information — Native American culture, which he had experienced to some degree firsthand — and then he turned to the descriptions he could find of African and Asian cultures.

---

[41]*DOS*, pt. 1, J IX:202 – 8, sec. 1.12 – 18.

[42]*DOS*, pt. 1, J IX:196 – 97, sec. 1.1 – 2.

[43]*LJW* 1:188, 225, 286; 4:67; 5:327.

[44]Edward Brerewood, *Enquiries Touching the Diversity of Languages*, 1614.

[45]*DOS*, pt. 1, J IX:210, sec. 2.2.

No one would consider Wesley to be a normative or even reliable interpreter of these great cultures, as he shared many stereotypes common to his generation. But it is evident that he was interested in bringing into his teaching what he knew of these cultures, even though limited by what we today would regard as relatively small databases and many conjectures.[46]

Among Native Americans with whom he had some immediate experience,[47] Wesley observed as evidence of sin their constant intertribal warfare. He was especially disturbed by their practice of torturing defenseless victims. As one of the few English writers of his day who had actually spent time in the immediate environment of Native Americans, Wesley did not share the distantly conceived inflated picture of the noble savage that prevailed among enlightened French literati of the eighteenth century. Wesley punctured this picture, providing a graphic depiction of how these natives were as deeply embedded in sin as the avaricious colonial British.[48]

Turning to Asia, Wesley was disturbed by what appeared to him as the complete immobility of Chinese society, unable to yield to any significant changes, trapped in cultural prejudices and oddities, such as the crippling of women by binding their feet, and their 300,000-character alphabet, which he thought debilitating to social progress and a means of social control by knowledge-and-power elites. He suspected that the aristocratic class benefited from this immobility, often in absurd and demeaning ways, such as being fed by servants and having feces preserved.[49]

Wesley's picture of eighteenth-century black African culture was shaped by contemporary stereotypes. He especially noted the constant warfare between tribes and the lack of intertribal justice, yet he was capable of appreciating many aspects of native African culture. Above all, he was implacably opposed to slavery, which he had personally observed in Savannah, as radically demeaning all who touched it. The antislavery movements in England and America would follow in Wesley's footsteps.

Wesley's purpose in all of this was to show not just a small slice of human history but the whole of it in a sweeping panorama. The whole of history is thoroughly saturated with corruptions analogous to those described summarily in Genesis 3 and Romans 1 – 2. There is, Wesley thought, a cohesion in the biblical description of sin that is illustrated at every turn of subsequent so-called secular human history.[50]

In "Thoughts on a Late Publication" (1789), a critique of a report by H. Wilson and George Keate on their travels to the Pelew Islands, Wesley took strong exception to the romantic hypothesis that the natives of Pelew constituted "a nation who

---

[46]DOS, pt. 1, J IX:208 – 9, sec. 2.1.
[47]See Wesley's journal accounts of interactions with Native Americans in his ministry to them in Georgia, JJW 1:156 – 62, 236 – 39, 248 – 50, 297 – 98, 406 – 9.
[48]DOS, pt. 1, J IX:210 – 13, sec. 2.3.
[49]DOS, pt. 1, J IX:213 – 15, sec. 2.4, 5.
[50]DOS, pt. 1, J IX:208 – 15, sec. 2.1 – 5.

are by nature free from sin, without any ill tempers, without anything blamable either in their words or actions."[51] Even this report shows that they murdered prisoners in cold blood and practiced polygamy and suffered frequent theft. "I have conversed, in fourscore years, (between forty and fifty of which I have, at an average, travelled four thousand miles a year,) with more persons than these two gentlemen[52] put together; and many of them Indians of various nations, Creeks, Cherokees, Chickasaws, and no ways infected with Christianity: But one such man as [described in the Pelew account] I have not found."[53] "If mankind are faultless by nature, naturally endued with light to see all necessary truth, and with strength to follow it ... revelation is a mere fable."[54] Homer fantastically supposed that the Ethiopians were similarly unblamable, but even Homer did little justice to humankind if the account of the Pelew natives be true.

2. The Universality of Sin in Theistic Cultures

If these problems with sin pervade the nontheistic history of humanity, to what degree are they mitigated in the theistic world, as one might hope? Wesley addressed first the Muslim world as he knew it, again by certain exaggerated characterizations. But keep in mind his purpose. It was to show the universality of corruption and misery — not to show that Muslims are intrinsically more corrupt than Christians and animists but equally prone to be so.[55] He decried Islamic holy wars undertaken with religious rhetoric disguising economic motivations. He said that Muslims had earned their reputation as "wolves and tigers to all other nations." He viewed the rigid attachment of Islamic followers to an untranslatable Koran as the height of immobile irrationality. He warned of the tendencies to fanaticism in Islamic determinism, whose exponents are prone to "beat each other's brains from generation to generation!"[56]

Wesley's views of alternative cultures are not to be taken as normative for our time. What we are seeking to grasp is his fundamental point of view toward the general corruptibility of human nature and how it correlates with the human condition everywhere.

3. The Universality of Sin in Predominantly Christian Cultures

Having addressed the universality of sin in nontheistic and theistic cultures, Wesley then proceeded to speak about the special forms of sin prevailing in supposedly Christian cultures, first Greek Orthodox and then Roman Catholic, leaving his most devastating disapproval for Protestants. With both the Orthodox and Roman

---

[51]"Thoughts on a Late Publication," J XIII:411.
[52]Captain W. Wilson and George Keate, *An Account of the Pelew Islands*; *JJW* 7:464; 8:29; *AM* (1790): 545; (1791): 38–39.
[53]"Thoughts on a Late Publication," J XIII:412.
[54]"Thoughts on a Late Publication," J XIII:413.
[55]For further reference to Islam, see *LJW* 1:277; 5:250; 6:118, 123, 371; *JJW* 5:242; 1:31–32; *CH* 7:608.
[56]*DOS*, pt. 1, J IX:215–16, sec. 2.6.

traditions, he was quick to see the abuses of sacramental teaching and the resistance to reformation. The Counter-Reformation inquisition revealed the layered hypocrisies that he thought were rife in Roman canon law.[57]

Given the withering power of his censure of these traditions, one might expect him then to have been a little softer on Protestantism. But again his critique only intensified. For in none of the preceding cultural criticisms would he be more stringent than in his own. He aimed squarely at the irascible Protestant tendencies toward divisiveness, how they had failed to become a tradition of continuing reform, and especially their failure to reform their own social abuses. Among key examples of the perennial injustices of societies shaped by Protestant religion were poverty, war, social oppression, prostitution, and litigiousness, with "villains exalted to the highest places."[58]

The court itself, sworn to uphold justice, had become an instrument for perverting justice. Honesty among lawyers was very thinly spread.[59] "If my neighbor has a mind to my cow, he hires a lawyer to prove that he ought to have my cow from me. I must hire another to defend my right, it being against all rules of law that a man should speak for himself. In pleading, they do not dwell on the merits of the cause, but upon circumstances foreign thereto."[60]

Wesley's point: sin is everywhere an empirical fact, even where civilized virtues attempt to shine brightest. Wherever we see the human will at work, we see its miserable products. There is nowhere to look in human history where we will not find a history of injustice, a dismal account of the social and interpersonal transmission of sin and misery.[61]

4. Whether War Is a Prototype of Social Sin

Wesley's most recurrent example of social sin was *war.* He examined realistically what happens when leaders become inordinately ambitious for power. Innocents are killed. He was stunned by the endless ways we deceive ourselves, pretending in our nationalism that we are exceedingly advanced morally—rational and well intentioned, all while promoting the enterprises of institutionalized horror.

> Now, who can reconcile war, I will not say to religion, but to any degree of reason or common sense?... Here are forty thousand men gathered together on this plain. What are they going to do? See, there are thirty or forty thousand more at a little distance. And these are going to shoot them through the head or body, to stab them, or split their skulls, and send most of their souls into everlasting fire as fast as they possibly can. Why so?... They do not so much as know them.... What a method of proof! What an amazing way of deciding controversies!

All our declamations on the strength of human reason, and the eminence of our

---

[57]*DOS*, pt. 1, J IX:217–19, sec. 2.7–9.
[58]*DOS*, pt. 1, J IX:219–21, sec. 2.9.
[59]*DOS*, pt. 1, J IX:228–30, sec. 2.11.
[60]*DOS*, pt. 1, J IX:219–21, sec. 2.9, quoting Abraham Cowley.
[61]*DOS*, pt. 1, J IX:230–38, sec. 2.12–15.

virtues, are no more than the cant and jargon of pride and ignorance, so long as there is such a thing as war in the world.[62]

5. Experiential Self-Examination Confirms the Universality of Sin

As if this indictment were not enough, Wesley invited each reader to "survey" her or his own behavior. Whatever may be the objective situation in human history, the question may be asked even more personally and inwardly by any serious person: Am I pleased with my own behavior? The last time I made a resolution, how long did it take to actually correct my behavior? Each hearer is called to press such questions in the most candid way directly home to the scenes of daily decisions.[63] How long has it been since my conscience told me that I did something contrary to justice? Who has not entertained "unreasonable desires" one knows are wrong? Who has not taken one's anger further than the cause required?[64] Only the hearer can answer in the depths of inwardness.[65] Few can honestly answer these questions without a tinge of repentance.

Hence those with any remaining doubt about original sin do well to examine themselves in complete honesty, scrutinizing skewed motives and the bad consequences of their good intentions. Wesley probed relentlessly into whether people had made promises that remained unfulfilled, whether their spouses were treated fairly, what children thought of their parents' fairness, how those closest to them judged their trustability. When guilt creeps in and we wonder where it came from, is this not the voice of conscience?

We resolve to change but remain the same. We say things contrary to truth or love that we later regret.[66] If all were honest, would written receipts be required? In any serious self-examination, those who look at their behavior know how far below the mark they fall.

Long before sociologist Erving Goffman spoke of impression management, Wesley was observing that "the generality of men do not wear their worst side outward. Rather, they study to appear better than they are, and to conceal what they can of their faults." We conceal parts of ourselves that others may not see the whole. Our modes of impression management always make us put on a face better than the reality.[67] For Wesley all such sociological truisms stand as empirical testimony to the universality of human corruption.[68]

Guilt plays a key role in bringing us to ourselves by helping us see where we are failing to reflect the goodness of God in human relationship. Guilt functions

---

[62]DOS, pt. 1, J IX:221–23, sec. 2.10.

[63]SS 2:215.

[64]This stands in the Puritan tradition of penitential self-examination of conscience. B 1:299; 2:215, 511; 3:124n.

[65]DOS, pt. 1, J IX:236–38, sec. 2.15.

[66]DOS, pt. 1, J IX:231–34, sec. 2.12.

[67]DOS, pt. 1, J IX:234, sec. 2.13.

[68]JWTT 56.

positively to call us to ourselves in God's presence. Conscience is that universally experienced human awareness that relentlessly notices whenever we fall short of the image of God trying to shine through our human finitude.[69]

6. The Unhappiness of Universal Human History Is Due to the Unholiness of Human Choices

"Universal misery is at once a consequence and a proof of this universal corruption. Men are unhappy (how very few are the exceptions!) because they are unholy....'Pain accompanies and follows sin.'"[70] As long as "vicious tempers" rule the heart, peace has no place there. "Sin is the root of trouble, and it is unholiness which causes unhappiness." Unhappiness is neither attributable to economic hardship nor prevented by frugality or abundance.[71]

No moment of human history is left unaffected by this misery. The ground of our misery is our lack of actually reflecting the holiness of God, the image of God originally given in human creation. We do not exercise our original capacity for proximately reflecting or imaging God. Our persistent unholiness is the basis for our unhappiness.

After untold centuries of actual and voluntary sin, human history is not rightly described as rather a bit unhappy. Much stronger terms are required: wretchedness, misery. "Sin is the baleful source of affliction; and consequently, the flood of miseries which covers the face of the earth — which overwhelms not only single persons, but whole families, towns, cities, kingdoms — is a demonstrative proof of the overflowing of ungodliness in every nation under heaven."[72] All of this we can learn rationally and experientially, from the study of history, society, and self. All of this we can learn from experience and historical observation, apart from sacred Scripture.

D. Learning from Scripture about Original Sin

Although Wesley found abundant evidences for original sin in historical, sociological, and experiential inquiries, it was chiefly from Scripture that he sought to counter the deistic[73] arguments against intergenerational guilt and spiritual death as a result of the history of sin.

1. From the Beginning

Original means "first." Original sin is the first form of sin in human history that dates back to the primordial beginning of the human story. That sin is original which is the archetype of subsequent sin, derivative from the first sin, and being

---

[69]B 1:301 – 4; 3:479 – 90.

[70]*DOS*, pt. 1, J IX:235, sec. 2.14; *culpam poena premit comes.*

[71]*DOS*, pt. 1, J IX:237, sec. 2.15; cf. B 1:197 – 98; 4:287 – 88.

[72]*DOS*, pt. 1, J IX:235 – 38, sec. 2.14 – 15.

[73]For Wesley's comments on deism, see B 3:452, 494, 499; FA, B 11:175 – 76; *LJW* 2:75, 96, 313; 7:263 – 65; *JJW* 1:357; 3:433.

configured from the fallen human condition becomes the formative pattern for other sins in history.

No sooner did God give humanity freedom than we managed to corrupt and adulterate it. This is what human beings have been doing from the very origins of human history. That is essentially what original sin means. Fallen human history has been molded by sin in ways that influence all subsequent communication.

The biblical way of portraying and corporately signifying the radical fallenness of humanity is by rehearsing the account of Adam and Eve.[74] They fell from holiness and happiness in a way that has decisively impacted the entire subsequent history of freedom.[75]

Each of us has become involved in their story. Their story has become our own — the human story, the history of sin. What they did has consequences for us, just as what we do has consequences for all who follow us. Broken freedom makes whimpers and howls that echo endlessly toward the future. The consequences of my sin do not end with me but impact others after me whom I will never see.

2. Whether One Suffers from Another's Sin

The evil lodged at the heart of human history cannot be explained merely in terms of having followed a bad example or being cursed by a bad environment or upbringing. It requires the more searching scriptural premise of the corrupted and corrupting will.[76]

The first scriptural evidence of original sin is that after Adam and Eve sinned, they were filled with shame, eliciting a sense of nakedness, fear, and guilt, and loss of the graces they had earlier received. And even their shame in the presence of the holy God was deceptively covered up because of their pride, which refused to acknowledge their guilt.[77]

Scripturally, the consequence of Adam's sin was death not only for Adam but for all his progeny.[78] In Adam all die as the consequence of the disobedience of one.[79] It is false to assert that Adam's posterity could not be justly punished for the transgression of the prototypical human sin. For that would be to deny the interconnected character of human history passed on from generation to generation.

This interconnectedness is evident in the fact that we suffer for each other. "So we do in fact suffer for Adam's sin, and that too by the sentence inflicted on our first parents. We suffer death in consequence of their transgression. Therefore we are, in some sense, guilty of their sin. I would ask, What is guilt, but an obligation to suffer punishment for sin? Now since we suffer the same penal evil which God threatened

[74]B 4:366.
[75]In *DOS*, pt. 4., Wesley developed this point by including a substantial extract from Isaac Watts's response to John Taylor: *The Ruin and Recovery of Mankind* (1741); *DOS*, pt. 4; J IX:397–415.
[76]*DOS*, pt. 2, J IX:238–39, sec. 1.1.
[77]*DOS*, pt. 2, J IX:241–42, sec. 1.4; cf. B 1:442–43.
[78]*SS* 1:157.
[79]*DOS*, pt. 2, J IX:240–41, sec. 1.3; Gen. 2:17.

to, and inflicted on, Adam for his sin.... Therefore we are all in some way guilty of Adam's sin."[80] But how does sin lead to death?

E. Sin and Death

1. Distinguishing Temporal Death from Spiritual Death

Taylor had argued individualistically that the only result of the fall was individual physical death for Adam. He did not grasp that it had vast consequences for the corruption of human nature socially. Wesley responded that death in Adam implies far more than the loss of his own personal bodily life. The death expressed in the original admonition and pronounced on humanity included a judgment on all evils that affect the temporal body: "death temporal, spiritual, and eternal," both a temporal death (dissolution of the body) and a spiritual death (loss of eternal life).[81]

The result of original sin was a continuing propensity to sin, which itself resulted in actual sins of individuals in human history. Taylor could not imagine how a just God could hold progeny accountable for their parents' sin. Wesley appealed to the corporate anthropology of the scriptural narratives that show that the sins of the fathers are often visited on their posterity.[82]

2. Whether Redemption in Christ Makes Up for Losses Suffered in Adam

By one man sin entered the world. The punishment threatened to Adam is now inflicted on all humanity, so that all are deemed sinners in the presence of God. By one offense, death reigned in human history. All human beings are involved in this single judicial sentence. Assuming social connectedness, all of Adam's progeny live in a default situation of enduring the consequences.

As by the offense of one many are dead, by one, grace is extended to all humanity. In one, Adam, many are made dead. In one, Christ, many are made alive. What is lost by one is restored by the other. Through our relation with Adam, we all suffer. But there is good news: through our relation with the second Adam, all are offered new life, and all who believe effectively receive new life.[83]

Though all humanity died spiritually in Adam,[84] humanity has nonetheless gained more blessings through Christ than it lost in Adam. Where sin abounds, grace abounds more.[85] The benefit we attain through Christ far surpasses what we mislay in Adam. For those who repent and believe Christ removes all sin, and not original sin only. Christ raises believers to a far happier state than that which Adam enjoyed in paradise.[86]

---

[80]*DOS*, pt. 2, J IX:242 – 43, sec. 1.5, with reference to Jennings's *Vindication*.
[81]*DOS*, pt. 2, J IX:244 – 45, sec. 1.6; on physical and spiritual death, see B 1:142 – 47, 227 – 28.
[82]*DOS*, pt. 1, J IX:244 – 46, sec. 1.6 – 7.
[83]*DOS*, pt. 2, J IX:255 – 57, sec. 1.16.
[84]*DOS*, pt. 2, J IX:257 – 61, sec. 1.17 – 18.
[85]*DOS*, pt. 2, J IX:253 – 55, sec. 1.14.
[86]*DOS*, pt. 2, J IX:242 – 46, sec. 1.5 – 7.

3. The Westminster Catechism on Original Sin

A detailed exegetical inquiry ensued into principal passages of Scripture on original sin, particularly those cited by six propositions on original sin of the Larger Catechism of Westminster,[87] which formed a useful structure on which to organize his exegetical study, though Wesley added, "To this I never subscribed, but I think it is in the main a very excellent composition, which I shall therefore cheerfully endeavour to defend, so far as I conceive it is grounded on clear Scripture."[88]

Taylor opposed all six propositions of the Westminster Confession because he thought they (1) demeaned human freedom and moral agency, and (2) intensi-fied the impasse of theodicy. Wesley answered both objections. Original sin does not imply that humanity lacks moral choice, for through prevenient or initiating grace, God is forever offering to lead humanity toward saving grace. As with Calvin's teaching of common grace, this form of grace gives the opportunity of restoring some measure of free will to all who seek it. It is not by their fallen nature but by common grace that rational moral agents are able to seek relative forms of justice in political society.

Sufficient prevenient grace is given to all humanity to enable us at least to pray for the grace further necessary to repent and believe.[89] Since God acted to redeem humanity, providing "a Savior for them all ... this fully acquits both his justice and his mercy."[90] The tensions created for theodicy by the doctrine of original sin are resolved not by human logic but by God's own saving deed — the redeeming action of God's grace on the cross through the Son and in our hearts through the Holy Spirit. A high doctrine of original sin is the premise and companion of a high doc-trine of grace. Since the whole of humanity is involved in guilt and punishment, having no possibility of self-salvation, we do well to cast ourselves solely on the grace offered in Christ.

F. Adam's Headship with Eve's Cooperation

1. Adam as a Public Person: On Federal Headship

Wesley defended Westminster Proposition 1: "The covenant being made with Adam not only for himself, but for his posterity, all mankind descending from him by ordinary generation, sinned in him, and fell with him, in his first transgres-sion."[91] Original sin best explains the universality of sin. All alternative explanations — example, custom, education, or the passage of time — are inept insofar as they skip over the decisive first cause, thus failing to grasp why sin is so pervasive in human history.

---

[87]*DOS*, pt. 2, J IX:261–88, sec. 2.1.
[88]*DOS*, pt. 2, J IX:261, sec. 2.1.
[89]*DOS*, pt. 2, J IX:273, sec. 2.9, 10.
[90]*DOS*, pt. 2, J IX:285, sec. 2.18.
[91]COC 111:679; *DOS*, pt. 2, J IX:262, sec. 2.2.

Adam stands at the head of human history as a "public person."[92] The divine command to "not eat" and the deadly consequence of its neglect were addressed not merely to Adam personally but to all humanity corporately.[93]

Neither *representative head* nor *federal head* are scriptural terms, hence for Wesley they were hardly worthy of lengthy disputation. Nonetheless, he argued that both Adam and Christ are portrayed in Scripture as representatives of all humanity. Both include both genders. Adam as a "public person" was an anticipative type or figure of Christ, for as all juridically die in Adam, all are by grace made alive in Christ. As God laid on all of humanity the iniquities of Adam, so God laid on Christ the iniquities of us all.[94] Though Eve's choice preceded Adam's, Adam by consenting became the representative figure for sin in the whole of the history that followed him.

2. The Consequence of Adam's Fall for Subsequent Human History

Wesley defended Westminster Proposition 2: "The fall brought mankind into an estate of sin and misery."[95] Adam's disobedience brought guilt and spiritual death to all, not just physical suffering and death to Adam. Humanity as a whole was swept into a corporate state of sin and suffering, making all people corrupt and guilty and subject to punishment.[96] In the fall, the image of God in all humanity was gravely damaged, though not entirely obliterated (Gen. 5:1–3; Eccl. 7:29). Romans 5 and 1 Corinthians 15 describe the situation as one of spiritual death. Before the fall, Adam was perfect, but his perfection was not absolute, since he could grow and change and alter his future by his own decisions. He was temptable as a result of his natural liberty. In response to Taylor's interpretation of death not as a punishment for sin but as a benefit to all humanity intended to increase the vanity of earthly things and abate their force to delude us, Scripture counters constantly that it is a punishment.[97]

Wesley defended Westminster Proposition 3: " 'Sin is any want of conformity to, or transgression of, the law of God,' given as a rule to the reasonable creation."[98] By the fall, such sin comes to be "of our nature," or a kind of second nature to all who share in human history. We are described as having a law of sin in our members (Rom. 7:23), being dead in sin (Eph. 2:1).

3. The Abyss into Which Humanity Plunged

Wesley defended Westminster Proposition 4: "The sinfulness of that estate whereinto man fell, consists in the guilt of Adam's first sin, the want of original

---

[92]*LJW* 4:98, 155.

[93]*DOS*, pt. 2, J IX:262, sec. 2.2.

[94]*DOS*, pt. 3, J IX:332–34, sec. 6. Both Adam and Eve are jointly responsible for the original fall of humanity into these syndromes of sin, but in Genesis Adam took on a headship or federal role in the debacle.

[95]*DOS*, pt. 2, J IX:263, sec. 2.3; COC 111:679.

[96]*DOS*, pt. 1, J IX:263, sec. 2.3.

[97]*DOS*, pt. 2, J IX:258–59, sec. 1.18.

[98]*DOS*, pt. 2, J IX:264, sec. 2.4; quoting Westminster Shorter Catechism, Q 14, COC 111:678.

righteousness, and the corruption of his whole nature, which is commonly called original sin; together with all actual transgressions which proceed from it."[99] "The LORD saw how great the wickedness of the human race had become on the earth, and that every inclination of the thoughts of the human heart was only evil all the time" (Gen. 6:5 NIV). "Now the earth was corrupt in God's sight and was full of violence" (Gen. 6:11 NIV).[100] It is not fitting to hedge with elaborate excuses the clear biblical description that "our very nature exposed us to the Divine Wrath, like the rest of mankind" (Eph. 2:3 TCNT, so that we "were by nature the children of wrath," KJV).[101] "The mind governed by the flesh is death.... Those who are in the realm of the flesh cannot please God" (Rom. 8:6, 8 NIV).[102] "Without supernatural grace, we can neither will nor do what is pleasing to God."[103]

Wesley corroborated David Jennings's subtle argument in response to Taylor's view that if sin is natural, it is necessary. "If by sin is meant the corrupt bias of our wills, that indeed is natural to us, as our nature is corrupted by the fall; but not as it came originally out of the hand of God.... A proud or passionate temper is evil, whether a man has contracted it himself, or derived it from his parents." If by sin is meant those sinful actions to which this corrupt bias of the will inclines us, it is not self-evident that these are necessary. "If a corrupt bias makes sin to be necessary, and consequently, to be no sin, then the more any man is inclined to sin, the less sin he can commit.... And so the man, instead of growing more wicked, grows more innocent."[104]

"Is God the cause of those sinful motions? He is the cause of the motion ... [but] of the sin, he is not ... otherwise you make God the direct author of all the sin under heaven." This view of original sin has ancient ecumenical conciliar assent, being held in the Greek East and the Latin West, and ecumenically, "so far as we can learn, in every church under heaven."[105]

4. Distinguishing Original Sin from Actual Sin

Wesley then defended Westminster Proposition 5: "Original sin is conveyed from our first parents to their posterity by natural generation, so as all that proceed from them in that way are conceived and born in sin."[106] Actual sins spring from within the context of original sin. Evil works proceed from an evil heart. We choose to follow a natural inclination to sin. As the psalmist expressed it: "Surely I was sinful at birth, sinful from the time my mother conceived me" (Ps. 51:5 NIV). Otherwise the work of saving grace in Christ would hardly be necessary, were there no insidious captivity in the human predicament. Wesley found empirical evidence

---

[99]COC 111:679; *DOS* pt. 2, J IX:264, sec. 2.5; on sin as indebtedness, see B 1:586.
[100]*DOS*, pt. 2, J IX:272, sec. 2.9.
[101]*DOS*, pt. 2, J IX:266 – 69, sec. 2.6.
[102]*DOS*, pt. 2, J IX:271, sec. 2.8.
[103]*DOS*, pt. 2, J IX:273, sec. 2.10.
[104]Ibid., in reference to *Vindication*, 68.
[105]*DOS*, pt. 2, J IX:274, sec. 2.11.
[106]*DOS*, pt. 2, J IX:275, sec. 2.13.

for this in the primitive egocentricities of neonates, and in the fact that some still sin without even being tempted, which he thought to be confirmation of an internally rooted rebelliousness against the giver of good.

One person's sin and its consequent punishment are in fact visited on others. This is the solemn principle of the social and corporeal nature and consequence of sin in human history. For progenitors' sins, descendants in fact often must suffer. This is a part of the high price we pay for the precious gift of freedom.

But by grace we are empowered to conquer this primordial inclination.[107] Even though we were "conceived in sin and shapen in iniquity," there is always sufficient grace in God's saving deed to remove whatever sin has been willed. That "my mother conceived me" does not refer flatly to sexual copulation but to the general history of sin in which my physical conception took place. Eve is the mother of us all.[108] "Who can bring what is pure from the impure? No one!" (Job 14:4 NIV).[109] Yet no one can plead being excused from culpability by appealing to another's depravity.

G. Answering Questions on the Insidious Spread of Sin

1. The Intergenerational Sociality of Sin

The premise of the sociality of sin is a deeply held scriptural assumption. It goes directly against the stream of naive individualism, which assumes that we are responsible only for our private, individual actions, not for others or for how our behavior touches others. Hebraic consciousness passionately held to the social nature of human existence. Wesley shared that assumption of relational humanity and translated it into eighteenth-century terms, controversies, and moral choices.

Your sin can affect me; my sin can affect my grandchildren; my grandfather's sin can affect me in ways difficult to understand exhaustively, yet to some degree subject to empirical analysis. These causal chains are not wholly mysterious or beyond inquiry, yet there remains a stubborn element of the mystery of iniquity in all human freedom, since these causal chains are often hidden in the complex history of freedom's outcomes.

Sin's effects reverberate from age to age. Wesley ruled out an individual conception of sin populated only by two parties, God and me. The individualistic fantasy is that my foibles do not affect anybody else, or if so, surely not all that seriously, or if seriously, surely not eternally. Wrong. Wesley viewed the human predicament as radically bound together in social covenant. This was ultimately symbolized by the notion of the federal headship of Adam representing humanity, and all whose life and breath derive finally from Eve, the mother of all living. All it took was one man and one woman to together lead all humanity astray.

Their choices, free choices, were not fated, not determined, but chosen, and these preferences were permitted by God as the one who originally offered and sub-

---

[107]*DOS*, pt. 2, J IX:275, sec. 2.12.
[108]*DOS*, pt. 2, J IX:275–79, sec. 2.13.
[109]*DOS*, pt. 2, J IX:279–80, sec. 2.14–15.

sequently honored human self-determination. God does not want sin but permits sin in the interest of preserving free, companionate, self-determined persons with whom to communicate incomparable divine love and holiness.

2. The Communication of the Sin of Adam and Eve to All Humanity

It is predictable that my generation is going to have its good and bad effects on the next generation, and the next on the next. No one begins with a clean slate, because all finite freedom lives in an actual history, not a fantasy world. We truly affect the destinies and possibilities of others. This is a highly realistic assumption about the moral consequences of human choices. Wesley found this doctrine of sin clearly attested throughout Scripture, Genesis to Revelation, especially in the prophetic and apostolic witnesses, and in no voice more definitely than Jesus'.

All other less realistic hypotheses for explaining sin are deficient. Some wish for a crafty escape hatch from responsibility in the notion that sin occurs exhaustively by social determination, that since we learn by example, custom, and social processes, sin is transferred *without our willing it*. Wesley answered that social processes obviously transfer sin but not without our willing it. Each of us reinforces and relives the history of Adam and Eve's fallenness.

3. Whether Loss of Communion with God Sharpens the Sting of Unexplained Suffering

Wesley defended Westminster Proposition 6: "All mankind by their fall lost communion with God, are under his wrath and curse, and so made liable to all the miseries in this life."[110] "The faded glory, the darkness, the disorder, the impurity, the decayed state in all respects of this temple, too plainly show the Great Inhabitant is gone."[111]

God originally created our natures pure. Evil is the absurd corruption of nature brought on by Adam's free choice under God's permissive will. Otherwise God would be guilty of authoring evil. God is the *primum mobile*, the spring of all motion throughout the universe, thus the first cause of every vegetable, animal, and human activity. Yet sin is not God's will but due to the willing of men and women. Even at our conception, we are drenched in the history of sin. That is not God's doing but comes as a result of that measure of human pride, envy, and rebelliousness permitted by God. God "who this moment supplies the power by which a sinful action is committed is not chargeable with the sinfulness of that action."[112]

To those who challenge the justice of God in allowing the history of sin, Wesley had an eschatological answer: the provision of "a Saviour for them all; and this fully acquits both [God's] justice and mercy."[113]

---

[110]*COC* 111:679–80; *DOS*, pt. 2, J IX:282, sec. 2.17.

[111]*DOS*, pt. 2, J IX:288, sec. 2.20; quoted from John Howe, *The Living Temple* (London: Parkhurst, 1703).

[112]*DOS*, pt. 3, J IX:335, sec. 7.

[113]*DOS*, pt. 2, J IX:285, sec. 2.18.

4. Whether There Remains a Natural Tendency to Sin

Are we now in worse moral circumstances than Adam? Yes, if by "moral circumstances" we mean the decline of religion and virtue. No, if by "moral circumstances" we are referring to some provision of spiritual improvement, for in that case we are far better off than Adam, due to the history of grace.[114]

We derive from Adam a natural propensity to sin, within the permissive will of God, but this does not make God the source, only the permitter, of wrongful acts of human freedom. All born into history's corruptions have "a natural propensity to sin. Nevertheless, this propensity is not necessary, if by necessary you mean irresistible. We can resist and conquer it too, by the grace which is ever at hand."[115]

In response to Taylor's arguments against a propensity to sin in our fallen nature, Wesley contended that we commit sinful acts because we are sinners: "I (and you too, whether you will it or no) am inclined, and was ever since I can remember antecedently to any choice of my own, to pride, revenge, idolatry."[116]

Do the vices of parents in fact often infect their children? The most common observation shows that they do. This cannot stand as a charge against the justice of God.

If we lack the premise of original sin, it is hard to account for the fact that children begin to sin so soon. As soon as their faculties appear, they appear to be disordered. The use and abuse of reason grow up together.[117]

Human freedom has always shown itself prone, given time, to espouse and implement this fallenness. The social history of sin inclines personal freedom toward harmful habituation. The inclination to evil appears inevitably with the gift of freedom. Individual, self-determining freedom finds its own distinctive ways to further distort the history of sin and subtly collude with temptations to choose the lesser good.

5. Whether Guilt May Be Imputed from One to Another

As guilt was imputed to the scapegoat in Hebraic sacrificial liturgy, so are our sins borne by Christ on the cross. No just God would punish the innocent, but "God does not look upon infants as innocent, but as involved in the guilt of Adam's sin," and at times suffering mightily from their parents' sins, even as they may benefit from their parents' righteousness.[118]

That all are under the curse of sin is evident from the fact that all suffer.[119] Suffering may result even where there is no personal, individual sin, but only indirect, corporate sin. Brutes and infants may suffer even without exercising their wills sin-

---

[114]*DOS*, pt. 2, J IX:289, sec. 3.
[115]*DOS*, pt. 2, J IX:284, sec. 3.
[116]*DOS*, pt. 2, J IX:294, sec. 3.
[117]*DOS*, pt. 2, J IX:295, sec. 3.
[118]*DOS*, pt. 3, J IX:316, sec. 1.
[119]*DOS*, pt. 3, J IX:317–19, sec. 2.

fully as individuals, because their lives are framed in the context of corporate sin.[120] Human toil and pain in childbirth are the prototype scriptural evidences that progeny suffer for the sins of their parents. However great their sufferings, "the best of men cannot be made unhappy by any calamities or oppressions whatsoever," for they have learned to be content in every possible state, rejoicing and giving thanks.[121]

The teaching of human nature as radically fallen does not indicate that one despises humanity, "since, whatever we are by nature, we may by grace be children of God, and heirs." Even when sinners have lost the power to perform their duty by nature, they still by grace may perform it, and thus it does not cease to be their duty.[122]

H. The Hidden Link between Redemption and Original Sin

1. Original Sin and New Birth

Regeneration does not mean the *self-initiated* process of "gaining habits of holiness," for that would locate it as a natural change, while it is a change enabled by supernatural *grace*. "The new birth is not, as you supposed, the progress, or the whole, of sanctification, but the beginning of it; as the natural birth is not the whole of life, but only the entrance upon it. He that is 'born of a woman,' then begins to live a natural life; he that is 'born of God,' then begins to live a spiritual."[123]

"There is no possibility of the power of godliness" without first understanding sin. "No man truly believes in Christ till he is deeply convinced of his own sinfulness, and helplessness. But this no man ever was, neither can be, who does not know he has a corrupt nature."[124]

Original sin, far from being a threat to moral endeavor, is a spur to the repentance that readies the will for faith active in love. Far from turning people away from God in moral disgust, it turns sinners toward God in the more radical sense of trusting in grace.

The doctrine, that we are by nature "dead in sin," and therefore "children of wrath," promotes repentance, a true knowledge of ourselves, and thereby leads to faith in Christ, to a true knowledge of Christ crucified. And faith works the love; and by love, all holiness both of heart and life. Consequently, this doctrine promotes (nay, and is absolutely, indispensably necessary to promote) the whole of that religion which the Son of God lived and died to establish.[125]

In the new birth, believers "put on the new man" (Col. 3:10) by a real inward change,

---

[120]*DOS*, pt. 3, J IX:320 – 26, sec. 3.
[121]*DOS*, pt. 3, J IX:324 – 26, sec. 3.
[122]*DOS*, pt. 3, J IX:327, sec. 4.
[123]*DOS*, pt. 2, J IX:310, sec. 3.
[124]*DOS*, pt. 2, J IX:313, sec. 3.
[125]*DOS*, pt. 2, J IX:312, sec. 3.

a renewal of the soul in "righteousness and true holiness" (Eph. 4:24), a renewal of the image of God in us—where God's love governs the senses, appetites, and passions, as was the case in the prefallen Adam.[126]

2. Reframing Wesley's Doctrine within Contemporary Culture

Wesley's views still haunt the present inheritors of the Protestant traditions, though they inhabit a society in which these assumptions seem easily dismissible.[127] Those who preach can no longer assume that modern Protestant audiences understand the premise of original sin around which other biblical teachings pivot.

To refix the pivot must then become a part of the teaching of discipleship. The responsibility to enter this arena falls to those to whom the teaching task is committed. They have a duty to teach this sober biblical truth to persons today, even and especially while the culture is resisting it. To do so requires an insurgency against the romanticist optimism of a modern cultural momentum that appearing sweet has gone sour.

We have watched drug abuse spread, trapping seeming innocents before they know they are caught in a syndrome they can hardly escape, feeling they must supply their habit, colluding with mixed motives, doing violence to remain addicted. This describes original sin. The key terms above are *seeming, hardly, feeling,* and *colluding.* They are not wholly innocent due to their collusions with evil, and their feeling of bondage is not absolutely unaffected by their own prior choices.

Wesley intuited (as Reinhold Niebuhr would later state explicitly) that the only Christian doctrine supported by extensive empirical evidence is original sin: "Original sin ... is no play of imagination, but plain, clear fact. We see it with our eyes and hear it with our ears daily. Heathens, Turks, Jews, Christians, of every nation, as such men as are there described. Such are the tempers, such the manners, of lords, gentlemen, clergymen, in England, as well as of tradesmen and the low vulgar. No man in his senses can deny it; and none can account for it but upon the supposition of original sin."[128]

What is today ironically called "news" sets forth this perennial evidence anew each day. The media function constantly as exploiters of human corruption, but few think of this as original sin.

I. Conclusion

Wesley did not think the problem of sin could be solved politically, but rather only by a drastic change of heart one person at a time. Many economic problems emerge

---

[126]*DOS*, pt. 3, J IX:339–45, sec. 8.

[127]Robert Chiles, *Theological Transition in American Methodism 1790–1935* (1965; repr., New York: University Press of America, 1983), argues that the trend of the Methodist theological tradition has been to move away from original sin, from free grace to free will.

[128]Letter to Samuel Sparrow, July 2, 1772, *LJW* 5:327.

out of sin but are not resolvable economically. Renewed humanity begins afresh with a new birth made possible only by response to the merciful love of God the Son, who entered our human scene and offered himself on the cross. The new birth reshapes the entire circumference of our lives. Though original sin is a massive subject stretching from the beginning to the end of human history, rightly understood it brings each sinner to a personal decision, a change of heart, an opportunity for repentance.[129]

There is no other or better way to explain the universal extent of sin if humanity has remained forever upright by nature. The only plausible explanation for the extent and depth of sin is the biblical account of original sin.[130] Our sinning, though the result of our fallen nature, is still our responsibility. We are responsible for sin's continuance, even if not personally responsible for its primal origin.

In the appendixes to *The Doctrine of Original Sin*, there are substantial extracts from Isaac Watts's response to John Taylor, *The Ruin and Recovery of Mankind*, 1741 (part 4); Samuel Hebden's tracts in response to Taylor (parts 5 and 6);[131] and Thomas Boston's *Fourfold State of Man* (part 7).

In a concluding letter to John Taylor, Wesley spoke of his deep motivation: "Were it not on a point of so deep importance, I would no more enter the lists with Dr. Taylor, than I would lift my hand against a giant.... I am grieved for you.... O Sir, think it possible that you may have been mistaken! That you may have leaned too far, to what you thought was the better extreme! Be persuaded once more to review your whole cause, and that from the very foundation."[132] Those who seek a remedy to this dilemma are invited to read the next volume.

Further Reading on Original Sin

Bainbridge, W., and M. Riggall. "Wesley and Dr. John Taylor of Norwich." *PWHS* 16 (1928): 69–71.

Baker, Frank. "Wesley and Arminius." *PWHS* 22 (1939): 118, 119.

Blaising, Craig. "John Wesley's Doctrine of Original Sin." PhD Diss., Dallas Theological Seminary, 1979, microfilm.

Burtner, Robert W., and Robert E. Chiles. *A Compend of Wesley's Theology*, 107ff. Nashville: Abingdon, 1954.

Collins, Kenneth. "Prevenient Grace and Human Sin." In *Wesley on Salvation*. Grand Rapids: Zondervan, 1989.

Dorr, Donal. "Total Corruption and the Wesleyan Tradition: Prevenient Grace." *Irish Theological Quarterly* 31 (1964): 303–21.

Hannah, Vern A. "Original Sin and Sanctification: A Problem for Wesleyans." *WTJ* 12 (Spring 1977): 47–53.

---

[129] *CH* 7:513, 550, 560.

[130] *DOS*, pt. 2, J IX:286–88, sec. 2.20.

[131] "Man's Original Righteousness," "Baptismal Regeneration Disproved," and "The Doctrine of Original Sin," 1740–41.

[132] *DOS*, pt. 6, J IX:431–33.

Harper, Steve. *John Wesley's Message for Today*, 27 – 30. Grand Rapids: Zondervan, 1983.

Joy, James R. "Wesley: A Man of a Thousand Books and a Book." *RL* 8 (1939): 71 – 84.

Keefer, Luke L., Jr. "Characteristics of Wesley's Arminianism." *WTJ* 22 (Spring 1987): 88 – 100.

Lindström, Harald J. *Wesley and Sanctification*. Nashville: Abingdon: 1946.

Miley, John. *Systematic Theology*. Reprint, Peabody, MA: Hendrickson, 1989.

Payne, George. *The Doctrine of Original Sin*. London: Jackson and Walford, 1845.

Pope, William Burt. *A Compendium of Christian Theology*. 3 vols. London: Wesleyan Methodist Book-Room, 1880.

Ralston, Thomas N. *Elements of Divinity*. New York: Abingdon, 1924.

Rose, Delbert. "The Wesleyan Understanding of Sin." In *Distinctive Emphases of Asbury Theological Seminary*, 7 – 30.

Slaatte, Howard A. *Fire in the Brand: Introduction to the Creative Work and Theology of John Wesley*, 115ff. New York: Exposition, 1963.

Smith, H. Shelton. *Changing Conceptions of Original Sin*. New York: Scribner, 1955.

Starkey, Lycurgus M. *The Work of the Holy Spirit*. Nashville: Abingdon, 1962.

Summers, Thomas O. *Systematic Theology*. 2 vols. Edited by J. J. Tigert. Nashville: Methodist Publishing House South, 1888.

Watson, Richard. *Theological Institutes*. 2 vols. New York: Mason and Lane, 1836, 1840; edited by John M'Clintock, New York: Carlton & Porter, 1850.

Williams, Colin. "Original Sin." In *John Wesley's Theology Today*, 47ff. Nashville: Abingdon, 1960.

Williams, N. P. *The Ideas of the Fall and of Original Sin*. London and New York: Longmans Green, 1927.

Alphabetical Correlation of the Sermons in the Jackson and Bicentennial Editions

The Bicentennial edition is represented by B. The Jackson edition is represented by J. Sermon numbers are often preceded by the pound sign (#). An asterisk (*) indicates that the homily was wrongly attributed to Mr. Wesley in at least one of its early editions, with the correct author supplied, or has varying titles or numbers in different editions.

The Almost Christian (#2, B 1:131 – 41 – #2, J V:17 – 25) — Acts 26:28

Awake, Thou That Sleepest (#3, B 1:142 – 58 = #3, J V:25 – 36) — Ephesians 5:14

A Call to Backsliders (#86, B 3:201 – 26 = #86, J VI:514 – 27) — Psalm 77:7 – 8

The Case of Reason Impartially Considered (#70, B 2:587 – 600 = #70, J VI:350 – 60) — 1 Corinthians 14:20

The Catholic Spirit (#39, B 2:79 – 96 = #2, J V:492 – 504) — 2 Kings 10:15

*The Cause and Cure of Earthquakes (by Charles Wesley — #129, Jackson ed. only, VII:386 – 99) — Psalm 46:8

The Causes of the Inefficiency of Christianity (#122, B 4:85 – 96 = #122, J VII:281 – 90) — Jeremiah 8:22

A Caution against Bigotry (#38, B 2:61 – 78 = #38, J V:479 – 92) — Mark 9:38 – 39

Christian Perfection (#40, B 2:97 – 124 = #40, J VI:1 – 22) — Philippians 3:12

The Circumcision of the Heart (#17, B 1 398 – 414 = #17, J V:202 – 12) — Romans 2:29

The Cure of Evil Speaking (#49, B 2:251 – 62 = #49, J VI:114 – 24) — Matthew 18:15 – 17

The Danger of Increasing Riches (#131, B 4:177 – 86 = #131, J VII:355 – 62) — Psalm 62:10

The Danger of Riches (#87, B 3:227 – 46 = #87, J VII:1 – 15) — 1 Timothy 6:9

Death and Deliverance (#133, B 4:204 – 14; not in Jackson)

Dives and Lazarus (#115, B 4:4 – 18 = The Rich Man and Lazarus, #112, J VII:244 – 55) — Luke 16:31

The Duty of Constant Communion (#101, B 3:427 – 39 = #101, J VII:147 – 57) — Luke 22:19

The Duty of Reproving Our Neighbor (#65, B 2:511 – 20 = #65, J VI:296 – 304) — Leviticus 19:17

The End of Christ's Coming (#62, B

2:471 – 84 = #62, J VI:267 – 77) —
1 John 3:8

The First Fruits of the Spirit (#8, B
1:233 – 47 = #8, J V:87 – 97) — Romans
8:1

Free Grace (#110, B 3:542 – 63 = #110,
J VII:373 – 86) — Romans 8:32

The General Deliverance (#60, B
2:436 – 50 = #60, J VI:241 – 52) —
Romans 8:19 – 22

The General Spread of the Gospel (#63, B
2:485 – 99 = #63, J VI:277 – 88) — Isaiah
11:9

God's Approbation of His Works (#56,
B 2:387 – 99 = #56, J VI:206 – 15) —
Genesis 1:31

God's Love to Fallen Man (#59, B
2:422 – 35 = #59, J VI:231 – 40) —
Romans 5:15

The Good Steward (#51, B 2:281 – 99 =
#51, J VI:136 – 49) — Luke 16:2

The Great Assize (#15, B 1:354 – 75 =
#15, J V:171 – 85) — Romans 14:10

The Great Privilege of Those That Are
Born of God (#19, B 1:431 – 43 = #19,
J V:223 – 33) — 1 John 3:9

Heavenly Treasure in Earthen Vessels
(#129, B 4:161 – 67 = #129, J
VII:344 – 48) — 2 Corinthians 4:7

Heaviness through Manifold Temptations
(#47, B 2:222 – 35 = #47, J VI:91 – 103)
— 1 Peter 1:6

Hell (#73, B 3:30 – 44 = #73, J VI:381 – 91)
— Mark 9:48

Human Life a Dream (#124, B 4:108 – 19
= #124, J VII:318 – 25) — Psalm 73:20

The Imperfection of Human Knowledge
(#69, B 2:567 – 86 = #69, J VI:337 – 50)
— 1 Corinthians 13:9

The Important Question (#84, B
3:181 – 98 = #84, J VI:493 – 505) —
Matthew 16:26

In What Sense We Are to Leave the
World (#81, B 3:141 – 55 = #81, J
VI:464 – 75) — 2 Corinthians 6:17 – 18

An Israelite Indeed (#90, B 3:278 – 89 =
#90, J VII:37 – 45) — John 1:47

Justification by Faith (#5, B 1:181 – 99 =
#5, J V:53 – 64) — Romans 4:5

The Late Work of God in North America
(#113, B 3:594 – 609 = #131,
J VII:409 – 29) — Ezekiel 1:16

The Law Established through Faith, 1
(#35, B 2:20 – 32 = #35, J V:447 – 57)
— Romans 3:31

The Law Established through Faith, 2
(#36, B 2:33 – 43 = #36, J V:458 – 66)
— Romans 3:31

Lord Our Righteousness (#20, B
1:444 – 65 = #20, J V:234 – 46) —
Jeremiah 23:6

Marks of the New Birth (#18, B 1:415 – 30
= #18, J V:212 – 23) — John 3:8

The Means of Grace (#16, B 1:376 – 97 =
#16, J V:185 – 201) — Malachi 3:7

The Ministerial Office (#121, B 4:72 – 84
= #115, J IV:72 – 84) — Hebrews 5:4

More Excellent Way (#89, B 3:262 – 77
= #89, J VII:26 – 37) — 1 Corinthians
12:31

The Mystery of Iniquity (#61, B 2:451 – 70
= #61, J VI:253 – 67) — 2 Thessalonians
2:7

National Sins and Miseries (#111, B
3:564 – 76 = #111, J VII:400 – 408) —
2 Samuel 24:17

The Nature of Enthusiasm (#37, B
2:44 – 60 = #37, J V:467 – 78) — Acts
26:24

The New Birth (#45, B 2:186 – 201 = #45,
J VI:65 – 77) — John 3:7

New Creation (#64, B 2:500 – 510 = #64,
J VI:288 – 96) — Revelation 21:5

Of the Church (#74, B 3:45 – 57 = #74, J VI:392 – 401) — Ephesians 4:1 – 6

Of Evil Angels (#72, B 3:16 – 29 = #72, J VI:370 – 80) — Ephesians 6:12

Of Former Times (#102, B 3:440 – 53 = #102, J VII:157 – 66) — Ecclesiastes 7:10

Of Good Angels (#71, B 3:3 – 15 = #71, J VI:361 – 70) — Hebrews 1:14

On Attending the Church Service (#104, B 3:464 – 78 = #104, J VII:174 – 85) — 1 Samuel 2:17

On Charity (#91, B 3:290 – 307 = #91, J VII:45 – 57) — 1 Corinthians 13:1 – 3

On Conscience (#105, B 3:478 – 90 = #105, J VII:186 – 94) — 2 Corinthians 1:12

On Corrupting the Word of God (#137, B 4:244 – 51 = #137, J VII:468 – 73) — 2 Corinthians 2:17

On the Death of Mr. Whitefield (#53, B 2:325 – 48 = #53, #133, J VI:167 – 82) — Numbers 20:10

On the Death of Rev. Mr. John Fletcher (#133, B 3:610 – 29 = #133; J VII:431 – 52, 1785) — Psalm 37:37

On the Deceitfulness of the Human Heart (#128, B 4:149 – 60 = #128, J VII:335 – 43) — Jeremiah 17:9

On the Discoveries of Faith (#117, B 4:28 – 38; #117, J VII:231 – 38) — Hebrews 11:1

On Dissipation (#79, B 3:115 – 25 = #79, J VI:444 – 52) — 1 Corinthians 7:35

On Divine Providence (#67, B 2:534 – 50 = #67, J VI:313 – 25) — Luke 12:7

On Dress (#88, B 3:247 – 61 = #88, J VII:15 – 26) — 1 Peter 3:3 – 4

On the Education of Children (#95, B 3:347 – 60 = #95, J VII:86 – 98) — Proverbs 22:6

On Eternity (#54, B 2:358 – 72 = #54, J VI:189 – 98) — Psalm 90:2

On Faith (#106, B 3:491 – 501 = #106, J VII:195 – 202) — Hebrews 11:6

On Faith (#132, B 4:187 – 200 = #122, J VII:326 – 35) — Hebrews 11:1

On the Fall of Man (#57, B 2:400 – 412 = #57, J VI:215 – 24) — Genesis 3:19

On Family Religion (#94, B 3:333 – 46 = #94, J VII:76 – 86) — Joshua 24:15

On Friendship with the World (#80, B 3:126 – 40 = #80, J VI:452 – 63) — James 4:4

On God's Vineyard (#107, B 3:502 – 17 = #107, J VII:203 – 13) — Isaiah 5:4

*On Grieving the Holy Spirit (by William Tilly — #137, Jackson ed. only, J VII:485 – 92) — Ephesians 4:30

*On the Holy Spirit (by John Gambold — #141, Jackson ed. only, VII:508 – 20) 2 Corinthians 3:17

On Knowing Christ after the Flesh (#123, B 4:97 – 106 = #123, J VII:291 – 96) — 2 Corinthians 5:16

On Laying the Foundation of the New Chapel (#112, B 3:577 – 93 = #112, J VII:419 – 30) — Numbers 23:23

On Living without God (#130, B 4:168 – 76 = #130, J VII:349 – 54) — Ephesians 2:12

On Love (#149, B 4:378 – 88 = #149, J VII:492 – 99) — 1 Corinthians 13:3

On Mourning for the Dead (#136, B 4:236 – 43 = #136, J VII:463 – 68) — 2 Samuel 12:23

On Obedience to Parents (#96, B 3:361 – 72 = #96, J VII:98 – 108) — Colossians 3:20

On Obedience to Pastors (#97, B 3:373 – 83 = #97, J VII:108 – 16) — Hebrews 13:17

On the Omnipresence of God (#118, B 4:39 – 47 = #118, J VII:238 – 44) — Jeremiah 23:24

Sermon on the Mount, 3 (#23, B
1:510 – 30 = #23, J V:278 – 294 —
Matthew 5:8 – 12

Sermon on the Mount, 4 (#24, B
1:531 – 49 = #24, J V:294 – 310) —
Matthew 5:13 – 16

Sermon on the Mount, 5 (#25, B
1:550 – 71 = #25, J V:310 – 27) —
Matthew 5:17 – 20

Sermon on the Mount, 6 (#26, B
1:572 – 91 = #26 J V:327 – 43) —
Matthew 6:1 – 15

Sermon on the Mount, 7 (#27, B
1:591 – 611= #27, J V:344 – 60) —
Matthew 6:16 – 18

Sermon on the Mount, 8 (#28, B
1:612 – 31 = #28, J V:361 – 77) —
Matthew 6:19 – 23

Sermon on the Mount, 9 (#29, B
1:632 – 49 = #29, J V:378 – 93) —
Matthew 6:24 – 34

Sermon on the Mount, 10 (#30, B
1:650 – 63 = #30, J V:393 – 404) —
Matthew 7:1 – 12

Sermon on the Mount, 11 (#31, B
1:664 – 74 = #31, J V:405 – 13) —
Matthew 7:13 – 14

Sermon on the Mount, 12 (#32, B
1:675 – 686 = #32, J V:414 – 22) —
Matthew 7:15 – 20

Sermon on the Mount, 13 (#33, B
1:687 – 98 = #33, J V:423 – 33) —
Matthew 7:21 – 27

The Signs of the Times (#66, B 2:521 – 33
= #66, J VII:409 – 19) — Ezekiel 1:16

The Signs of the Times (#66, B 2:521 – 33
= #66, J VI:304 – 13) — Matthew 16:3

Some Account of the Late Work of God
in North America (#113, B 3:594 – 608
= #131, J VII:409 – 29) — Ezekiel 1:16

The Spirit of Bondage and of Adoption

(#9, B 1:248 – 66 = #9, J V:98 – 111)
— Romans 8:15

Spiritual Idolatry (#78, B 3:103 – 14 = #78,
J VI:435 – 444) — 1 John 5:21

Spiritual Worship (#77, B 3:88 – 102 =
#77, J VI:424 – 435) — 1 John 5:20

The Trouble and Rest of Good Men
(#109, B 3:531 – 41= #109,
J VII:365 – 32) — Job 3:17

True Christianity Defended (#134,
Jackson ed. only, VII:452 – 62) — Isaiah
1:21

The Unity of the Divine Being (#120,
B 4:61 – 71 = #114, J VII:264 – 73) —
Mark 12:32

The Use of Money (#50, B 2:263 – 80 =
#50, J VI:124 – 36) — Luke 16:9

Walking by Sight and Walking by
Faith (#119, B 4:48 – 59 = #113, J
VII:256 – 64) — 2 Corinthians 5:7

Wandering Thoughts (#41, B 2:125 – 37 =
#41, J VI:23 – 32) — 2 Corinthians 10:5

The Way to the Kingdom (#7, B
1:217 – 32 = #7, J V:76 – 86) — Mark
1:15

What Is Man? (#103, B 3:454 – 63 = #103,
J VII:167 – 74) — Psalm 8:4

Wilderness State (#46, B 2:202 – 21 = #46,
J VI:7 – 91) — John 16:22

The Wisdom of God's Counsels (#68,
B 3:551 – 66 = #68, J VI:325 – 33) —
Romans 11:33

The Wisdom of Winning Souls (#142,
in Bicentennial ed. only, B 4:305 – 17)
— 2 Corinthians 1:12

The Witness of the Spirit, 1 (#10, B
1:267 – 84 = #10, J V:111 – 23) —
Romans 8:16

The Witness of the Spirit, 2 (#11, B
1:285 – 98 = #11, J V:123 – 34) —
2 Corinthians 1:12

Bicentennial Volume Titles Published to Date

Note: Volume 1 was published in 1984. Subsequently, ten more volumes have been published. As of this date of publication, nineteen Bicentennial volumes remain to be published. They are marked with an asterisk (*). Here we have used the Jackson, Sugden, Telford, Curnock, and other editions to supplement the preferred Bicentennial edition.

1. Sermons 1 – 33
2. Sermons 34 – 70
3. Sermons 71 – 114
4. Sermons 115 – 51
*5. Explanatory Notes upon the New Testament I
*6. Explanatory Notes upon the New Testament II
7. A Collection of Hymns for the Use of the People Called Methodist
*8. Forms of Worship and Prayer
9. The Methodist Societies, History, Nature, and Design
*10. The Methodist Societies: The Conference
11. Appeals to Men of Reason and Religion and Certain Related Open Letters
*12. Doctrinal Writings: Theological Treatises
*13. Doctrinal Writings: The Defense of Christianity
*14. Pastoral and Instructional Writings I

*15. Pastoral and Instructional Writings II
*16. Editorial Work
*17. Natural Philosophy and Medicine
18. Journals and Diaries I
19. Journals and Diaries II
20. Journals and Diaries III
21. Journals and Diaries IV
22. Journals and Diaries V
23. Journals and Diaries VI
24. Journals and Diaries VII
25. Letters I
*26. Letters II
*27. Letters III
*28. Letters III
*29. Letters IV
*30. Letters V
*31. Letters VI
*32. Letters VII
*33. Bibliography of the Publications of John and Charles Wesley Letters VIII
*34. Miscellanea and General Index

Subject Index

Scripture Index